I MET GOD IN HELL

TIM EHMANN

with DANA EHMANN

BroadStreet
PUBLISHING

BroadStreet Publishing Group, LLC
Racine, Wisconsin, USA
www.broadstreetpublishing.com

I MET GOD IN HELL!

I MET GOD IN HELL! SERIES

Cover by Dan Pitts and Chris Garborg
Interior by Katherine Lloyd

Stock or custom editions of BroadStreet Publishing titles may be purchased in bulk for educational, business, ministry, fundraising, or sales promotional use. For information, please e-mail info@broadstreetpublishing.com.

Printed in the United States of America

15 16 17 18 19 20 5 4 3 2 1

DEDICATION

To my Papa-Yahweh, Jesus, and Holy Spirit—my best friends,
and Your amazing power that keeps me alive!

Also to my family, children, and grandchildren,
and all those who encouraged me to finally write my story—
I'm forever grateful.

CONTENTS

PART ONE: OUT OF THE DARKNESS

PART TWO: INTO THE LIGHT

PREFACE

In this book some names have been changed to protect the privacy of others, though the story of my life is true.

Because Almighty God, the creator of everything seen and unseen, often chooses to reveal Himself to me at different times through one of the distinct persons of His Divine Godhead—the Father, Son, and Holy Spirit—I have chosen to mainly refer to Him as "God" in order to simplify the flow of the story. However, at times I will specifically refer to one of the distinct persons because He chooses to interact with me through that person.

God is the "One God in Three Persons," otherwise known as the "Holy Trinity." Each person of His Godhead is coequal, coexistent, and coeternal as revealed throughout His written Word, the Bible, from the first pages of Genesis where He said, "Let us make man in our image and likeness" through to Revelation, where he defines Himself as "the First and the Last." Often referred to as "a mystery," difficult to grasp through human reason alone, He becomes more understandable and knowable only through His personal revelation of Himself to you.

This book shares things that God personally taught me about Himself after He got a hold of me— yet there is so much more to God than just what I know and have experienced. Get to know Him. Let Him teach you personally. Use spiritual discernment on your journey. Most importantly, make your life a love affair with the Lord!

At first, I didn't want to add Scripture references to this book or fill it with "Christian-ese" language because that's not how I usually speak. It's also never what God wanted from me or how He intended for me to represent Him. He wouldn't even allow me to be seen carrying around a Bible or wearing a cross around my neck, displaying typical Christian symbols to the world. For the majority of my walk, He's asked me to stay out of most churches so there was little chance of confusion that could hinder the already pure and accurate words of the revelations I receive from Him—just as I've received from the very beginning.

My call from Him is not to address the church but the world, those not even looking or asking for Him, just as it had been with me when He made His first astounding unannounced grand entrance into my life—for which I'm forever grateful!

God is in hot, passionate pursuit for this world, which He loves with an outta-control love! Prop items, popular Christian-speak, and the usual status-quo Christian representations tend to turn people off after they've seen and experienced what's been popularly modeled to them as "Christian." Much misrepresentation of God and who He really is has been commercialized, institutionalized, drastically watered down, and stripped of its truth and dynamite power; it's not at all what God originally intended.

Many people have bought their "fire insurance" by saying the typical salvation prayer, thinking they're saved, packing their suitcases, and getting ready to go in a self-centered, quick escape that leaves behind what God truly yearns for. His heart cries out for the world to know Him, and He wants His children to love and trust Him enough to put their relationship with Him first and start walking in heaven's unlimited supply and eternity with Him now—to change *this* world. Yet so many live in fear, unbelief, cowardice, compromise, and false assurance, propped up by religion, religious systems, false beliefs, and good works. That's just false light that looks good; it only serves to extinguish the Spirit of God, the true saving relationship with Him, and what He's really saying and trying to show and teach us personally.

The Scriptures, also known as the Holy Bible, are the reliable, inspired Word of God (in their original form). God's Word is alive and powerful, sharper than any two-edged sword, and a hammer of Holy-Spirit-breathed truth that will never fail and will always stand the test of time. God even says, "If they speak not according to this Word, it is because there is no light in them" (Isaiah 8:20 KJV). The Bible brings absolute truth and light that you can trust and learn from, because God's Word never changes. It's also His initial love letter to a world that He wants to know Him, but it's meant to lead us to know what's most important, the living author and "Word" Himself, in a personal relationship.

God also speaks to us in our everyday language in amazing ways. Without that one-on-one, two-way personal relationship with Him, we'll never really know where our true eternal position stands, and we'll never know our true identity or reach His great destiny for us in this life.

Hearing and discerning His voice to *you* is the primary reason for a relationship with Him, and it is absolutely vital in these days more than ever. God was always meant to be your primary teacher, encourager, helper, and personal friend above anything else that calls for you, your heart, and your attention.

Everything in my life story "passes the test" for those who require scriptural backup of the validity that it's really God who's been working in my life. But then again, some of it may be new to you, and it may leave some staunch theologically bound Bible bangers ready to lynch me for telling it like it is. That's okay. I learned a long time ago that it's only God's opinion of me that matters.

God will never contradict His already spoken Word, but the layers of personal revelation He wants to give you, communicated directly by His Spirit, go to much deeper levels than you could ever imagine. He is a *big* God, and what He does is ever creative, new, and different, but always redemptive and founded in truth and love. It's who He is and what He's all about, and that will never change.

Let God out of your box and beyond the limits you may have confined *yourself* in, and let God stretch you into the depths, layers, and realms of revelation of who He really is. Many of you are going to need it as you read my story.

My best advice is always to ask God for yourself and let Him personally teach, confirm, and show you Himself. What He'll show you will be completely accurate—and He *wants* to share Himself with you.

I finally relented and added Scripture in this book, only to serve as confirmation of my experiences with God as a solid foundation for those who want trustworthy validity that it is truly Him speaking to me. For you:

> I keep asking that the God of our Lord Jesus Christ, the glorious Father, may give you the Spirit of wisdom and revelation, so that you may know him better. I pray that the eyes of your heart may be enlightened in order that you may know the hope to which he has called you, the riches of his glorious inheritance in his holy people, and his incomparably great power for us who believe. That power is the same as the mighty strength he exerted when he raised Christ from the dead and seated him at his right hand in the heavenly realms. (Ephesians 1:17–20 NIV)

The walk of a true child of God is always a faith walk. That's all that truly pleases God. It's an exciting, risk-taking adventure founded in step-by-step trust of who God is and what He wants to show you through what He is personally saying to you.

May my story stretch your faith and stir you up to new levels to dare to believe God for, as you experience the goodness, trustworthiness, and faithfulness of this amazing, almighty God who knows no bounds, in ways you never thought possible.

With regard to all of what God is about to do on this earth, one thing I know for sure is that "you ain't seen nothing yet, baby!"

– Tim Ehmann

INTRODUCTION

I see both realities: heaven and hell.
I've been there.

— Tim Ehmann

On the night of September 1, 2000, I overdosed from shooting too many successive speedballs of heroin and crack. I collapsed in my upstairs bedroom, my heart stopped, and my spirit left my lifeless body. Within moments, I was in hell. It is without a doubt the most dreadful place to experience—and it is *real*. But it was where I belonged. After all, it really was my choice at the time.

I met God in hell.

I wasn't looking or asking for Him, nor had I ever cared to. He made it no secret, though, that all He wanted was just me. That alone surprised me. Why would He want *me*? What could He possibly see in me? I was just a hell-bent, self-centered show-off rock 'n' roll musician who lived only for all the drugs, women, and possessions I could obtain. By that time in my life, I didn't care about anyone or anything—especially about looking for God.

Everyone I knew back then is shocked that I'm alive today. Most of my rock 'n' roll friends died way too young. Untimely deaths. The lengths God went to just to get me were crazy and wild! This God truly is 100 percent love, and I can assure you there are no bounds that can hinder Him and no place He cannot go to find you. There's no way you can hold Him back or stop His outrageous love for you, no matter who you are or what you've done. His is a persistent, pursuing love that's totally radical and unintimidated by anything—even your unbelief in it.

My life is a miracle story. It started with miracles, and the miracles have continued all the way through it. What I've learned is, no one else has the power or authority to save you from that awful place, hell. In fact, God is the only one who can save you from yourself too.

My story is just one example of so many that reveal the true character of God and the depth of His passionate, unrestrained, and unstoppable love for us. God *is* love, and I am living proof that His love is *always* outta control!

Part One

OUT OF THE DARKNESS...

"Old life" rocker in the 1980s

1

ENCOUNTER

This is for you, son. Use it, use it!
I'm giving you My very heart.

– GOD

It was March 2010, ten years after the fateful day I died and went to hell. I was spending a quiet evening alone at my home in Dormont, a suburb of Pittsburgh, Pennsylvania. The cold weather had finally eased after a long, bitter winter, and the beginning of spring was melting the last of the snow and liberating the trees and flowers to bloom again.

I anticipated a trip to Chicago for a meeting I'd been invited to attend by the speaker. After packing my bags, I reviewed the itinerary one last time. The trip would start with an eight-hour drive, and I planned to leave that night so I could arrive in time for the first early morning session. Satisfied that I was ready, I lay down to get a few hours of rest.

I settled onto my bed, a simple air mattress on the floor at the time, and talked with God for a while, praying over the trip ahead. But as I wondered what might be ahead for me, my mind wouldn't relax. Finally, a thick blanket of peace fell over me. That's when I noticed that a tiny angel had come into the room. It flew over and sat on my left shoulder. I'd seen this same angel before, just sitting there quietly and hanging out with me.

God had been letting me see His angels quite often by now,

and their presence always reminded me that He was with me and watching out for me. As well, they also came for special purposes. As I lay there pondering why this particular angel had come and what God might be up to, the bedroom door behind my head suddenly flew open with a loud *thwack* against the wall.

I looked back to see what had happened. To my astonishment, the entire doorway was illuminated with a brilliant white light, and it emanated powerfully into my small bedroom. I squinted, trying to see into the near-blinding light, and there I found the awesome being of a big, beautiful angel. It stood right on the threshold of the doorway, its size filling the entire doorframe. I lay there frozen, not daring to move and wondering what would happen next.

Then I became aware of the sound of music coming into the room. I followed the sound, turning my gaze back toward the foot of my bed, and saw the window on the opposite wall also radiating brilliantly. As I looked into it, I could see what looked like hundreds of angels outside the window, jockeying for a position to peek into my room. That's when I realized they were the ones singing. The music was unbelievably beautiful, and it flowed effortlessly right into the room. As I listened more intently to their amazing unearthly song, I distinctly heard the words of their repeated chorus. Covered in a supernatural peace, I lay there still, trying to take it all in. Soon I just *knew* the name of their song. It was called "Eulogy," and they were praising Jesus.

The music itself filtered right through the light beaming into the room. Its sweet rhythm flowed through the light like it was alive. *Yeah! This is pretty cool!* I excitedly thought. Then I became aware of movement directly above me. I looked up and saw a giant hand slowly come into the room—right through the ceiling. I was in awe but felt no fear; the atmosphere was too full with such tranquil peace. I recognized this familiar hand, as I'd seen it before on several occasions. It was the hand of God.

His hand was cupped and in it He held a huge multi-faceted white diamond. It too was brilliantly lit up, and it glowed with sparkling brilliance, pulsating and vibrating with a life all its own. Probably two feet wide by two feet deep, it was cut in the shape of a heart. Slowly and steadily, God's hand floated down from the ceiling toward me in a soft, rhythmic flow in perfect time with the angels' serenade and paused right above my belly. It opened wide to reveal the gem's wondrous living beauty to me, and I gazed at it in awe, my heart beating wildly with excitement.

I heard the voice of God say, "This is for you, son. Use it, use it! I'm giving you my very heart." Then His hand just dove seamlessly into my belly and He released that heavenly gem directly inside of me!

When He gently pulled His emptied hand out, it again floated slowly, rhythmically back up and right through the ceiling. The motion of His hand flowing with the angels' chorus was so tranquil, smooth, and free, just like the flow of Heaven is, with nothing out of sync. The angels outside watching through the window still sang their beautiful Eulogy song, and the angel in my bedroom doorway continued standing there, still emanating that brilliant heavenly light powerfully into the room. About eight minutes later it all faded away, with the big angel leaving last.

There I was on my bed, alone again. The bedroom door remained wide open though. That in itself was a revelation to me: the sign of the "Open Door," another name for Jesus—and a message God often repeats to me.

God often gives me love gifts like these, but this one was quite special. After that awesome divine appointment, I was intrigued. I know from experience that there's *always* profound and precise meaning in every minute detail of what God does or says. It's full of revelation and layers of more treasure gifts from Him. Sometimes He even continues to give more understanding of those deeper layers over years throughout life.

God's far from boring, and He likes to play treasure hunt games with His children. Like a big kid having the time of His life, He'll entice you along with wildly creative clues to lead you to the grand reveal of each and every treasure from Him, if you'll just stay in the pursuit. He doesn't hide His treasures *from* us; He hides them *for* us. Sometimes I don't know who gets more excited when I figure them out. He loves to watch us have those "aha" moments when we discover them, and He doesn't make His treasures too hard to find. It's all part of the fun and adventurous love relationship He wants to have with us.

After this special encounter with God, the more I thought on every detail, the more He revealed. I just needed to find a dictionary to look up the word "eulogy." I wanted to see if it provided further clues to what the word really meant. I learned that its root meaning is "to praise" and that a eulogy is typically an event performed in order to express words of love, gratitude, and remembrance of someone on a special occasion. This only added to the wow factor of it all. I'd discovered another deep layer of what God was saying to me. Then I realized that God had considered this gift-giving event such a special occasion that He sent a stunning herald angel with a backup choir to celebrate it with Him. God is *really* cool!

Even the angels love to watch in awe of the things God is currently doing. They're especially curious and still ever learning themselves about the creative ways He continually showers His love, mercy, and grace on His most beloved creation—people. His love for us never stops, and everything He does is new and different just to specially reveal Himself to us. God loves to give His children gifts, and with them always comes some sort of special impartation of Himself. He'll lets us have, see, and use His gifts even before we go to live in heaven. These gifts are meant for the individual, and often for others as well.

There's no way I could describe in a book all that I've experienced so far. I've had so many encounters with God; they're innumerable and perpetual. How do you describe twenty thousand or so encounters with God per year? They come when I'm awake, and they come when I'm asleep—in visions, dreams, and awesome events where I know I'm actually there. Some mornings I wake up in heaven. Either I'm caught up in heaven with God, or the realm of heaven is with me, encompassing me in my bedroom as I first open my eyes. That familiar bright heavenly light surrounds me, and God's awesome presence and peace fills the room. It's one of the many ways He likes to greet me first thing in the morning.

What many people don't know is that God is not only righteous and holy, but He's also wild, free, and fun! He has a great sense of humor, even telling jokes sometimes, and can be incredibly funny. He *loves* laughter and joy. He also loves adventure and sharing with us the things of His heavenly kingdom, where all things are possible on a daily basis—and it's available to us now.

I've learned to stay open to what God wants to show me, because I've found it rarely comes close to what my limited mind or natural reason can understand. He most often teaches me about Himself and His ways by choosing to vividly show me what He sees, thinks, and knows.

One thing I know is, God's heart is crying out for His children to come home to Him. Perpetually seeking after each one of us is the full-time most important task on God's agenda. Sometimes it's hard to understand that we are truly His main focus; we don't realize what great worth we are to God. He's always demonstrating how deeply He loves and cares for me, but He also shows me His love for this world and its people, which He made for such a great purpose. God loves us with an outta-control love. It's like He can't help Himself.

Because He places such a high value on us, we are a major prize, caught in a mostly unseen battle between two kingdoms, light and dark, good and evil, and we are fiercely contended for. But God has a place available right inside Him that's safe, peaceful, and pure, where we can know the truth of what's really going on, walk in His protection, and rest in complete assured trust that we're forever loved and already home.

2

THE UNSEEN PERIMETER FENCE

He is the God who does it all—
that's a true salvation!

– TIM EHMANN

My life didn't start out with my knowing and experiencing all these things. My story is one of an outrageously determined God who wouldn't stop chasing after me my whole life—though I sure wasn't looking for Him or asking for any of this. While I went about my days doing things my own wild way, He pursued me, sovereignly protected me, kept calling me, and patiently waited…for a long time. He gave me a lengthy amount of rope to run on (much more, it seems, than He gives many others), and I ran it out all the way to the end—and then some. But no matter what I did or how much I didn't believe in Him, He never stopped chasing after me.

It was kind of like having a loving, protective dad allowing his wild, rambunctious kid to run himself silly in every direction, getting away with all kinds of things, for as long as he needed to, but in a yard so big that he couldn't see that he had a high protective perimeter fence keeping him safe the whole time. I took my unhindered freedom to the max; that is, for forty-four years I ran and my watchful, heavenly Dad patiently waited until I was all run out doing things my own way. I believe the bottom line to my story is that if God could save me, He can save anyone.

Throughout my entire life of running at breakneck speed down the wrong roads, I was continually covered by an unseen hand of protection through peril after peril, most of which were admittedly self-inflicted. The protection He had around me defied any natural explanation for how I could have survived them. Most of the events were just surreal.

Yet even in all my stupid stuff, I was allowed to run. My life-long vocation of being a touring rock 'n' roll musician only added to the crazy opportunities and trouble I could find. I got away with a lot. Nothing ever seemed to touch or stop me, no matter what I did. Because of this, eventually a godlike complex took a hold of me, and this made me even more brazen and bold. I started to believe I was just invincible. I should have died multiple times through those first decades of my life. Even when I saw some of my fairly young friends dying, I never thought that would happen to me. I never gave much consideration to death, though everything I did, every day, was always on the edge of it.

Unbelievably, this relentless God who had been chasing after me my whole life—the one I didn't even want to know—also chased after me straight into hell, which is where I went after I overdosed on drugs and died. Somehow He was determined (peculiarly confident, in fact) that He was going to get me, and to get me to the planned destiny He had intended for me since before my birth. His stubborn, outta-control love for me just wouldn't let me go.

Many people believe God is all about judgment and condemning people, but that certainly wasn't the way I came to know Him. I knew who I was and what I stood for, and I lived it every day to the max. That included writing and performing some pretty nasty songs about Him and inciting others through my music and lifestyle. I loved the shock reaction it brought, and many in the crowds really ate it up. I didn't believe in God. I didn't know Him, and most of all, I didn't care to.

Despite who I was and the wild way I was living, this unseen

God kept patiently drawing me in, piece by piece, with His never-to-be-out-done, relentless love. He didn't do it with judgment, which no doubt would have made me run even farther from Him. Though I was living so wrongly and even ignorantly inciting hate against Him, it was His consistent, repeated demonstration of love for me over and over that finally proved irresistible in the end. God's steadfast love is the only thing I know that can truly break the hardest, most crusted over, cold or apathetic rebel's heart to Him. Yes, God even loves wild rebels! He knows and understands them well, because they are so much like Him.

Most people eventually give up on the wild rebels in their life, but God often sees these people as having the greatest potential and providing His best opportunities. In fact, I'm convinced He made me with this type of personality. Rebels are passionate about their independence and freedom to do whatever it is they believe in. They also tend to be adventurous and don't like to be restrained or controlled. They question everything and have no problem going against the status quo, and they usually don't care what others think of them or what it costs.

But God just sees all the juicy possibilities waiting right in front of Him. When God gets a hold of a wild rebel's passionate, determined heart and turns it toward Him, there's no end to what He can do with that person. He's thrilled, and He greatly enjoys the entire process even when He has to wait a long time.

The Bible is full of rebel types. Not many of the great Bible personalities started out as what you'd call "good people." Some were outright rotten. But these people once considered "rebels, rabble, and rubble," often throwaways, discounted or maybe even odd ones to the world, were the very ones God specially hand-picked to train up for His front stage. They are examples of some of His greatest work and became known as His champions of the day once He got a hold of their hearts. He even chose to record His-story of some of their lives in His great love letter to us, the Bible. It shows us some examples of who He is, how much He loves, and what amazing things He can do with *anyone's* life. The rest of those stories have also already been written—but they are still being lived and played out every day.

There is no "case" too hard for God, though I believe I had to be one of His toughest. In fact, I'm sure I wore out the guardian angels He assigned to me. I'm glad that when everyone else gives up on the rebels, God never does. He relentlessly calls to them until the last possible moment. I'm so ever grateful that, with me, He even went beyond that final moment.

It's vitally important to never, ever give up hope and trust in God as you pray for the rebels you may know too. Let me assure you, I've learned God is limitless and extremely creative in the ways He chases after them. Our prayers are way more powerful than we think.

God has a dynamic unseen "perimeter fence" around everyone born into this world. Though its work may be misunderstood or seem harsh at times in the circumstances of your life, it's inherently a fence of God's great love at work. It's designed to help move you right into the place where God wants you, to lead you into opportunities to finally hear and recognize His voice in His relentless, personal call for you. It seems this fence is much stronger when there are others praying on your behalf, even if it's only one person. My life story revealed here is just one example to help you recognize what this "perimeter fence" of love can actually look like.

I thought I was wild, but let me tell you, I discovered pretty quickly that God is way wilder than I ever dreamt of being! He's a revolutionary rebel in His own right. This alone was what first caught my attention at the time, and it brought me a lot of deep respect for Him. I've always thought big in my life and I don't give up easily, but I knew when I was finally one-upped in the wildness department. God always goes against the usual, popular flow. He doesn't play by our rules. In fact, He's totally into anticonformity to "normal" rules, and He can bring shock value better than the wildest rebel ever known. Sometimes, He'll even allow things that will purposely offend you, just so He can show you what's off in *your* heart. Even so, no matter how creative or outrageous He needs to be to get your attention, everything He does is always in love and for a redemptive value.

One day, I think a lot of people will be surprised to see many "once-hard-core rebels" in heaven—people written off and thrown away by the world, considered no good or marked as hopeless cases. In contrast, what a surprise it will be when they see what they thought were some really good, moral, ethical people (even regular church-going people) in hell.

For God, it's all a matter of your heart and what you're *really* trusting in. This wild God loves to use what looks like foolishness to this world, to pull the carpet out from under those who think they're wise and know it all already. And He loves to turn things upside down. He'll purposely choose what looks utterly weak or even offensive to this world, and use it to reveal Himself.

I've found that God thinks a lot differently than we do. His thoughts and ways are completely way-out-there different from ours. In fact, this seems to be a signature mark that it *is* Him. So we'd better pay attention and be willing to take a second look at the things that don't make sense to our natural reason or that scream, "That couldn't possibly be God!" You'll never get to know Him through your faculty of everyday natural reason anyway.

All I ever want to talk about are heaven and this incredible, personal God. That's the real deal and the only thing worth talking about. Close friends and family who've seen my life and what I've experienced have urged me to write my story—that is, the whole story, the bad and the good. But it's really all God's story. Some things many people may have never heard of before, and He's urged me to put it all out there anyway, just so others can know more of who He is and what outrageous things He can do—with anyone.

I resisted it for a long time, simply because I hate talking about my past before I knew God. I don't like to give the Devil any more credit by speaking about all he did; he took enough years of my life. But at the time, I didn't know it was really him driving it all. I didn't believe in the Devil or hell, let alone God or heaven, nor did I believe that all I was trusting and believing in were just lies.

A prophetic friend of mine once told me he had a vivid vision where he was shown a scene deep in Satan's lair. There he saw a spectacle of the Devil in his bedroom, fuming with anger and entirely frustrated. He said it was obvious how much he intensely hated me because he saw a big riddled dartboard with my picture on it over the head of his bed. With a familiar understanding of what it meant, we both laughed it off, though it was with deep and noted respect for what God was really saying. The Devil is always lurking about like a prowling lion, "seeking whom he may devour" (1 Peter 5:8), and this was just another loving warning revealed by God to remind me to stay vigilant and close to Him. Even so, the Devil can't have me anymore now. I belong to Jesus. He's my best, most-trusted, and all-powerful friend. The only safe place for me is *in* Him.

Nevertheless, to show the depths of what God can pull any individual out of and how greatly He loves, pursues, saves, and desires to bring us into a love-affair relationship with Him, I press on in sharing my story. It will reveal something of who this amazing, almighty God really is, as well as His true heart, incredible character, and great grace and mercy toward us all. He alone gets the credit for it all, though, because I've found He is the God who does it all—that's a true salvation!

3

UNWELCOME "FRIENDS"

But the way of the wicked He turns upside down.

– PSALM 146:9C

I grew up with great, loving parents. Our family was considered middle class in the '60s. Dad worked as a superintendent for the US Postal Service, and his job was to train all the new postal workers. Mom was a homemaker who took care of the family. My older brother Mickey, younger sister Maryanne, and I were born and raised in Pittsburgh, Pennsylvania, and lived in a comfortable two-story house in a great neighborhood.

Dad loved and trusted in God and participated faithfully in the Catholic Church, but Mom wouldn't go to church because she felt church people were all hypocrites. She had a pretty defined relationship with God herself though. She kept it between her and God alone, but she knew and loved Him very much. God would prove to be her unquestionable lifeline through some unbelievably tough years ahead.

Mom and I were always close. We had a great relationship and could talk for hours and hours, even when I was older. She didn't judge me, and that's why we could freely talk. We laughed a lot and discussed everything, like good friends. She truly was, in many ways, my best friend at the time, and I relied on that relationship a lot.

When I was nine years old, Mom started to suffer severe on-and-off psychosis-type episodes where she thought she was losing reality at times, though she couldn't figure out why. It was something that wasn't discussed with children during that time period, and my parents kept it between themselves as much as possible. The fact was, Mom had spent years taking experimental fertility drugs after a series of miscarriages. Later, the use of these drugs became a worldwide scandal as the news broke out of the devastating problems they caused. Mom was one of the many guinea pigs used in testing these experimental drugs, and the side effects were utterly debilitating. When she reached menopause, the strong hormonal drug's lingering side effects sent her body wildly out of balance and she couldn't understand what was happening to her or why. At the time, the doctors didn't know why either. Nobody understood it.

Dad was faced with the dilemma of seeing Mom greatly suffering and having doctors tell him that the best option for her was intense professional help that required institutionalizing her in a specialty hospital. My parents loved each other, and Dad was pretty torn, but after multiple consults and strong advice from the doctors, he believed they knew best. My parents discussed it and she finally agreed. Mom then went through a nightmare over the next three years, in and out of institutions that conducted further experimental treatments on her.

The first time she had to leave us, she was gone for about two years before coming back home—but she stayed only for a short time. Then she left again for another year of more "treatments." What was most tragic was that all the new trial regimens tried on her were in an attempt to fix what the first treatments caused, all at the hands of doctors and so-called "experts" trying more new experiments on her. These included shock treatments to her brain that proved devastating and almost killed her. In the end, finally dismissed from the treatments, she came home but wasn't the same person. She remained in a daze, barely able to speak, and was only a shell of who she'd once been. She'd often sit alone for hours at the kitchen table just staring off into space, smoking cigarettes and sipping a drink, not saying a word to anyone.

Amazingly, though, about a year later she somehow snapped out of it and came back stronger than ever. When she learned that it was the infertility drugs that were the initial cause of her problems, it was like a light went on. This made her so mad that she became fiercely determined to fight her way back. And her long journey in all that deep, dark desperation led her to reach out to God with a wild, fierce faith like never before. She leaned on Him with all she had because she first-handedly learned that He was the only one she could trust. He didn't let her down.

While Mom was away for those long periods, Dad had to raise us kids by himself while working full time. Struggling with three of us, he thought it best to send Maryanne to live with my aunt. With our family further broken up, Mickey and I spent a lot of time home alone with no supervision.

The hurt of losing my mother and best friend in those formative years hit me hard. My strong emotions quickly turned to misunderstood anger toward Dad, as I placed the blame on him for "putting Mom away," not understanding all that was involved. A spirit of intense hurt and offense seated itself in my young heart. Once I welcomed and harbored it there, it grew and began to invite its friends: sadness, depression, bitterness, anger, and then others. Over time, it so intensely internalized that I didn't know how to deal with it at my young age. I mention all this because, looking back, I believe this was one of the major pivotal points that began the successive and long course of my own self-destruction.

I remember back to one of my first strange "seeing" incidents when I was just seven years old. I was in my upstairs room, tucked in bed for the night, and my parents were asleep in their room down the hall. As I lay there in the dark, with my bedroom softly lit by the streetlight outside the window, I saw something fly into my room—but it came in through the closed window. It looked like a black crow, and it wildly flew around and around my room over my bed. I laid there in awe, watching it for almost ten minutes and wondering how a bird could possibly get into my room through a closed window. Once in a while it would land on the old mantle on the wall opposite the foot of my bed. Then it would take off again and make its rounds circling over my bed.

Finally, I yelled out at the top of my lungs to my sleeping parents, "There's a bird in my room! There's a bird in my room!" My parents hurried to my room, threw open the door, and flipped on the light. But the moment they opened the door, the bird simply disappeared. At my crying insistence, they looked through my entire room—my closet, cupboards, and in every corner—but found nothing.

Only after I came to know God, when I was much older, did I understand the unique discernment language He uses most often to speak to me: he just shows me. I now know it was a warning vision back then, though it was as real looking as anything physical. God was showing and warning me, even in my younger years, that I was being targeted by the Enemy, but I didn't understand it at the time. Spiritually speaking, when God symbolizes black crows to me, they're generally a sign of rebellion and witchcraft, which He calls one and the same (1 Samuel 15:23a).

By the time I'd entered eighth grade, I became quite unruly and mischievous. Dad, who was a committed Catholic, was really proud of me, though, because I agreed to serve as an altar boy during the Masses at Holy Innocents Catholic Church. Being an altar boy included learning a lot of practiced rituals, and we carried out our learned routines well.

One Mass I served for was particularly large, as it was Christmas and the church was filled with people. All the teams of trained altar boys were required to serve for this special Holy Day service, and we were dressed in matching altar boy garb: black pants and shoes, the traditional long black robe to the ankles, and a shorter white vestment layered over it. However, because this was a Christmas Mass, we were required to also wear long red matching ties, which hung down on the outside of our garments.

At the middle of the service, the altar boys had to pick up their own tall lighted candle and line up in two rows on either side of the altar as three priests continued the service. But waiting there for what seemed like an eternity in this particularly long Mass made me extremely bored, and I was getting fidgety. That was when I came up with another of my harebrained ideas. I glanced out the corners of my eyes at the altar boys standing in line on either side of me, their eyes glazed over in an obedient, mesmerized daze. Then I discreetly tipped my candle sideways, touching my flame to the bottom tip of each of their ties. *Ahh. Some fun and excitement at last!* I thought to myself.

When they finally realized flames were starting to lick up the length of their ties, they jumped around frantically, pounding at their chests while trying to keep as quiet and unnoticed as possible. It was like watching an old silent slapstick comedy show. I just stood stock still, holding my candle tightly upright and trying to look like I didn't know what was going on. But inwardly I was deviously thrilled at the fun of being mischievous and outrageous once again.

Eventually, the boys got the flames patted out and stepped back in line. The Mass continued on, though the atmosphere was now electric with some excitement. I waited, hoping I'd somehow gotten away with it, but Sister Mary Giles, the nun who headed the team of altar boys, could hardly wait for the Mass to end. She was fuming mad and had been impatiently pacing in the dressing room, pausing every couple of minutes to peer with intense anger at me through the cracked-open back door.

When the Mass ended and we headed out the back stage door, she grabbed me and lit into me. Of course I was fired on the spot. Later, I somehow got through the lecture from Dad, and that ended my days as an altar boy. I loved getting attention, and it didn't matter to me how it came.

Sometimes I think I was born to be on some sort of a stage and that's what first attracted me to music. Writing and playing music became the passion of my life after I picked up a guitar at the age of thirteen. I'd first thought learning keyboards was what I was destined to do, and I tried a few lessons, but that was short lived. At school I would lie, telling everyone I was already a keyboard player in a band, while in reality I had just started lessons. With my growing major-show-off-type personality, I loved the extra attention it got me, especially from the girls.

I had only two short periods with guitar lessons, each lasting about a year. One was with Bill Clydesdale, a famous and very structured teacher. The other teacher was a jazz player, and I'll never forget his advice to me: "Whatever you do with your life, don't make this your career!" That statement devastated me as I struggled along, learning to play the best I could. But I was determined that the guitar was what I wanted to do with my life. So I decided to keep at it on my own and spent hours and hours practicing at home. Before long I invited friends who also played instruments to jam with me. Then I started up experimental bands.

It was the late '60s, and in those early days I loved the popular rock music at the time. My favorite guitar players were Alvin Lee, Jimmy Page, and Richie Blackmore, and I tried to come up with a sound that was my own but also emulated them.

My older brother, Mickey, also played the guitar, and for a couple of years he was in different bands. They would practice downstairs in the basement, but I would never go down to watch. Mickey was a big, muscular guy (unlike me), and he frequently got in fights at school. He was known as the "baddest muscle guy" in his class, and he'd often practice on me. I'd go to the fights to watch just so I could root for the other guy. This started some major sibling divisions between us.

Mickey was the first person to sell me drugs. They were black beauties (speed), but later he turned me in to Mom and Dad for doing drugs. I couldn't believe it—and that turned me against him even more at the time. Our on-again, off-again brotherly friendship lasted a long time, though I do love my brother dearly.

At that time, the hippie scene was big in downtown Pittsburgh.

It was an atmosphere of "peace, love, and rock 'n' roll." British bands were big too, and groups like the Beatles, The Byrds, The Who, Rolling Stones, Black Sabbath, The Doors, and Grateful Dead were coming out and taking off like wildfire. The older generations mostly looked on it as wild, rebellious music, but the younger generation loved it.

The Vietnam War dragged on, and peace sit-ins and activist protests, especially against the war and government, spread throughout the country. Hippies loved to protest, but there were also some groups with way more radical ideas. They'd try to recruit some of the hippies at the park. These were people, I found out later, who protested through outright mayhem and destructive violence.

One day, I went with a group of my hippie friends to Oakland (part of Pittsburgh), where some of these convincing recruiters offered to take us to one of their underground meetings. I was only about fourteen or fifteen at the time. There they shared plans for unleashing riots at a whole new level, including major destruction of property, attacking police, bombing public buildings, and even murdering innocent people—anything to bring attention to their cause. But when the leaders then incited everyone there to go home and kill their parents, I balked. They were much too radical for me.

Those days were also a time of hitchhiking. Everyone seemed to be doing it. We'd hitchhike to get to concerts, then someone there would give us a ride home, with everyone getting high on the way back. The growing population of young "long hairs" hanging out in the city weren't trusted by many people—and by the cops even less. Police would yell brash remarks at any guy with long hair, and the guys were greatly mistreated, looked down upon, and considered "no-good rebels."

With plenty of spare time on my hands after school, if I wasn't playing my guitar, I'd walk down to the city's downtown park and hang out there with the hippies. I partied with them, doing drugs, and spent more and more time there. I'll never forget a scene that really caught my attention at the time.

Huge crowds would come in droves during certain times of the month, meeting in a big old stone church, called the First Presbyterian Church, across the street. Traffic was always heavy, and huge crowds would gather outside the building's doors and down the sidewalks. Everyone looked desperate to get into that building, so something was obviously a big draw. Many of these people were in wheelchairs, with canes, or using other medical devices. Some even lay on stretchers carried by their friends. It looked so bizarre, and I wondered with great interest what was going on in there.

Finally, I asked a couple of the hippies if they knew what it was all about. They said some sort of minister lady came to hold so-called "miracle healing services" there. I later learned that lady was Kathryn Kuhlman, a well-known healing minister, and she had been regularly holding the meetings there for years.

I've often thought back to this scene. I now believe that it was God tapping me on the shoulder, even back then. Only much later did I come to know and respect Kathryn Kuhlman. She knew the Holy Spirit and the voice of God; she had a real-deal relationship with Him, and God used her powerfully. A lot of people came out of those services miraculously healed.

At the age of fourteen, I started using heroin, and then reds and acid too. Before long, heroin became a daily need. I'd buy it from one of the hippies at the park, then practically crawl back home to sleep for hours. I used the money Dad gave me for weekly allowance, and soon after, began to steal spare change from his dresser too.

Over time, I grew bolder. I once stole three hundred dollars from a lady's purse that was unattended in a back room during a church service at my school. It was too easy, and I needed money for drugs, so I risked it. I never really liked thievery though. Instead, I became a great swindler, manipulating people so they would give me what I wanted. I became good at persuasive manipulation, but years later it turned into a need for control—and it became a *big* problem.

By the time I was in ninth grade, I wanted to let my hair grow long, but it was against the rules at the strict Catholic school I attended. I let it grow longer, and one day the school contacted my parents telling them I simply had to cut my hair to their code or I wouldn't be permitted in school anymore.

My hair had become part of my identity, and I absolutely refused. Mom and Dad used their authority, though, and were ready to make me get it cut. On the day they were going to take me to the barbershop, I packed a bag to run away. I went to the park to meet with my older hippie friend Boo, and together we decided to hitch-hike our way to Georgetown, in D.C., about four hours away.

While there we did a lot of acid and tripped out the whole time. We found an old mission that took people in and let them stay for free, so we spent the nights there. After a few days, though, I decided it was time I went home and hitchhiked back to Pittsburgh.

My frantic parents were so utterly shocked and shaken by my running away and how determined I was to keep my long hair, that they made a deal with me and then ran it past the school adminis-tration. If I was willing to wear a short-hair wig to school, keeping my long hair stuffed up underneath it, I could keep it. The deal was agreed upon, and that's when I started wearing a brown short-haired wig to school every day, which I did for three years. As soon as the bell rang at the end of the day, I could be "me" again and let it all hang down. Eventually, my hair grew to my waist.

In those high school years, my friends and I got into a regular get-together routine. Right after school most days, I'd come home and play music with a friend or two till bedtime. On Wednesdays the school held a weekly dance night, and we'd all go to Crafton, a town a few miles away, for the dance. Out on the dance floor I'd do this thing I called the "Air Guitar." I didn't know that anyone else was doing that back then, but it quickly caught on. We'd wait until the end of the night because they'd finally loosen up and let us play the hard rock stuff. I'd get a few of the guys to step out with me in the middle of the dance floor, and we'd start doing our thing, just wailing on our pretend guitars to the music. Kids would gather around until the crowds got huge. They would all scream and cheer us on. The Air Guitar thing became a hit with everyone after that—a phenomenon, even famous.

Thursdays were lake days, and we would all hang out at the nearby lake. It was a total party scene with drugs, drinking, and girls. Then Fridays were blast-it days. My parents always went grocery shopping on Friday, and I would turn the volume up on my amps and rock out big-time in the house.

It was around this time when Dad became concerned that I had an ongoing drug problem. He forced me into a teen drug rehab program that held night meetings in Dormont. A long-haired college-age guy who was an ex-addict himself ran the meetings. (This was a time when drug and alcohol counseling centers were just starting to open.) The meetings ran anywhere from two to four hours long. I went to a couple of them, then dropped out with excuses and lies to my parents that I was still attending them. But that's where I met one of my guitar teachers. He was teaching anyone who wanted to learn to play or improve their skills, for free.

When I was fifteen, I played my first gig at a nightclub called the Casbah, on Walnut Street in Shadyside, an artsy boutique kind of area. I was the lead guitar player for an acoustic guitar player who sang lead, and we played there weekly. Not long afterward, by age sixteen, I was getting a lot more gigs and started to regularly play at nightclubs with various groups. This furthered my being gone from home even more.

I had my first real girlfriend a little before I turned sixteen. Her name was Glory, and she was twenty-four. I met her through my drummer friend Allen, who was dating Glory's sister. Glory was the former girlfriend of rocker Leon Russell, and was into New Age religion and reading tarot cards. She would pick me up from school in her sporty red Corvette.

As my time with Glory progressed, my parents suspected I was in a serious relationship with a girl they didn't know. They eventually became so concerned that they asked me to set up a meeting with her parents (they didn't know her real age and that she had her own apartment). I answered them with, "Okay, I'll set it up." But every time they were ready for the meeting, I told them that her parents weren't available at the time they picked. Eventually, they gave up asking.

One day, Glory took me to a Lou Reed concert held at an ice rink in the Forest Hills area of Pittsburgh. It was there I was introduced to David Bowie. We had third-row seats, and my seat was right next to his. At the time, Bowie was doing his Stardust tour and still playing at small venues, before he got big and started doing arena events. We smoked weed together and talked throughout the whole concert. The type of music he and others like him were doing at the time got my attention.

I had sex for the first time when I turned sixteen. It was my birthday, and Glory and I did speedballs (crack processed down with added heroin), smoked cigarettes, and had sex at her apartment. She said it was "time to give me my birthday present." But after six months together, our relationship ended. Later, I heard Glory had left town and got married to some guy who owned a bakery shop in San Francisco. I never saw her again.

Right before my last year of high school, the Catholic school I'd been attending closed and I was moved to public school at Langley High, which had a whole new set of rules. But I could finally lose the wig and wear my hair how I wanted. Strangely, even though I was able to wear it long, I cut it short to "clean up" for a girl I wanted to take to the senior prom. Our relationship ended up lasting only a couple of months, but the short hair a lot longer. I'll never forget my friends taunting and railing on me. They thought I was stupid for cutting my hair just for a date with a girl. I knew they were right.

Getting my driver's license increased my independence and freedom more, and I finally earned enough money playing gigs to buy my first car. It was a green '68 Oldsmobile station wagon with plenty of room for packing in my music equipment and friends. I drove them everywhere.

One of those days, I was out cruising a main city street in Pittsburgh with two friends, Allen and Whoopie. We were all getting high smoking hash. As I was driving along, everything suddenly turned upside down. The street, the buildings, the cars, and even the people were upside down as we cruised by. I was going nuts seeing this plain as day with my own eyes, but no one in the car understood what I was frantically trying to tell them. I kept trying to explain it to them, surprised they couldn't see it too, but they thought I'd gone crazy, even joking I had gotten too high and was just "out of it."

By then I was familiar with the effects of certain drugs, and I *knew* this wasn't the drugs! This was different. After a while, everything turned back to normal and I gave up trying to get my friends to believe me. But bizarre things like this began to happen more and more to me throughout my life. I even thought it was normal and the way everybody saw things.

I didn't understand until nearly thirty years later that this also was a vision from God. He was trying to speak to me, even back then, but I had no understanding of it or Him. Then years later I picked up a Bible for the first time in my life. While I was casually flipping through the pages, my eyes landed on a passage that read "but the way of the wicked He turns upside down" (Psalm 146:9c). It was then that I heard the distinct voice of God speak audibly to me, "Do you remember when I showed you this, Timmy? That was Me!" The scene in the car with my friends instantly came to mind.

This was another of His gentle warnings that I was walking on the wrong path, but again, I didn't recognize it was Him. I just didn't have any understanding or belief in God at the time.

4

SEX, DRUGS, AND ROCK 'N' ROLL!

You've got to do this!

– GOD

During my midteens, my music preferences changed and darker music started to attract me. Growing up in the late '60's and early '70s, I was influenced by hard rock and heavy metal, then punk, shock rock, and glam rock. I idolized musicians like Alice Cooper, David Bowie, Mick Ronson, Ian Hunter, and bands like KISS and Uriah Heep when they were new and original (before they got big and their sound became more commercialized and mainstreamed).

In later years I got an invite to the Nixon Theatre in Pittsburgh to see the New York Dolls, a glitter-punk band that was a big influence on later all-out punk bands. The Dolls had been fairly new when they won a "Best New Band" title in '73, just a few days earlier. Though they were controversial for many, they had a growing following because of their new and wild originality. The show they played at the Nixon Theatre had a crowd of only about one hundred in the approximately seventeen-hundred-seat place.

Every one of the empty seat bottoms in the theater was flopping up and down with the sound they were putting out. I thought the whole building would shake apart. The show was utterly outrageous, and everyone there was all-out partying. They also had a light show with laser guns that they shot out into the audience, which was a pretty new thing at the time.

During this particular show, the band sent out a fancy large crystal container to be passed around through the rows of the theater. In it were complementary drugs of just about any and every kind of pill you could think of: reds, whites, blues, black beauties, morphine, and who knows what else. People would take whatever they wanted and pass it on down, complements of the band.

Everyone there agreed that it was the wildest and probably best show they'd ever attended. The Dolls were pioneers for some of the darkest bands that would soon follow, pushing music, shock, and outrageous entertainment beyond limits ever seen before. It was one of the bands that helped bring beyond-control, purely demonically influenced bands to the forefront—bands that many record companies didn't want to touch with a ten-foot pole at the time.

The Dolls, along with the emerging punk-rock-movement bands that came out during the '70's, like the Sex Pistols and the Dead Boys, were bands I'd really come to admire because their music was similar to what I'd been writing and playing, though these bands had a style that was totally new. The music was raw with original sounds, and their shows were performed with an outrageousness that pushed any previous boundaries. It was totally out-of-the-box, wild, and rebellious stuff, and the attitude of it all fit right in with who I had become. It helped spur me deeper into the blackness of my life, and I spent a lot of time hanging out and playing with these friends.

Many of the British bands coming up in this movement became popular too. Punk rock was considered a subculture, born from the underground movement because they were completely independent of the monopolized music industry. In fact, most were totally hostile and outspoken against it. They saw that the public was being fed only commercially packaged and censored music that was syndicated by exclusive corporations and record companies controlling all airplay, distribution, and TV airing.

(The intension, of course, was to make a profit, but it also allowed them to keep control of what the world could and couldn't hear.)

Punk rock was a total revolt and backlash to this entrenched monopoly. It quickly grew into a rebellious, anticonformist, even anarchistic type movement that was determined to break barriers no one had ever shattered before. Later, when glam rock became popular in the '80s, bands and music were more highly commercialized. It brought big hair and makeup, with many bands following the same format and sounds.

By the time I turned eighteen, I was gone from home so much that I decided to move out. For a few months, I stayed in an apartment located above a punk rock club in Swissvale, a small town outside Pittsburgh. I met and hung out with a lot of the bands that flowed through that place. We played shows and partied together. I began to write new songs and continued to put bands together. Soon I was back out, hitting the road heavy and playing everywhere I went.

By the age of twenty, rock 'n' roll had become my entire life and I was living the full-on proverbial "sex, drugs, and rock 'n' roll" lifestyle. That included endless traveling, practices, gigs, nightclubs, bars, and party houses till the early morning hours—day after day, night after night.

One of those nights while going to a party after a late-night gig, I had another strange incident happen to me. I was driving through a long tunnel, going through the bottom of a mountain, when my whole car lit up with this brilliant light all around me. I heard an audible voice say with determination, "You've got to do this!" I was stunned and kept wondering to myself, *What...in the world...is going on?* In shock, I spoke back to the unseen voice, "I've got to do *what?*" But there was no answer. Then the light faded away and everything went back as it was.

I often wondered over the years what that voice was and what it meant. But again, it wasn't until much later, after I got to know God and His familiar voice and light, that I realized the voice was also Him. By that later time, I understood exactly what He was talking about too; He was referring to answering the call He placed on my life and walking toward the destiny He told me He had for me after He personally came and pulled me out of hell.

It wasn't long after this that I got into a relationship with a beautiful woman named Nikki. I ended up moving into an apartment with her in Pittsburgh as a home base. Of course, we went out and partied a lot together, and Nikki often came with me to my local gigs. However, I was still gone from home without her a lot.

Touring is part of a musician's life, but it also became a good excuse to get away for a while when we started having contentions. It was a good escape, allowing things between us to simmer down. Ours was a relationship filled with partying, alcohol, drugs, and rock 'n' roll—and inevitable volatility. I became verbally abusive as well as controlling and would often fly off the handle over little things. Eventually our fighting became physical too. In my industry, there was no faithfulness—and there were always accusations, jealousy, and suspicions. I expected faithfulness from my woman, though that was not always the case with either of us. Then not long after our live-in relationship began, Nikki got pregnant with our first child.

We worked at the relationship the best we knew how, but we lived in an endless sick cycle of partying, suspicion, mistrust, fighting, making up, repeat. Of course, we were living the way of the world at the time; that was all we knew. Later, when our daughter Hannah was born, Nikki's need for me to stay closer to home became more of an issue—and it also became a hot point in our arguments. So I enrolled in a local computer management school to learn computer programming and started a part-time commercial house-painting business on the side. Tired of the arguments, I thought that would somehow give us more stability with me in a job closer to home.

The computer school gave me a great education and the work came easily to me, even though I was always high. Over time, though, the predictable routine of sitting at a computer for hours made me so bored out of my mind that I got restless. I began to step outside my classes to smoke a joint and try to get my mind off of it. Eventually, one of those times outside, I realized I was so entirely frustrated and feeling out of place that I knew this line of work wasn't for me. I dropped out of the school.

I knew I had learned enough to get a job as a programmer, and still trying to do what I thought was the right thing with my girlfriend and a child to consider, I found a job at a local microfilm company. Again, it wasn't long before the monotony, boredom, and feeling out of place had me miserable. I lasted only eight months before I quit.

Finally, I decided to give up trying to fit myself in a mold I knew I couldn't be happy in. I went back into full-time entertainment, trying my best to stay as close to home as possible. Nikki and I worked things out so I could be back by the early morning hours to sleep till noon, then watch Hannah when she got home from preschool. Later, when Nikki came home from her day job, she'd take over and I'd leave for my all-nighter.

As Hannah got older, there were times I had to take her with me to scheduled band practices or shows. She grew up crawling around on stages through the musicians' feet and equipment, becoming the darling of the stage crew. Friends would always help me out, even playing with her backstage when I had to go out to perform. But a couple of times, Hannah somehow slipped away from her babysitter on a mission looking for me, crawling right onto the stage in the middle of a show—but it was to cheers of endearment when she was found and whisked backstage again.

My relationship with Nikki went through many periods of good and bad, as well as on-again-off-again chapters, as we tried to make it work. During that time, our second child came along. I had this strange but sure "knowing" the very night he was conceived. Even unsaved and drugged out, a level of this gifting God had put in me was always working. I just *knew* that I had another child coming and that it would be a son.

I had just finished playing another late-night gig when I got the call that our son, Tee, was on the way. Thankfully, I was local so I could be there at the hospital with Nikki and see my second child born too. I have to say my kids are the best things that have ever happened to me, though regrettably my relationship with their mother eventually deteriorated beyond repair within about five years' time. Nikki was a great mother, but we were both living a life mostly for self, and a foundation like that doesn't lead to a healthy, lasting relationship. Knowing no other remedy, and to stop all the fighting and hurt we were causing each other, I determined it was best to leave the relationship for good. Eventually I moved out, this time for the last time.

5

HOLLYWOOD DREAMS

I will instruct you and teach you in the way you should go;
I will guide you with my eye.

— PSALM 32:8

Unsatisfied and searching once again for my place in life, I poured myself into my music. I moved to the West Coast to live in Hollywood, California, looking for new opportunities with my music and wanting to hook up with other musicians in the famous town of rock 'n' roll.

I played, partied, and hung out with musician friends in the area's busiest rock 'n' roll clubs. Rainbow Bar & Grill, Whisky a Go-Go, The Viper Room, the Roxy, the Coconut Teazer, Gazzarri's, and others were all on the two hottest blocks of the Hollywood strip, and these places were where most of who's who in rock 'n' roll congregated. Drugs, drinking, women, and business opportunities flowed nightly. I set up new bands and performed in the area clubs as well as in some away venues as I kept waiting for a bigger break. But I also drowned a lot of my frustrations and pain in new excesses of drug use and craziness.

I lived in the Echo Park area of Hollywood, and on Mondays we musicians would head to the "doctor's counters." These were little clinics in town where doctors would freely give prescription drugs to actors and rock stars. We'd hand them fifty bucks and they'd give a prescription for whatever we wanted, no questions asked. Most of us were getting perks, vikes, or some sort of cough medicine with heroin in it. One day when I went in to pick up a prescription, the doctor was shooting up heroin in one arm while writing out prescriptions with the other. After getting our prescriptions, we'd go hang out in Venice or Malibu Beach for the rest of the day.

In the middle of West Hollywood, most of the rockers congregated at Ralph's Market on Sunset Boulevard where we did our grocery shopping. In the afternoons, we'd run into each other there after getting up after our long night out. We knew who the starving musicians were because they were picking and eating their way through the produce aisles or stuffing lifted items under their shirts or into their pants. The Hollywood clubs didn't pay much, if at all, and most of them charged us to play their clubs and showcase our music.

While I'd been doing heroin daily since fourteen years old, I was now also doing a host of other drugs, as well as smoking and drinking. My habits ran me a steady average of about five hundred dollars a day. Living high was not just a necessity for me; it had become all I knew. It was my "normal," and I didn't know how to live any other way.

I did almost every drug out there, depending on what was popular at the time. Along with heroin, I used acid, peyote, pot, cocaine, meth, crack, PCP, reds, Quaaludes, Valium, Vicodin, hydrocodone, ecstasy, and any other club and prescription drugs I could get a hold of. I needed drugs to get up, and drugs and alcohol to try to go to sleep—an endless daily cycle. I took them every way possible, by shooting, toking, snorting, or eating them. I was averaging a daily base of ten to twenty bags of heroin and seven grams of cocaine, along with whatever else I could find.

Once in a while I went off on excess binges, shooting speedballs every couple of hours all day long. As soon as I could get up off the floor, I'd go for another one. This proved difficult at times because the speed had me shaking all over, and aiming for a vein and keeping the needle there was next to impossible. Missing the vein would occasionally produce a large, excruciatingly painful abscess in my skin. I'd sleep once every three to four days when on jags like this, and getting to sleep would require an extra-large dose of heroin, often while downing a fifth of whiskey to knock myself out. I abused my body terribly every day, though I just didn't care.

From time to time, the veins in my arms would collapse from shooting them up so much. The pain from this made it unbearable to even move my arm. When this happened, or when I'd get an abscess, I'd hit a point where I couldn't bear the pain anymore, but only as a last resort would I go to the emergency room. Once there, the hospital staff weren't at all kind. They looked down on me with utter disgust and judgment when they saw the obviously self-inflicted track marks, bruises, and scars on my arms and hands. I avoided the ER at all costs, but sometimes the raging agony was so bad that it outweighed the additional pain, dirty looks, and comments.

The quantities and types of drugs I was doing and mixing daily defied any reason for how a person could survive them at all. This alone was deemed a major miracle of God's protective covering on my life itself—every day. But on and on it went, day after day, year after year, decade after decade—drugs averaging five hundred dollars a day, to what ended up being thirty straight years of abuse. I was a walking death wish for a long time, though I never admitted it to myself. Strangely, all through those periods of my life, nothing seemed to be able to touch me or take me out, and I didn't know why. I functioned pretty well, and I came to believe with a false but very self-assured confidence that in some way I was "invincible" and nothing could take me out. I got away with so much, never getting in any real trouble even though many others did for much lesser offenses.

In this vocation, fans often idolize "stars" and we were treated with much favor. Even businesses, bankers, and cops would give indulgences not afforded to most. Endorsers offered free equipment and nice clothes for our bands, and we were often invited to free backstage events, parties, and VIP rooms. One of those invites was VIP access to a Victoria's Secret lingerie show. We were escorted right into the models' backstage dressing rooms where drinks and hors d'oeuvres were served while the models openly changed and were readied for their show.

There were always after-parties and get-togethers, with open orgies even breaking out. Some of my friends got involved in way-out kinky stuff, but that wasn't my thing. I'd always been a straight one-woman man with whatever woman I was with at the time. Of course, that didn't make me any better than anyone else; we were all living the way of the world, everyone to his or her own beliefs or excesses. When I look back on this, though, I find it interesting that there was always *something* inside me that drew the line at certain things.

We also had access to many beautiful women. We could pretty much pick and choose whom we wanted. Women, even married ones, would throw themselves at us. Friends and acquaintances were jealous, saying I dated some of the most beautiful women in the world. My confidence and cocky arrogance only grew with the recognition and favorable treatment. There were times when, after ending a wild show, I'd jump off the stage, confidently walk over and grab any beautiful woman I desired, and start kissing her. It didn't matter if she was with her boyfriend or husband. When the guy would protest, I'd just ask the woman, "Do you wanna leave with me?" Inevitably she would—even if the guy was her husband.

Despite my ruthless audacity, it really bothered me that none of the women were faithful. Ironically, that only added to the distrust that I had for most women. As well, there were a couple of times when I left out the back doors after a gig, only to be met by big, angry dudes—like two hundred and fifty to three hundred pounds plus—who were waiting there for me. They threatened to take my head off for something I said or did to them, a friend, or a woman during the night. Despite the starkly obvious odds, nothing ever came of these confrontations. After only a few words, the guys left me alone and I walked away unharmed. There never seemed to be a natural explanation for not getting what I deserved, but escapes like this were happening on almost a daily basis. But even though I acted invincible, inside I was extremely insecure.

I ended up living in Hollywood for a couple of years, though I took occasional short tours with my band and some trips to Pittsburgh to see my kids. Even so, nothing big was breaking for me and I reached a point where I needed to make more money. Eventually, I resorted to doing something I'd never done before: auditioning with a couple of big-name rock bands that were looking for a lead guitarist.

My first audition was for a group called Lost Boys. I got all prepped, found the address, and walked into a room with a long line of people waiting for their call into the audition. I stood at the end of the line with my guitar, but I wasn't used to this. I became more and more uncomfortable and then frustrated, wondering why I had actually come to this. I surveyed the scene around me and looked ahead through the long line. *Man,* I thought, *everyone here looks exactly the same!* In fact, every guy in line was wearing similar rocker clothes and had straight long hair combed perfectly down to his butt. Standing in that line really bugged me. I started feeling disgusted, finally seeing it all for what it was—and for how fake it looked. What I had become was staring me right in the face.

While I didn't want to stay in the room any longer, my pride wouldn't let me leave either. So, with ego intact, I made a go for the audition door. I walked past those waiting, right up to the door, and knocked impatiently. They opened the door, I said, "Hi, I'm Tim," and they let me in. I did my audition, got interviewed by some TV crew, and took off out of there.

Another audition call-in came days afterward, as I was just getting home from one of my Monday beach days. The phone was ringing when I stepped in the door, and I answered it. "This is Sharon," the caller stated.

"Sharon who?" I barked, not really in the mood to talk.

"Sharon Osbourne," she shot back. "I have an audition for you with Lita Ford at Mate Studios on Wednesday at noon. Go pick up the album and learn the songs. I'll see you there." And with that, she hung up without an answer from me.

I didn't know how to copy others' music; I'd never done it before. All I ever played were my own songs, and I'd always run my own bands. I couldn't stand playing other people's music. To me as an artist, that was like being fake, and I didn't see the purpose in it. It also felt like I was selling my soul to play other people's dreams. But I was getting short on money, and my daily needs required cash. I decided I had to give it another try.

So there I was, getting ready for another audition I thought I needed—in two days. I ended up asking for assistance from Jo Satriani, a friend who was a well-known rock guitar player in town. I knew he could quickly write out the chords and the lead parts they'd want to hear from me. He had it done by Tuesday afternoon, I practiced, and on Wednesday I pulled up to the audition building, ready.

The audition took place in a big arena room complete with stage lights, and there were already semi-trucks full of equipment parked outside for the pending tour. My roadie friends had helped set me up beforehand, and I walked into the audition ready, dressed out, and full of confident, cocky attitude. I went down toward the stage and threw my long black leather coat off onto the floor, then reached out to shake Sharon's hand and introduce myself. Sharon was a manager for a lot of artists and bands, including her husband, Ozzy Osbourne. I thought if anything, she might be able to hook me up elsewhere if this band wasn't a good fit for my style.

Then Lita Ford called from the stage, "Hey, you wanna jam?"

Sharon sat down in the front row to observe along with two of her little girls. Lita and I jammed wildly for ten minutes, which was my thing, and it was intense. She was a great guitar player, and she actually made me work to try to shine past her. But our music collided a bit because I was too hard rock/metal for what she was playing. She was more of a structured player.

We then moved on to playing her band's songs. That went smoothly, and I had a pretty decent audition. Most of all, I had a blast playing with Lita. The band put me in their top five for their lead but warned me that they were close to going back on tour. That meant I might have a big decision to make—quickly.

I left with a stand-by for a final callback pending at any time and a notice that if I was picked, I'd better be ready to hit the road with them right away. But as I drove home, discomfort crept in on me again. It got so strong I could hardly stand it, and I knew I needed to pinpoint what was eating at me. There wasn't really anything wrong. In fact, things looked like they were going fairly well. I considered the possibility of endless long-haul touring again, where my life was heading, what I was really doing in Hollywood, and the possibility of spending the next year or so playing somebody else's songs and dream. I had thought it was what I needed—what I wanted—but now I wasn't so sure.

As I look back on those days, I now know that discomfort feeling was God again tapping me on the shoulder, even before I knew Him. At that point, though I didn't understand it, I had learned to pay attention to it. In addition, I was also feeling uneasiness about where I was living, wondering what I was *really* after in Hollywood. The pretense and fakeness bothered me. It seemed I couldn't trust anybody at their word. My eyes were being opened to see what my life had become and what I'd been doing with it. The more I thought about it, the more I realized that I didn't want to head in that direction.

Although I had just paid my next month's rent for my Echo

Park house, I decided then and there that I was done. I packed my things, got in my car, and left. Without enough money to even make it to the East Coast, I got on the road and started driving in that direction. I made it as far as Las Vegas, Nevada, with only twenty bucks left in my pocket. I pulled into a casino, went in, and put my twenty bucks on the twenty on the wheel. Amazingly, it hit and I got four hundred dollars in that one shot. Now I had enough money to make it back East.

Years later, I *knew* this also was God's work. He agreed with that move and supplied the means for me to leave. If I'd stayed in Hollywood or on another track in my career, my life would have taken a much different and longer road to get me where He wanted me.

6

REBELLION AND ANARCHY

Do you not know that those who run in a race all run,
but one receives the prize?
Run in such a way that you may obtain it.
— 1 CORINTHIANS 9:24

D ays later, I arrived in Pittsburgh and pulled up to a gas station
with my tank pegged on empty and not a dollar left. As I was
walking around my car at the pump, wondering what I was going
to do next, I noticed an old painter friend standing by his car on
the side of the station. He looked over, recognized me, and came
over to say hello and see what was up. We began to talk, and he
soon realized my dilemma, though I didn't say a word about it.
He not only offered to supply me with some gas but also asked if
I needed a place to stay. Of course I took him up on it since I had
no idea where I was going to go stay at the time either.

That stay turned into an equal partnership in the painting business again. Knowing the trade well, good money began coming in
for both of us. Soon I was able to rent a house on my own. After
several months in business, though, I realized I was the one doing
all the work while my partner, also a drug addict, stayed home too
high to be able to get up. I couldn't help him (I was in the same
place myself), but I was at least functioning and able to work. So I
politely exited the partnership and went out on my own.

In no time, I built my business up, with plenty of big commercial and residential jobs coming my way. I even had to hire crews to work with me. It was easy to find workers because I hired mostly other drug addicts or alcoholics who were on downtime from the construction business. I knew how to supervise them well and paid cash at the end of each day. I kept at this for another three years, and with steady relief crews it allowed me to play gigs most nights.

With the money I was making, I bought a new house on Chapel Street in Pittsburgh and started accumulating other toys too: sport cars, boats, expensive clothes and jewelry, and even a limo I bought for a side business. But none of it really made me happy. A great emptiness and restlessness stirred inside me, and I wanted something more.

I had once toured and played in London, England, which I'd loved, so went to live there for a while. I rented a small upstairs loft in West London, right on the notorious Kings Road (the birthplace of the British punk rock movement). I played and hung out with friends and musicians who were in the underground bands there, steeped in the popular counterculture movement of the time. I was looking again for new connections and opportunities in music, but I mostly loved just hanging out with the culture of rebellion. Those days fueled my outrageousness even further.

In my younger years I'd spent time with hippies, shunning the more hardcore activist groups, but now I buckled, finally gravitating toward those who acted out a lot of hate and mayhem—even hate against God.

The underground music cultures associated themselves with rebellious causes, loosely or otherwise. I naturally gravitated to hanging out with some of the most hard-core friends and groups around, even neo-Nazi types. I was naturally drawn to it because I identified with the hate, though it was senselessly targeted at many things. I even had a swastika tattooed on my back (though many years later I had it changed to a cross with a heart in it). The hate and mayhem poured out in the music I wrote, and I became very outspoken about it.

Dark, rebellious music made the crowds go wild. The movement had a mind-set all about independence, rebellion, anticonformity, and anarchy, and it always manifested at different levels with different people. It carried an in-your-face attitude and provided an outlet to make outrageous shock statements that would force people to have to react in one way or another.

I wrote an anarchy-themed song that we played nightly. Part of the song's act was to fire up a chainsaw and violently cut off the head of a mannequin dressed up to look like a senator in a suit and tie. The crowds *loved* this stuff. Since we played the act nearly every night, before long we ran out of our supply of cheap mannequins. The band and I found a specialty supply store that sold them and told the owner we were sent from the local fire department to pick up dummies to be used for fire department trainings. With that, they began giving us the dummies for free.

One night during that song, one of my band members was really high and nearly killed me. Right after I jumped off the stage into the crowd to do my "wild thing" on my guitar, he jumped off holding the dressed up mannequin and fired-up chainsaw. He accidently dropped the dummy into the frenzied crowd of people, and as he was feeling around for it, he grabbed me by mistake and started aiming that roaring chainsaw right at my neck. I put my hands up, trying to duck away from him, yelling as loud as I could above the crowd's roar, "No, no, no! It's me!" But it was only at the last moment that he recognized that. Yeah, we used real chainsaws back in those days. It was a close call.

Most of us were high when we performed, and I was so often drugged out of my mind that I don't remember most of the things I did. I was driven by the wildness and mayhem. Every night was just utter out-of-control madness into the early morning hours with each night's escapades designed to top the others, and I was most always the ringleader. The demonic realm I'd ignorantly given myself over to incited me into utter craziness and perpetual self-destruction, but I didn't understand that stuff was real and that I'd given it full right to control my life. I didn't believe in the Devil, hell, or anything but myself—and I certainly didn't believe anyone or anything else could ever have control over me.

Because of the all the darkness I walked in, the rebellion, senseless hate, and rage became deep-seated in me. Abuse of myself turned into abuse of others because it made me feel like I had more control, but really, I was totally out of control and always hanging with others of the same mind-set. My extreme lifestyle fueled senseless fires raging inside me. I'd scream at or curse out anyone I didn't like. At times I'd push or punch people walking by on the sidewalks—for no real reason. It might have been the way they were dressed or looked. I'd say whatever was on my mind to anyone, just to ridicule, shock, or provoke them. But no one ever retaliated.

Sometimes before going into a gig, I'd pick up whatever I could find in the parking lot—a big club, metal rod, or hammer—and start smashing car windows, slashing tires, or lighting cars on fire. These were cars of the patrons or friends I was going in to play for or later party with. To me it was just having some fun and getting ramped up for my show. I became pretty abusive with my band mates at times too, yelling at them when things didn't go as I thought they should. I'd even throw empty beer bottles at other bands in nightclubs, verbally shouting them down if I thought they didn't sound good. It didn't take much to set me off.

Unhindered egotism mixed with all the drugs made me difficult to live with too, and that meant many women came and went in my life. A lot of them were first attracted not to me but to my money or what I represented as a rock musician. I had high expectations of my bands and high expectations of the women in my life—and I really didn't trust women. Unfaithfulness was rampant in the industry and though I didn't always practice faithfulness, I expected it from my woman—and didn't always get it. That resulted in intense jealousy and more need to control. I was always suspicious and often accusing. If something didn't go perfectly right in my eyes, even if it was something small, I first took it out on the easiest target—a woman.

I would impulsively smack a woman in the face, sometimes blackening her eyes or bloodying her nose, or throw her down or across tables—or just out. Punching or pushing your woman when you felt she was "getting out of hand" was something bystanders in bars would gather around and cheer on at that time, and that came from both men *and* women. I couldn't get off the perpetual abuse cycle. My woman and I would start off in the honeymoon period, then abuse would begin, I'd apologize profusely, we'd make up, and she'd come back. Over and over again, week after week, month after month, year after year. Some women rightly left. The smart ones did. But the women still kept coming my way, night after night.

Tim's Note on Abuse

I don't condone abusive behavior at all, and only an act of God was able to deliver me from this. It was another of His great miracles in my life. God later showed me I had terrible hate and abuse demons (among others) influencing and controlling me. When God came into my life, He took them away in an instant, even though I never asked Him to.

Inability to control or understand why you feel compulsions to have such thoughts or do such acts is a key marker of a spiritually sourced (demonic) influence. There are a few different ways people can open themselves up for this to enter their life, and it can happen knowingly or ignorantly.

Only God has the authority and power over the very real demonic realm and can truly deliver people from oppressions, influence, torment, control, and destruction. When outside a saving relationship with God, people remain in the spiritual "kingdom of darkness" and by automatic rights they belong to the enemy of the human soul and of God, whether we believe it or not. This gives the spiritual Enemy (Satan) full rights to a person and allows him to enter and wreak havoc in that person's life.

The Enemy's nature and acts are always to deceive, oppress, torment, steal, lie, abuse, and even kill. He hates God, and he hates us with a passion because we were made by Him and in His image as a special creation to lavish His great mercy, grace, and love upon. As well, we're a potential great threat to him and his dark kingdom if we learn the real truth of our great identity, freedom in God, and given authority over him.

Abuse, just like any other continuous sin, will increase over time and can end in death. Women caught in this cycle need to get help or get out, but they too are caught in a dark grip that only increases in dangerousness over time.

Only the power of God can truly free people from abuse. What I know without a doubt is that it's not only demonically sourced, but it's also foundationally based in unbelief of who God says we are. This results in self-identity, self-esteem, and self-respect problems—on both sides. Outside God, we're trapped by the Enemy and his deceptive lies about who we are. God made us and knows us, and has already given us our greatest and true identity, but we must know it, believe it, step into it, and walk in it.

As one given a strong seer gifting whereby God shares with me through His eyes, showing me what's going on in the spiritual realm, I often see these horrific evil spirits oppressively attached to certain individuals' lives, as they were to mine. These demonic entities remain mostly hidden to the natural eye, though anyone can see and experience the manifestations of what evil and havoc they bring.

If people saw and knew the truth of this evil, they would do everything they could to find the freedom from it. As one who's been there, I know that freedom is found only in God through Jesus Christ, His Son. When we step into Him and His kingdom of light through belief and trust in Him, and know and believe the great identities He says we already have, God's amazing, powerful Spirit—His light living in us—then chases the darkness away.

7

JUST LIVIN' THE LIFE

Don't you know who I am?
– Tim Ehmann

One night I was out with one of my band mates, in his back seat as he drove me home after some late hours partying at a nightclub. Both of us were quite high and drunk, and feeling especially wild and crazy. As we neared one of Pittsburgh's many long mountain tunnels, he decided to step hard on the gas and race through the empty tunnel reaching a speed of one hundred and fifty miles an hour. I was so high out of my mind that I started trying to kick out his car's back window with my heavy boots. When I couldn't break the window, I turned around and slapped my hands over his eyes, trying to blindfold him. He tightened his grip on the wheel, somehow keeping the car driving straight as we both screamed and he struggled to get free. When I saw that wasn't working, I grabbed the steering wheel, trying to put the car into the tunnel wall. I couldn't, because I couldn't overtake his firm grip on the wheel.

I couldn't understand why I felt driven to do things like this, but they were all part of the daily unadmitted death wish that was my life. But time after time, almost predictively, it just wouldn't succeed—no matter what I did. I totaled twelve different sport cars I owned, one after the other. Each time, I was alone and driving well over one hundred miles an hour. In fact, I plowed one

58

of my nicest cars straight into a concrete bridge base. Others I wrapped around poles, rolled multiple times, or spun out before crashing. I even went off a bridge once. Only a couple of times did I hit other cars. Astonishingly, I was never hurt beyond scratches or bruises, nor was anyone else hurt. At the time, I could afford to just go buy a new car, but inevitably that would happen again and again—and for some unknown reason, I'd always walk away.

One night, after I played a gig in a Pittsburgh nightclub called the Graffiti, a few friends and I continued our usual partying by heading to a punk club called the Electric Banana. I was already high, and I finished another fifth of Jack Daniel's there. When I left, I ran a red light that I didn't seem to notice, and T-boned the side of a police cruiser going through the middle of the intersection. The two officers came out of their car shook up and angry but unharmed.

As they took a first look at the damage, I opened my car door and came out stumbling to my feet, still dressed in my extravagant glam-rock stage clothes with messed-up long hair, running face foundation, wild-colored eye shadow, and fading red lipstick. The cops took one look at me and burst out laughing. I tried to walk, tripping and weaving toward the front of my car, while they bent over howling with so much laughter that they could barely speak. When I finally fumbled my way to the front of my car, I puked right onto the back of their cruiser.

The scene was obviously pretty bizarre, but the cops couldn't get a word in because they were laughing so hard. No doubt, I was their best entertainment of the night. Unbelievably, they ended up simply asking if I had insurance and then telling me to go park it on the curb and sleep it off. Unreal. I pulled over to the side of the street, waited till they left, and then drove home in my still-running car with the smashed-up front end.

Bar hopping after gigs was a steady activity then, and I was always looking for trouble to stir up. The night I made a stopover at a local hard-core biker bar was no exception. Again, I was still dressed in the night's stage clothes with sweat-streaked, messed-up wild makeup and hair. I was in a cocky mood and didn't really like bikers; I just stopped there to harass them. Before heading inside, I walked to the back of the bar where all the bikes were neatly parked in rows and knocked them all down. They fell like falling dominoes.

When I went inside where the bikers were drinking and playing pool, I started to taunt them. I hurled verbal insults at them, so high and out of it that I didn't care what they might do to me. Picking out one huge tattooed, bald-headed biker sitting on a stool at the bar, I walked over and put my cigarette butt out right on his shiny head. When he stood up, he looked about six feet six and was as wide as a refrigerator. I cockily walked right past him into the bar's john, pulled out the red stage lipstick I still had in my pocket, and proceeded to write crude insults about them on the bathroom mirror.

Just then, about thirty enraged bikers came into the john, trapping and surrounding me inside. Their muscles rippled and the veins popped out of their reddened faces as they told me how many ways they were going to kill me. I laughed out loud, grabbed one of them by the collar, put my face right into his, and shouted, "Don't you know who I am?"

They came in for the kill.

Somehow, despite the obvious impossibility, I walked right through the furious group and out the door of the bar. It was like they didn't even see me! I always, for some reason entirely unknown to me at the time, walked away untouched. Things like this were just not natural by any means; they were surreal—even freaky.

There was another night when I was out on the town with my band's singer. After a couple of hours in a bar, a group of women came over wanting to hang out with us. The guys they'd come in with weren't happy about it and began to taunt my band mate for a fight. When he got up, I didn't notice that they followed him out into the back parking lot. There they got baseball bats from somewhere and started swinging at him.

When I finally went to look for him, I found him outside the back door, surrounded by the five angry men trying to teach him a lesson. He had armed himself with the only thing he could find—a big tree branch—and he was swinging it wildly, trying to hold them at bay. The scene was actually quite comical, because with every swing he took at them, another piece of his branch broke off, until he was fending off the well-armed mob with a pitiful little stick.

Standing there, I stuck my hand inside my long black leather duster coat and shouted that I was going to shoot every last one of them if they didn't get out of there. They looked back with sudden surprise, unaware that I had come out behind them, then their surprise turned to a terrified look in their eyes, and they ran.

However, things like this only proved to embolden me all the more, and I was not through with my entertainment for the night. My friend and I ducked into his Charger, and with me driving we followed them down the street. We found them rummaging through their cars and assumed they might have gone to get real guns and planned on coming back for more. Circling the streets, I crazily mocked them through the rolled-down windows every time we passed. Soon they went into another bar up the street.

Noticing an empty parking space right in front of one of their cars (a nice silver Ferrari), I pulled into it. I shifted hard into reverse and floored it, backing up and over the front of his low-slung car, and then repeated that four or five times. The men saw the whole thing from the bar's window— including my getting so high up over the Ferrari that I smashed the hood and windshield—but I think they were too shocked and scared to come out.

When I drove off, I went to pick up my own car to head home. Still extremely high, I entered the freeway going the wrong direction. The cars with their lights in my face were swerving every direction to get out of my way. I got off at the next exit (entrance) and pulled into a boarded-up abandoned gas station, not seeing the old exposed pipes sticking up where the pumps had once been. I ran right over them, taking out the underneath part of my car's transmission. As I wandered around by my car, looking up at the dark starry night sky and trying to figure out what to do next, a cop car drove up with its headlights on me.

Soon the officers were questioning me about the report they got of "some crazy guy going the wrong way on the freeway." I never copped to any of it. They couldn't help but notice my dilemma, though, not to mention how drunk and high I obviously was. Even then, they simply offered to give me a ride home. Not long afterward, I was thanking those nice cops for their kind lift as they delivered me safely to my home's curb.

Every night of my life things like this happened—and I always got off. I'm glad I never had to fight. I never worked out and was too scrawny from all the drugs. Though I never had to fight, there always seemed to be this constant, unexplainable favor and protection around me, no matter what stupid stuff I did.

• • •

The years 1981 to 1985 were probably my best music years back then. I found my niche playing my own style of alternative hard rock 'n' roll, and I was always on the road touring. My music was dark and rebellious, and songs would just pour out of me. Sometimes I'd write ten new songs a day, all about what I had to say at the time. Sometimes people would approach me after my shows and tell me I was a just a big promoter of sin. I was, but they seemed to like it. They kept coming back again and again.

I started and played in numerous bands over thirty-five years in the industry. I once put together a new band that I named City Boy. We practiced together for only a week before I booked our first gig at a nightclub. When we got there, we were shocked because the place was packed out, with lines down the sidewalk. We were still an unknown band, and it was our very first night out. What I didn't know was there was a New York band that went by the same name and was more established; that's who the people thought they were coming out to see. When I realized that, I quickly changed our band name to City Child. Our first gig helped get that band off to a great start, though, and our success continued for a long time.

I had another band called Ezbat (named for a witch holiday). We played large outdoor glitter music concerts for a year, wearing silver astronaut-style outfits, wild makeup, and knee-high six-inch-platform boots, and performing pretty dramatic shows. I had an excellent keyboard player, and Marshall was delivering free equipment for this basically unknown band at the time, and we had favor all around. Even so, we had a lot of in-band fighting going on. My drummer had a big head, and we also had problems with the bass player. None of us were in it for the money in this one; instead it was all about seeking fame.

One night I agreed we would do a private house party as a favor to my drummer. That night I broke three strings being wild on the guitar (not like that was something new), but then my drummer made some smart remark in the middle of a song—about my guitar sounding bad—and I went ballistic on him. Egos were high in everybody, and that night was the end of that band.

It didn't bother me that much though. I'd just run another newspaper ad for musicians, have my own auditions, and start up a new band. I'd know within a month if a band was going to get off the ground. One week's practice of about eight songs a set with professional musicians was all I needed to get started to play two sets a night. Then I'd make bookings to play and find back-up bands for us. I'd look for bands with established names and would place them as our opening act, knowing they would draw crowds and give us a good start.

In 1994, I decided to open my own nightclub in the Duquesne area of Pittsburgh. I was soon booking over twenty-one bands throughout seven nights a week. All the bands were original song artists, which was where my heart was really at. Pittsburgh didn't have a place that offered showcasing of new original artists and bands, and I believed it needed one. I knew I had a good niche. I also wanted to encourage other artists and bands by giving them a place to help them get off the ground.

I ran that club for about two years, and it was pretty successful and always busy. But the club hours were long and wore on me, and over time I burned out. Really, though, I couldn't handle it anymore because my drug problem had swung to new heights and I was too strung out all the time to keep up. Eventually, I put the business up for sale and got a great deal for it. I took some of the money from that sale and bought a second, much bigger house in Pittsburgh.

The Lovelace Street house was a large two-story with five bedrooms, seven fireplaces, and a large yard, and it needed a little work on it. Not long after I settled in, I decided to start my side painting business again, but this time I set it up differently. I hired bigger crews so I didn't have to work much. All I had to handle was bidding the jobs. This allowed me to stay home most of the time, so I could get high with enough money coming in to keep up with my expensive daily needs.

The Lovelace Street house needed some upgrading, though, and I had some of the guys on my crew help me totally refurbish it. I had the wood floors, stairs, and railings sanded down, stained, and lacquered like new. Then we painted the interior walls and ceilings with bright white paint and I furnished the house with beautiful antique furniture. With the yard fixed up as well, the place looked classy and the property value increased.

Even so, my life was still increasingly falling apart.

8

ADDICTION 24/7

Give it all up—and die!
(NEVER YOUR FATHER GOD'S VOICE)

Most of the money I brought in now paid for drugs. I got so strung out that I couldn't play gigs anymore, though I did try to get into the studios to record. But when staff saw me, they balked and turned me away. I was way too high.

I spiraled deeper into discouragement, frustration, and hopelessness. I even started hearing voices in my head telling me I was "nothing" and "worthless" and that my music career would never amount to anything, so I might as well "give it all up and die." But then at other times I'd hear another voice saying just the opposite. That voice would inspire me, saying I had a great gifting and plenty of experience, and that I was still going make it big. Even so, I plunged deeper into confusion and despair. Of course, the myriad of drugs and the alcohol didn't help.

Within a couple of years, I couldn't run the painting business at all. On a whim of the moment, I agreed to sell my Chapel Street house, which I was renting out, for a mere twelve thousand dollars to the neighbor next door. I was simply desperate for drug money. The house had nearly an acre of property and was worth far more than that, but he couldn't pass up such a great deal. He bought the house and razed it so he could plant a big garden.

Then that money ran out pretty quickly too, and soon I was

down to pawning anything I could for much less than its worth: the cars, boats, jewelry, and even the limo that now sat mostly forgotten. As my drug needs raged on, eventually I was down to pawning my most precious possessions: my music equipment, amps, and then, inevitably, my beloved guitars. I owned twelve really nice guitars, some electric and others acoustic. Each one had its own unique sound, and some carried precious history and memories. Many I sold outright, but my last, best, and favorite guitars and amps I rotated in and out of the pawn shops for as long as I could.

The pawn brokers were like loan sharks. They charged a 20 to 25 percent loan rate on top of whatever amount they'd loan me for an item. Then they'd hold the item for me for a few months. If I didn't pick up the item with the amount they loaned me plus their extra interest percentage within the specified time, I lost it. Then, of course, they sold the item for much more.

This alone became a lot of work in my condition, and all the pawn dealing took a toll on me. I could get only a one-hundred-to two-hundred-dollar loan for a nice Les Paul guitar. I ended up losing treasured five-thousand-dollar guitars for two hundred bucks, just for a fix. In fact, most of my guitars ended up lost to pawn shops. In the end, I had just my favorite, a Dean V-body electric guitar that toured everywhere with me. (That's only because my sister, Maryanne, found out about it and rescued it for me, paying off the fifty dollars due on it at the last moment. She kept the guitar and gave it back to me much later, for which I'm forever grateful to her.)

At the pawnshops, the staff knew what was up. They noticed that my musician friends, also junkies down to doing the pawn routine, were dying. When I went in, they would say things to me about it.

I had one old musician friend named Paul, and at one time we were considering a music project together. He was a rock star who played with a couple of notable bands in Los Angeles and London but eventually became too strung out to reliably work. A few years later, he overdosed on heroin or coke and died. (I'd been the one who'd taught him how to shoot drugs four to five years earlier at his insistence; he never shot drugs before then.)

My friend Sam, a drummer, also overdosed and died. Next was my friend, Willy, a singer who used to sing in the Nashville bands. I first met him around 1982 when I was running auditions for new musicians for City Child. He showed up to the audition with a guitar case filled with crank (speed), dropped the case down on the floor, opened it, and said, "Wanna do some?" I hired him on the spot—then didn't sleep for thirty days. He died in London after finishing a drug deal. When he turned to walk back across the street, he was hit by a car.

Another friend, "Bummer," a drummer in a Pittsburgh band, pulled out of a gas station one night in his little Chevette, high on heroin. As he entered the highway, he was hit head-on by an eighteen-wheeler going full highway speed. He never saw it coming. I was supposed to be with him that night, but at the last minute I chose to stay at the house where I was partying instead. When I received the phone call from one of the roadies telling me that he had just been killed, I laughed and hung up on him. I thought he was playing a sick joke on me. But the next morning I received another call confirming it. I was in total denial and couldn't believe it.

During those years, I never thought about death. I certainly didn't believe it pertained to me, although everything I did was right on the edge of it. Bummer's was the first funeral I ever attended in my life. When I saw him there in that casket, it hit me like a ton of bricks. I cried so uncontrollably that friends had to take me out of there. They tried everything they could to calm me down and comfort me, so they took me to a bar to get high and drunk. It was the only thing they knew to do for me.

Over a decade, I lost many of my other close friends in the music business. One by one they died, even many of the friends I'd known in Hollywood and London. All were untimely deaths: drug overdoses, accidents, AIDS, and the like. Soon I realized that I was one of the few who were left—and I was only forty-four at the time.

For a while, I had a girlfriend living with me in my Lovelace Street house. She was a junkie too, my first girlfriend who was deeply into drugs. Of course, it was a predictably tumultuous relationship. Once, during an argument while driving home from a bar, she wouldn't stop trying to start an argument with me. I wasn't in the mood to argue and kept asking her to stop, but she was high too and wouldn't relent. As I drove my little sports car sixty miles an hour down a highway, I hit a point where I couldn't take it anymore. I reached across her lap, flipped open her door, and shoved her out on the highway. I saw her rolling down the side of the road in my rear-view mirror. Later, after I came down and realized what I'd done, I was so relieved that she was all right. Incredibly, she had nothing more than a few minor bruises and scratches—but she came right back to me.

Every day was rife with out-of-control craziness like this in one-way or another. One morning I woke up to her straddled on top of me with a gun pointed at my face. She needed heroin and demanded I get up and get some for her. I didn't want to, so she fired a couple of shots into the bed right next to me. They were very near misses, only by a few inches. I grabbed a hold of her and the gun and we wrestled over it on the bed. Windows were shot out as I tried to get it away from her, but this was nothing new. I ended up beating the heck out of her after I chased her out into the yard. She had such a grip on the gun that I had to knock her unconscious to pull it from her hands. Then I had to drag her, still passed out, into the house. After that, I left to get the heroin.

I threw her out not long after this. She was doing way too much heroin and crack anyway, and I had a hard-enough time supporting my own habit. So I gave up on live-in girlfriends for a while. About five years later, she also died, although it was from cancer (she died still a heroin addict).

By this time I was in total isolation, a recluse in my own home except for when I needed to get my daily cop. The people in my life were only there for selfish reasons, so I could "borrow" money or drugs from them. I learned how to manipulate money or drugs out of people in a friendly way. Old friends and family quickly tired of me showing up just to ask to borrow money. I had burned them all out. I also wasn't hanging out or partying with anyone anymore, and I never attended friend or family get-togethers. With my business ended in '98, my addiction was all I lived for.

There was a period when I regularly went to my parents' house, asking Mom for money and giving various stories for why I needed it. One time I went to her door with the same story every day. I told her I needed the money for a broken alternator on my car and requested "a little help to get it fixed" so I could get to work. I was so out of it that I didn't know I was using the same story for thirty days straight. She never said anything to me at the time. She just gave me the money.

Later, Dad would answer the door when I showed up two to three times a week. He was on a fixed income from retirement from the post office, but he kept giving me money. In this desperate stage of my addiction, I think they feared I would do something *really* stupid, like get shot or something. Ironically, I believe they thought it better just to give it to me, rather than see me dead.

Both my parents, strong believers in God, were really praying for me. They knew about my drug problem and had some serious talks about it with me over the years. They even gave me money for programs to try to get off heroin. One clinic in Pittsburgh offered a new drug called Suboxone, a lozenge used every couple of hours and then decreased in dosage over a month to assist in detox. I tried it, but by week three or four, I still craved the heroin.

Twice, for about a year each time, I tried methadone to get off heroin. I would go to the clinic on Mondays to pay the one hundred dollars for a week's supply. Then I'd go in daily and get in line for the prescribed dosage of pills that were mixed with some kind of juice. The methadone helped cure the large daily heroin cost, but it didn't change my addiction desire. While I got my heroin-type needs down to only one hundred dollars a week, this allowed me to use any other money I had to go buy crack.

Eventually, I started asking for my weekly doses and telling them I didn't have the money to pay them anymore. I hoped they'd still give it to me as a "charity case," but they caught on that I was doing other drugs. I looked so bad that it was obvious. One day, they flat out told me they couldn't help me anymore. I was smoking ten grams of crack per day and looked awful. My bones were visible, my eyes were yellow, and my skin had turned a yellow-gray. There were black and blue-green bruises up and down my arms and at times festering abscesses from shooting up with dull needles.

I shook for thirty days straight from withdrawal from the doctor's methadone "solution," much longer than with heroin, which makes you shake for four to seven days at the most. I was often filthy because all the utilities at my Lovelace Street house had been long shut off due to nonpayment. It was during this time that I showed up for one of my regular visits to my parents' house, thin, yellow-gray, and really dirty. In addition, I hadn't shaved for days and had just come down off a full week of smoking crack and not eating or sleeping.

When Mom answered the door, she took one look at me and shuddered, jumping back with a look of horror on her face. She screamed at me, "Don't you ever come over to the house looking like that again!" and the frightened, angry tone of her voice and the expression on her face was something I'll never forget. I really scared her. Through all I put her and Dad through, Mom talked like this to me only once though.

I didn't stay away from my parents' house until one day Dad refused to answer the door anymore. It was because the last time I went there, I found nobody home and let myself in.

I noticed Dad's checkbook on the kitchen table, and I reasoned he was eventually going to give me money anyway, so I took a blank check. Later that day, Carl, my brother-in-law who was a sergeant for the Pittsburgh Police Department, came banging on my door at the urging of my sister, who tried everything to help me. When I opened the door, he said, "Either kill yourself or get help! But don't you ever go to your dad's house again or I'll have you arrested!" Then he further threatened to send his SWAT team right into my house.

Carl also asked to come into the house even though I didn't want him to. He stepped right in past me and stood there looking around with a look of shock on his face. Taking a walk through the house stunned him as he saw the broken windows with glass still on the floor, swastikas and foul graffiti written on the walls, and trash and dirt strewn everywhere. When he continued up the stairs, he found burnt bedrooms with blackened floors, walls, or ceilings.

One room was entirely blackened and still had a burnt bed in it. That happened on a terribly cold night when the wind chill hit twenty below zero. With no heat in the house, that bitter winter cold could make anyone despair—even of life. But the fact was, I had hit a point where I no longer cared about anything anymore—especially if I died. In a desperate attempt to get some warmth, I took a lighter to the foot-end of the blankets covering me on the bed. The last things I remember seeing were the blankets slowly catching fire, then the flames licking all the way up to the ceiling. Then I passed out.

When I next woke up, it was morning. I was choking and could barely breathe because the bedroom door had been closed and the fire had spread through the bedroom, leaving it filled with thick smoke. The floor, walls, and ceiling were blackened with thick soot, and charred finish and paint curls hung off the walls and ceiling. All the curtains were burned away, and the windows were entirely blackened too—all except for a sliver of daylight coming through one of them. That was the only way I knew it was daytime.

I rolled myself off the bed onto the floor, choking for air, and crawled to the bedroom door. When I finally got it opened, I managed to get a few feet into the hallway and collapsed. I just lay there trying to gulp in fresh air between coughing fits. The thick soot was up my nose, in my mouth, down my throat, in my eyes, ears, teeth—everywhere. When I looked down at myself, I was completely black from head to toe. I couldn't help but wonder how neither I nor my clothes had been burned.

I lay on the floor as I pondered once again the impossibilities of what I had survived. *This was a close one!* I thought. I couldn't believe how I could still be alive. Eventually, I pulled myself together, got up off the floor, and went back to take a look at the charred bedroom with smoke still wafting off the walls. Only ashes remained of the bed covers, and the bed was entirely blackened—all except for where my body had lain, which was white.

I finally decided to sit outside on the porch so I could breathe in the fresh morning air. I tried to wipe the soot out of my eyes and nose and off my face, but my hands were just as blackened. I had no water to get cleaned up with, or even a mirror to try. They had been broken at one time or another while I was alone, high, and in a drug rage. Even so, it wasn't long before my thoughts turned to figuring out that day's drug buy; that was really the only reason I ever stepped outside my house anymore. Unable to get cleaned up, I ended up going out just as I was. The few people I saw that day just handed me what I needed and never said a word.

After that, I moved to the spare bedrooms to sleep, though some of them also had burned areas in them too from one time or another. My once lovely Lovelace Street house had come to reflect my own condition— a completely ravaged crack house, a house of death. I had resorted to throwing my beautiful area rugs into fires to keep warm—and then even my prized antique furniture. After they were gone, I began pulling up big strips of the carpeting in the house to burn. The place was dark and dirty, and the yard was overgrown, making it look deserted, abandoned, and forgotten.

One night, while sitting on the floor in front of a fire I got roaring in the living room fireplace, I went and got my last unopened box of one hundred bullets and threw it into the fire. I sat down on the floor cross-legged, just enjoying the warmth with my eyes closed. Soon the bullets ignited one by one, exploding and flying everywhere. I sat there calmly, unmoved and not caring at all if I died. I could feel the bullets shooting past by my head, ripping through my hair, and grazing my legs and arms. Oddly, none of them hit me.

I can't imagine what the neighbors thought. They watched my house go downhill. I'm sure they could see the bright glow coming from upstairs windows, as well as hear the gunshots, screams, and beatings in the yard. And then they'd see me—the dirty skeleton of a man—going outside only to head out for my daily cop.

One day when I happened to be in the yard, one of the neighbors came over wanting to chat. He told me that he and his wife had noticed a bullet hole through one of their windows and he was wondering about it, asking if I'd seen anything going on in the neighborhood. Thankfully, no one was hurt.

By this time, the only people I saw were whomever I got money from, the drug dealer for crack and heroin, and the lady who sold cigarettes and lighters. Every day I'd go to her little corner store to buy cigarettes and three to six lighters (it took a lot of lighters to smoke crack because they had to be altered so they lit like a torch). She had to know why I was there each day, especially with how thin and dirty I looked.

Every now and then, I'd find a home-cooked meal left on my doorstep by the kind neighbors next door. Occasionally, they would come over just to say hello, see if I was all right, and give me a warm meal. They even invited me over once in a while to shower at their house. A couple of times, when winter temperatures hit single digits or below, they asked if I wanted to stay the night in their home, though I politely declined. Their caring concern, love, and mercy on me without judgment really touched me.

Then my precious sister, Maryanne, began to come over every Friday. She'd pull up in her car and honk the horn, urging me to come out with her for dinner somewhere. She'd also shove a bag or two of non-perishable groceries into my arms, begging me to eat. Maryanne had a big, compassionate heart, and she kept urging me to care about my life and get into a rehab. She tried to take care of me the best way she knew how, refusing to give up on me when everybody else understandably couldn't take any more. Finally, it nearly drove her off the deep end. She was entirely spent and frustrated. But her love for me was fiercely tenacious, and she just wouldn't let me go without a fight—no matter what I did. She gave up a lot of her own valuable time to keep checking up on me, and I knew she was praying desperately for me. I owe her the world, even my life, for what she did for me.

One day, she said something that finally hit home with me: "Don't you know that your body is a temple of God?" For some reason, I couldn't get those words out of my head. At the time, I had been feeling, hearing, and even seeing demons for about seven years. They appeared as dark or black shadows but with form, and sometimes I could see their menacing faces. They'd taunt me, peeking around corners, appearing and disappearing, and leading me on wild goose chases around the house as I fruitlessly tried to chase them away.

On one of my last, very desperate days in the Lovelace Street house, I was huddled on the dirty, stripped-bare floor in a corner of an upstairs room, trying to strike a single match on a paper matchbook. I was trying to light my expensive black leather pants on fire to keep warm, but my hands shook so wildly that I couldn't steady them enough to get the match to strike. Finally successful after countless repeated attempts, I watched my favorite stage pants curl up and burn.

They amounted to only a pitiful thirty seconds of heat.

9

INTO HELL

Where can I go from Your Spirit?
Or where can I flee from Your presence?
If I ascend into heaven, You are there;
If I make my bed in hell, behold, You are there.
If I take the wings of the morning,
And dwell in the uttermost parts of the sea,
Even there Your hand shall lead me,
And Your right hand shall hold me.
If I say, "Surely the darkness shall fall on me,"
Even the night shall be light about me.
Indeed, the darkness shall not hide from You,
But the night shines as the day.
The darkness and the light are both alike to You.

— PSALM 139:7–12

Friday, September 1, 2000, was a peculiar day. It was exceptionally cold for September in Pittsburgh, colder than I had remembered in a long time. The atmosphere in my house also had an exceptionally dark and eerie feeling about it.

As I went about getting high and trying to entertain myself in the house, I heard this beautiful, sweet celestial music that seemed to come out of nowhere. It faded in and out on occasion, but it continued throughout the day. I'd heard a lot of music in my lifetime, but this sound was so different and otherworldly— a soothing, slow, comforting sound with obscure chords, and I could hear soft angelic-sounding voices singing a beautiful melody in a captivating perfect harmony. I just wondered with awe about that unusual song and where it was coming from.

By the time evening turned into nightfall, I was restless for another fix, so I headed upstairs to my bedroom, lighting the big candles I kept in the hallway and the room so I could see. As I stood there at the little table by the mattress on the floor, preparing my fifth speedball of the day, the strange celestial-sounding symphony started up again.

I sucked the amber solution into my needle, chose the least painful spot left on my arm, and with welcome anticipation plunged the liquid into my vein. But no sooner had I pulled the needle from my arm, the room swirled, my knees buckled, and I collapsed, landing hard on the mattress with a loud thud I could hear but didn't really feel. Everything went pitch black.

Within a few moments, the beautiful music abruptly stopped. The hollow blackness deepened darker and darker to where it was literally palpable. I could feel it penetrating my entire being. It was then I realized I was no longer in my room anymore—but in a place of sheer horror.

I lay flat on what felt like a dirt floor, and an intense, tangible fear fully infiltrated the atmosphere around me. I shuddered at what sounded like millions and millions of voices screaming in random waves of shrill volumes. They were beyond frightening! Those desperate, dread-filled screams and wails of despair pierced right through me. I can only describe them as the sound of millions of humans screaming in terror—but their voices carried no life in them. They chilled me with a fear that went through every part of me.

It took all I had to take in part of a breath, because the stench was so awful that each breath I attempted was like breathing in, then tasting, something far worse than rotten and putrid. It was like tasting death. I tried to see around me through the deepest, blackest darkness I'd ever known, and then I began to dimly see things. Standing right in front of me were big ancient-looking gates made of heavy iron-like bars—and they were open inward.

I could hear a lot of activity going on in this place, and none of it was good.

Through the terrifying shrieks and wails, I also heard what sounded like chains far off in the distance. Heavy chains being dragged and scraped along, like on concrete. The sounds and thick, penetrating fear paralyzed me so much, I couldn't move, and with all of my senses heightened to new levels, I could smell, taste, hear, and feel dread with an intolerable intensity. I sensed what I can only describe as lifeless spirits all around me. Yet, they weren't really... dead. And then those chains sounded like they were coming closer and closer to where I lay.

Soon voices—much closer and through moans and cries— started calling out my name. That's when I began to realize those voices sounded familiar. Listening in shock and confusion, I recognized these were the voices of old friends—so many! People whom I'd known from my years in the music and entertainment industry. I had partnered, played, or partied with them at one time or another. When I turned my gaze toward their inviting calls, I could see more through the darkness. There against a backdrop of a dim fire-lit glow just inside the gates, a pile of skeletal-looking gray bodies lay stacked in a tall heap against a dark earthen wall. Their gaunt forms were moving, and with beckoning motions they tried to reach their hands toward me as they called out to me.

My mind raced trying to sort it all out. Some were those taken too soon by drug overdoses, accidents, or risky lifestyles, but most all of them were people I considered far better than I. In fact, some were pretty good, responsible, honest people with great families they took good care of. I wondered in puzzled disbelief, *What are* they *doing here?*

Their inviting, friendly calls to me seemed to offer some sort of a sick glimmer of hope, but then their cries began to change— into ever-increasing, imposing, even angry, demanding calls for me. They began to grasp and pull at me through the gate's bars, and then they attempted to claw and tear at me. They were trying to hurt me—even consume me—and drag me in with them!

Further waves of despair and hopelessness overcame me. I felt such an overwhelming sense of betrayal, and tried to shrink back away from their awful scratching, but I had no strength to even try to get away. At the same time, through the shrill noise, the dreadful things happening to me, and all the horrible things I could hear going on in this busy place, I distinctly heard those dragging chains coming ever closer. Soon arrived a scene beyond what I could take!

One by one, a big group of demons came into view. They were dragging those chains with them! I could literally feel the heavy metal already confining and holding me bound before they even came near. The demons were dark, ugly, horrific-looking creatures of various sizes, types, and colors. I'd never seen anything so absolutely hideous before! They had bulbous bodies, large, grotesque heads and big, puffed-out cheeks on distorted faces that looked almost like melted wax. Their teeth were huge, and they had long, sharp claws. The stench reeking from them overwhelmed me. In fact, I could smell them coming before I even saw them—a far worse stench than the original suffocating smell. My lungs burned for air as I tried to not breathe it in.

The skin on some was like thick elephant hide, and some were black while others were dark brown or brown with black spots on them. Their heights ranged from four feet tall to seven or eight feet tall. About a dozen of them surrounded me, their panting, sickening breath so close that I reeled with nausea. Panic left me unable to fight.

By now, it had sunk in where I was—but I didn't want to face it. The stark realization gave me no hope of escape. I knew I had died. My time was up. And beyond a shadow of a doubt, I knew I was lost for eternity in this awful place I'd often been warned about—and I even joked about—but never really wanted to believe in. This is hell—and it is *truly real!*

I tried to sink into a place to hide, wishing I could just cease to exist. I desperately craved with all my being to retreat into total insanity just to escape my consciousness and senses. But that was impossible. *This is death?* I thought. *This is what I've ignorantly been trying to escape to—from what I thought was such a horrible existence?*

What shocked me more was that I was completely conscious of everything going on. In fact, every part of me—my consciousness, my senses, everything that was "me"—experienced this horror at a height and sensitivity much more keen than I'd ever experienced anything on earth. I knew I had no chance anymore. No ability. No sliver of hope of ever getting away from any of it.

The hideous demons began hungrily readying the clanking chains, about to take me. So paralyzed in doom and terror, I didn't even think to cry out for help. Who would I have called to anyway? I'd never trusted in anyone other than myself. But here I was. And somehow, I *knew* this was my just fate, fair and deserved. You just *know*.

Suddenly, a brilliant white light appeared from some place high above me. Its blinding rays pierced the thick darkness and radiated down on me like a spotlight. The demons shrieked in terror and retreated as far from the light as they could get. The light illuminated my surroundings, showing even more of the ghastliness surrounding me. The demons crouched fearfully in the shadows, and I also saw many more of those pitiful imprisoned lifeless human souls. In the distance, a vast, cavernous terrain was dotted with countless pits of fire for as far as I could see. The inconsolable screams and cries of hell's tormented prisoners lost in their eternal nightmare echoed everywhere. And I knew it was forever.

At that moment, I felt something like big hands gently pick me up. I was caught up and pulled out of hell, rising higher and higher into the light. Then my vantage point abruptly changed from being on the ground in hell, to looking down on my body still lying in that awful, dark place. I too was a gaunt and gray skeletal victim.

Mercifully, the dreadful atmosphere of horror and terror—the putrid smells, the inability to breathe, and all the intense, over-whelming fear—just melted away. Instead, I was filled with an overwhelming calmness and peace. It flooded right into me and around me as I was suspended inside the brilliant light. The ter-rifying sounds of hell faded far off into the distance, replaced by that sweet, melodic music I'd heard in my house. The music filtered through the light, flowing and swirling in a living, rhyth-mic cadence through me. I could feel I was being held with big, comforting arms around me. Peace and love like I'd never known before emanated through me like waves. All I could do was lie like a limp rag, so thankful to be pulled out of that terrible place. At first I could only make out an outline of who was holding me. The light was emanating so brilliantly directly out of His entire being. Then I caught a glimpse of His face.

He radiated with such beauty, goodness, and purity. His eyes were like deep pools of liquid love as He looked upon me with such tender sincerity, love, and compassion. I knew He could see right into me—and that, somehow, He *knew* me. I was looking into the face of the Lord Jesus Christ. No other introduction was necessary.

There was no understanding of time, because we were in a place somewhere outside time. The flow of love and life coming from Him filled and revived me as I drank it all in. Soon I heard His voice, and He spoke to me in such a soothing, reassuring tone. "Son," He said, "I have called you to be a voice for Me since the day you were born. When are you going to turn?" Then He reached down as if to pull something from the pocket of His bril-liant, sparkling robe. Gently, He lifted a tiny string—the size of a single thread pulled from a strand of yarn—between His fingers and held it before my eyes. "This," He said as he looked at it, "is how much time you have left."

Being held there so tenderly was like being in the home I always belonged in but never knew how to find. I was all at once wrecked and in awe. The vibrating life of that realm of heaven kept swirling in, around, and through me in wonderful wave after healing wave. He looked deeply into my eyes again, right into my being, with unconditional love. He said, "I love you, son!" and though His words had such certainty and strength, they were spoken with great tenderness. I never wanted Him to let me go.

He talked with me in gentle and casual conversation about so many different subjects. I couldn't help but feel His words like they were going right into me—as if they were being deposited deep inside me. Every word had such depth, meaning, and life. To this day even, I still get deeper revelation and understanding of the things that He said to me then.

I knew that He knew everything about me, but He never once spoke like I was the wretched, wicked person I truly was. I couldn't believe He spoke so assuredly and highly of me. Everything He had to say had only pure life in it. He treated me as if I were already that so-valuable, lovable, good, and highly favored person He made me to be. He called me as He had made and saw me, not as I saw myself—or *knew* I really was at the time. He was calm and His words had confidence that He was going to get me where I was supposed to be. He then told me, in detail, all about what my life was meant to be.

He took His time talking with me, and it seemed like hours passed. The words were so full of life. I can only liken them to mass amounts of information downloaded quickly to a computer, though the conversation was casual and real-time for me. Later I would realize that the amount of information I was given would have filled libraries of books. Many of the words He had said I would later find verbatim in Scripture. He had put it all right inside me.

He talked a lot about the plans He had for me—about my destiny and how He was going to use me. He told me He had a high calling on my life and that He was the one who had been protecting and saving me through so many of the close calls in my life. With a smile, He added that it was just because He wanted to get me where I belonged. He even told me it was Him who had put a love for music in me.

He shocked me further when He said, "And I'm going to put you on a tour like you've never seen before." After pausing a moment, He added with another smile, "But this time, it will be for Me." He rattled off in detail the cities, places, and nations He was going to send me to, and revealed, "I am going to send you places where no one else can go." With deep affection, He again looked into my eyes and said with a gentle earnestness in His voice, "Timmy, I saved you. Now you go and save my children. Just bring them to me, and I will do all the rest."

I was undone. God really knew me! He knew everything about me. My thoughts, my life at the deepest levels. He knew all my secrets, my sins, even my hopes and dreams. And most of all, he knew my hopelessness and despair. My failures were right before Him, though He never mentioned them once. The fact was, He knew I was a living death wish and wanted to kill myself—though I lied to myself about it—and He knew I didn't care about my life or really anything anymore. He also knew I had no clue how to live. Yet with confidence He spoke of only good things, as if everything else didn't matter. It was pure life when He spoke about His grand plans filled with such hope and a great future for me—and He spoke it all as if it were already done.

I learned a lot about Him in that time too. Most of it came as a *knowing* just by being with Him in His amazing presence. When Jesus, still holding me securely in His arms, finished with all He wanted to say to me, we quietly continued to gaze down on my body still way down in hell. Then He spoke again, this time in a firm, commanding tone. He ordered, "Now move your right arm!"

I exerted effort and watched as the right arm on my body in hell moved. Suddenly, the demons somewhere in the shadows around my body shrieked in terror, "It's a bomb!" and frantically scrambled away.

Jesus looked amused with pleasure; it seemed almost like a fun game to Him. He ordered, "Now move your left leg!" I tried again—and saw the left leg on my body in hell move. I picked it up and watched myself move it up and down. He then commanded me to move each of my body parts separately one by one: feet, hands, and neck—everything—as we both watched. Then with finality, He commanded me, "Leave your head. Now get up and go!"

I jumped up with all my might, and the next thing I saw was myself coming down and through the ceiling of my bedroom, right back into my lifeless body still lying on the bed.

When I opened my eyes, I was looking up at the ceiling. I could hardly believe I was back in my body. I instantly jumped up off the bed as if a strong force had shot me effortlessly onto my feet and stood there looking around the room at the scene I had last left: the empty syringe on the floor...and then myself. I was amazed and so grateful to be back—and alive!

So overcome, I laughed out loud with ecstatic joy and relief. And that wonderful comfort and security hadn't left; I could still feel it encompassing me. As I thought about the unbelievable events I'd just been through, feelings and emotions flooded me as I tried to wrap my mind around it. It was just too much to take in!

I stayed in my bedroom for a while, trying to collect myself. Not knowing what else to do, I finally decided to head downstairs to make a fire in the living room fireplace so I could sit there and think awhile. But as I stepped out into the hallway, I was stopped in my tracks. At the other end of it, superimposed on the wall, I plainly saw a big, man-sized black shadow. It was shaped in the silhouette of a robber with beady eyes staring through a black eye mask and a mugger-type cap on his head—just like you'd see in an old-time cartoon. But it was pointing a big gun held with both hands—directly at me!

I jumped behind the doorway as the horrific terror I'd experienced in hell tried to sweep through me again. Then, slowly, I dared to peek back into the hallway. Yes, it was just a shadow, I assured myself after studying it, but it stayed there unmoving, still aiming at me. I could sense an intense, evil feeling all over it.

I looked for every probability of what could cast a shadow like that. In all the years I'd been in the house, it had never been there before. But there it was, and it was extremely dark and menacing. Chills ran up and down my spine as I tried to figure out what was going on and what to do. I ducked into the bathroom right off the hallway, shut the door and locked it, and lit the candle I kept on the sink for light.

Such a clash of thoughts and emotions overwhelmed me. I didn't know what to do next, even thinking I was going to come unglued. I didn't yet understand everything at this point; I hadn't had time to sort it all out. But somehow, I knew I was caught in the fighting clash of two different realms—light and dark, good and evil—and I was the prize being contended for!

I stayed locked in the bathroom, trying to decide what I was supposed to do. But the bathroom also happened to be where I stashed most of my drugs. Instinctively, I reached for the only thing that had ever helped me cope with anything up to this point in my life. I didn't leave the bathroom until I had smoked about twenty hits of crack. Oddly, though, I couldn't get high like I had before. Instead of the normal heightened feeling that usually accompanied smoking crack, I felt a totally different high—one totally enveloped in comfort and peace.

When I finally ventured out of the bathroom, the shadow was still there aiming at me. I tried to ignore it and cautiously headed past it and down the stairs. (It remained there for a couple of hours. though, because I'd go back once in a while to peek up the stairs to check on it.) In the living room, I made a small fire in the fireplace and sat down on the floor to try to process everything. My mind was overwhelmed just at the thought of it all.

Then suddenly, that same amazing light of heavenly atmosphere I was in with God dropped down into the room and surrounded me. The dark living room brilliantly lit up, and with it came the thick blanket of peace, wrapping me up in perfect waves of comfort and security. Within a couple of hours, daylight streamed in through the windows. That's when I realized how long I'd been gone. I had gone upstairs to my bedroom about an hour after nightfall, so I'd been gone most of the night. It had been at least seven or eight hours.

I cried like a baby and laughed with utter joy, basking in the wonderful, peaceful light and trying to take in everything. I had been a goner, and this Jesus personally came, pulled me out of hell, took me up in His heavenly realm, told me beautiful things that filled me with such wonder, and then brought me back to life. Though my encounter with Him didn't stop there.

Vivid visions began to appear right in front of me in the living room. My eyes, ears, and other senses remained opened to new heights. I saw and heard many things I knew were going on behind the scenes of the natural realm. God was showing me everything else He wanted me to know—things that were happening in the spiritual realm around me and in heaven.

Other times, I'd hear His voice talking to me again, often in answer to my thoughts. I spent hours pondering what He said to me. Then I would get a deep understanding of it all—in that I just *knew*—and I knew it was the truth. He would repeat wonderful things to me, but occasionally would also repeat His gentle warnings—that I still didn't have much time left.

My intense encounter with God continued for twenty days. It would ebb and flow randomly throughout the days and nights but never fully stop, no matter what I was doing. He just wouldn't leave me alone. I felt like I was living in two realms at once—the natural and the spiritual. I saw, heard, felt, smelled, and even knew things that were going on, things I couldn't have known naturally. God was revealing more and more of Himself to me. But He was also showing me things about my life, truth by truth. I listened and watched intently, wondering deeply.

At times when I was sitting in my living room, the realm of heaven would open up above me and I would see Jesus there in brilliant light, with glory and angels around Him. He'd look down at me with great love and contentment. Other times, He'd pull me back up in His heavenly atmosphere to talk with me. Sometimes, I'd strongly feel His familiar presence with me wherever I was, and I knew He was right there with me. No words were necessary at these times. Our communication was so rich, pleasant, and comforting that it went much deeper than words.

When I slept, I dreamt like crazy. Such realistic dreams, they were as real as if I were awake. I'd be shown and fully experience many new things. Then every morning the atmosphere of heaven would fill my room. Some of those times, I saw and heard Jesus and His angels right in my room with me.

One morning, I woke up feeling an especially strong presence in my room. I turned over to see Jesus standing next to my bed engulfed in intense blue, white, red, and gold flames that shot out at least three feet all around Him. Powerful lightning bolts of energy came from within Him, and His hair was white with light and His skin glowed a color like glistening golden brass. Even His eyes were blazing torches of fire. He was right there, as solid as you or I, yet the fire was so intense and pure that it made His form almost transparent. I was overwhelmed by His majesty. Had He not contained it to such degree, I'm sure it would have obliterated me.

Then more of the angelic music would come at times too, but these were new songs. One song was called "Hallelujah." It had a beautiful melody with the word "hallelujah" sung over and over with an emphasis on the h. It kept flowing on and on. Another song had the repeated phrase, "Jesus loves you," and when the angels softly sang it over and over, a 3D-movie-like vision would open in front of me. I'd see a cross, then a heart, and then a letter u would come swooping toward me with each word it symbolized.

Other new songs came too. I was getting so many that I had to write them down. I looked around for whatever I could find to write on. I ended up pulling apart old cereal boxes, making strips from paper bags, and even pulling long pieces of toilet paper off the roll. There wasn't much else left. The songs flowed right through me, and I wrote as fast as I could, trying to keep up with it all. This continued for days and days. Later, some of these songs and words ended up on new albums I recorded. "Far Much Better Life," "Best Friends," and "Black Crow" (now on my album *Prophesy*) came out of those first heavy-encounter days. But a lot of those songs never made it out of the house because the fragile scraps I had written them on were just lost.

It wasn't until after the twenty days that the intensity started to subside. It was then I realized I hadn't ate or drank—not even water—for the entire time. I had no thought, need, or desire to. It didn't seem to matter, though, because I was totally sustained by the presence around me.

Ironically, even through all of this, I continued my daily routine of drugs. They hardly affected me, but I still craved them—and I still didn't care enough about myself to stop. I didn't know how to. At this point I still didn't understand or truly believe the identity God kept telling me I had.

Interestingly, out of all the things He said and did with me, He never once directly addressed my drug use. Apparently, it wasn't that big of an issue to Him at the time. What was evidently more important was that He establish a relationship with me first. Though I never looked for or asked for any of this, He wasn't about to let go of me. Unbelievably, He kept showing me that I was too precious to Him.

I only learned much later how this was possible. God is spirit, and He mainly deals with you directly from His Spirit to your spirit. Things like drugs, for the most part, affect only your natural mind and body. But God totally bypassed my messed-up mind and body—even my still only world-trained, polluted way of thinking. Instead, He was revealing Himself to the core part of my being that could only begin to truly hear, see, or know Him—to my spirit. And I was receiving it all unhindered.

From the moment He brought me back, He took the liberty to step inside me and light me up in His light. I received and experienced Him with perfect, unhindered clarity—no matter what I did.

I know that will ruin some people's theology, but that's what happened. He came to live inside me by His Spirit—and I hadn't even asked Him to. Nothing I could do would make Him leave me alone!

On one of the intense encounter mornings, I woke up startled to find girl standing at the foot of my bed. She was as real as you or I, not like a vision. She had a big knife in her hand and kept stabbing herself in the head, plunging the knife into it over and over. She cried out in great anguish, trying to kill herself, but she wouldn't die. She looked just like one of the lifeless human spirits I'd seen in hell, but I have no doubt she was a real individual. God was letting me see her exactly as she was in that particular moment of her great distress. She was in hell, trying to escape her own existence in it, but there was no way out. I also knew it was another of God's repeated, yet loving warnings to me that I didn't have much time left either. One of those times He reminded me of this, He matter-of-factly added, "The world doesn't have much time left either."

As God dealt with me, there were also times I could hear some of the taunting demonic voices trying to speak to me. They posed carefully crafted statements or questions about the reality of what I was being told and shown by God, and they kept trying to sell me on the idea of reincarnation and the rest of the lies I'd believed for so long. Though I began to realize that what they said was in total opposition to what God was saying and plainly showing me. They wanted me to doubt and question it all. But God was using it all as a tool to teach me how to recognize and separate His voice from the others—and to know which voice I could trust.

I learned that everything with a voice that can speak to you is some sort of spirit. When God's familiar voice spoke to me, I chose to trust it; I knew my very life depended on it now. God warns us to "test the spirits" to see whether they're really from Him or not (1 John 4:1). This was the beginning of my discernment realm training by Him. I didn't learn any of this from a man, church, or organization; it all came directly from Him, from day one.

After those initial twenty encounter days, something else

incredible happened. All the deep-seated hate, rage, and outward abusive tendencies—which had overwhelmed me for decades—just left. God just took them all away. I never thought to ask Him for this, and it certainly wasn't accomplished by my own effort or capability. I later came to understand that these weren't my own "personality tendencies" either. They were actually demons I had! Through my own ignorance, I had opened the door of my soul to them. But it was over time He dealt with other major issues in my life one by one—and He had to do it all. Establishing relationship with me first was all He wanted at this point. He knew I was hardheaded, and He knew my rebel heart. It seemed I didn't have much choice in the matter though. He just wouldn't leave me alone to myself anymore.

I realized that God not only has the power to call the dead to life, but He also calls those things that are not, as though they already are (Romans 4:17). Little did I know at the time that the continuing journey still ahead of me would begin to fall into place just like He said.

These were the first things God did and took away in my life after saving me from hell. I was so grateful to Him for pulling me out of that awful place. Words cannot describe what a horrible place it is! I also began to understand why God told me, "Leave your head," back in hell. There was nothing good He could use in my natural mind and way of thinking. It had been steeped in decades of lies and skewed half-truths, especially about Him. Of course, I was natural-sense trained and knew only the way of the world up to this point in my life. But He wanted to give me a whole brand new start, with a heart and mind trained solely by Him, and made new—by the Spirit of Christ.

Now I better understand this truth, that our natural selves can't really know or experience God, because we're naturally—just natural. It's our world-born "flesh" nature and mind that's in total rebellion to God and the things of His Spirit, like He plainly says (1 Corinthians 2:14; Galatians 5:17; Romans 8:7). When God reveals Himself to us, it's not a "natural" event. Flesh and blood don't reveal it to us. It comes only from the Father in heaven— just like Jesus said to Peter (Matthew 16:17). It's an event that's entirely supernatural. It's a miraculous thing from the outset, and when it happens, we experience Him and hear His voice.

God is the one who started this relationship. He was determined that I would know Him. But this would take time as His relationship with me continued on. He spoke, nudged, and whispered to me in the days ahead. He'd talk to me in my own language, in friendly, creative, and even funny ways. He'd often use encouraging statements like "Hey Timmy, you're on the wrong path. Come on over here," or "This is where I am. Come on over this way." Sometimes He'd say, "Hey, your heart is off a little bit in this matter. Look, I'll show you a better way," or He'd incite me with, "Let's go have some fun! I want to show you some things."

Many times I heard Him speak, but more often He'd outright show me something. I liked that. Though I was still a messed-up individual and wasn't sure how to live or what I really wanted, He intended to show me piece by piece and truth by truth just who He is and all He was going to do for me.

He had to do it all. I was incapable of being or doing anything without Him. But that's the way it's meant to be. Frankly, it seemed I didn't have much choice anyway. He wouldn't stop interrupting me to show me just who He is and try to draw me closer to Him. Though I was still running in the wrong direction, that didn't intimidate Him. He never left me no matter what I did.

As I thought about all the things God had personally said to me, I realized what He was saying had to be true. All my long-held thinking and beliefs had the carpet pulled out from under them, piece by piece. I recognized and saw that His fingerprints had been all over my life. There were no other reasonable explanations for why I had come out of so many impossible circumstances. Everything was finally beginning to make some sense.

Intrigued, I couldn't help but wonder about this outrageous

God who had chased after me my whole life, even right into hell. Who was He to have such power, authority, and ability to not only save me from that sure eternal death trap, but also to make demons tremble and flee in terror at His presence? And why would He show such mercy and love for someone like me, who certainly didn't deserve it? Certainly, God knew I had to be one of His worst, most messed-up, uninterested, and hardest cases—though that didn't make it impossible for Him to reach me.

But one thing I did know unmistakably now: I met God in hell. And there are no bounds or limitations that can hold God back or keep Him from getting to anyone.

10

HE'S A KEEPER!

I revealed myself to those who did not ask for me;
I was found by those who did not seek me.
To a nation that did not call on my name,
I said, "Here am I, here am I."

– ISAIAH 65:1 NIV

For a year after God first introduced Himself so spectacularly
to me, I lived mostly isolated in the Lovelace Street house.
God's break-ins continued regularly. I heard His voice and saw
vivid visions and dreams through which He'd show and teach me
things. I also still often saw His amazing heavenly light. Even so,
my drug use greatly worsened through that year.

I became even more physically weak and frail. People tried to
persuade me to get help, but it was Maryanne, with her caring,
tough love, who wouldn't take no for an answer anymore. She
never gave up on me, and her stubborn persistence finally paid
off. I agreed to try a rehab.

Gateway Rehab was known as one of the best rehab facili-
ties at the time. A lot of famous and influential people had been
treated there, including big-name rock stars. My sister set everything up with their administration and I prepared to drive myself
there, but right before I left, knowing this was it, I finished off my
drugs. I slammed my last bags of heroin, downed all my pills, and
then climbed into my old painter's van.

On the drive there I smoked my last two grams of crack, and

when I arrived, they were already waiting outside expectantly for me. When they came over to pull me out of my van, my head and arms shook so wildly that I couldn't control myself. The staff tried talking to me, asking me questions, but I couldn't put words together in a sensible sentence. They carried me right into the center's medical quarters.

First they weighed me. Even wearing my long black leather coat and thick platform boots, the scale read 90 pounds. My heavy clothes alone constituted at least 10 of those pounds. When healthy, I'd weighed 165 pounds, though that had been many years prior. Right away they drew blood for testing, then carried me to the exam room to see the doctor.

The exam and interview were lengthy, and I did my best to get through them. The doctor shook his head in disbelief as he examined my trembling skeletal body. The whites of my eyes were yellow, and my skin was yellow-gray with bruises, open sores, scars, and track marks riddling my arms and hands. He reviewed my long drug list, the quantities, mixes, and twenty nine-year history of abuse. Then he got up and left the room for a while.

When he came back, he sat on the stool and rolled it over to the exam table. He looked down at the floor, then blurted out, "'Tim, you are the worst case we've ever seen here. We just can't understand how you're even still alive." He went on, "We don't understand how a human body taking the types of drugs, the quantities, and the mixes you've been taking could even survive a day, let alone all these years! I mean, we've never seen anything like this. It should be impossible." Totally perplexed, he searched for how to say his next words. "Tim, I'm sorry. We've found that all of your organs are beginning to shut down. You maybe have but thirty days left to live." He hesitated a moment, then added, "If you're lucky."

Before he left the room, with his hand still on the doorknob, he paused, looked back over his shoulder at me, and candidly remarked, "If you do make it, send me a postcard." Then he went into the hallway where the staff were waiting. "He's a keeper!" he told them. And with that, I was checked into a room in Gateway Rehab.

The staff there treated me with great compassion and care. They supported me through the difficult withdrawal process, but I did it without the additional drugs they encouraged me to take to ease the symptoms. I'd made up my mind, because I knew something they didn't. I knew God was with me, and I knew He would help me through it all. They fed me healthy meals, something I hadn't had in a long time, let alone regularly. They checked on me around the clock and encouraged me daily. Over the weeks there, the cloud in my head began to clear and the shaking subsided to controllable levels. I stunned the doctors when I started putting on weight and the sick pall color began leaving my skin.

Gateway was a twelve-step type of program, and one of my counselors was Rodney, an ex-addict who happened to be an amazing drummer. He was a believer in God, and when he learned what I'd gone through, including dying, going to hell, and being rescued by God and taken to heaven, he was intrigued. He would sit and talk with me about God for hours. Rodney and I became close friends, and he became one of my greatest encouragers.

With a lot of time on my hands and a clearing head, one day I picked up the Bible in my room just to pass the time. I was shocked to find the things that I read matched what God had personally said to me or shown me over the previous year. The first passage I read said, "I am the resurrection and the life. The one who believes in me will live, even though they die; and whoever lives by believing in me will never die. Do you believe this?" (John 11:25–26 NIV). It awed me, even made me cry. Emotions convicted me as I realized more of who this really was that had been protecting and chasing after me my whole life, rescued me, brought me back to life, and now talked with me.

At the time, I still didn't understand what God saw in me or why I had any worth to Him. As I read John 1:1, I saw that

Jesus Christ is also called the "Word of God." I'd been talking to the "Word of God" Himself, while holding His book called the "Word of God." And it was in perfect agreement with what He'd said and done with me all along.

While at rehab, there were times I got together for group meetings with the other addicts. Everyone would get their turn to talk about their story or ask questions. When my turn came, what I later learned is called "the gift of prophecy" would randomly pour out of me. "Prophecy" is basically the ability to clearly hear or see something God is saying or showing you, and then repeating it when and how He tells you to. Sometimes it's just "knowing" things not recognizable by natural means; God shares them with you.

Here I was, such a broken, sick man still—and the Spirit of God was using me to encourage others. What I spoke were precise, accurate words about their lives that I was getting from Him—words that neither I nor anyone else there could have possibly known. It was absolutely wild!

Sometimes God would open my "spiritual eyes," and I would plainly see what was going on in the lives of the people around the room. It was like I was reading their private mail. The accuracy of my words shocked everyone. Frankly, it stunned me too. However, God was only giving me "previews" of what would later come from Him. He was teaching me, if I listened to Him He is always completely accurate.

I don't know why God used me even before I fully surrendered my life to Him. But I learned that's just the way He works. He already knew who He had made me to be, and He already knew my future. He was determined He would bring me through to it. My rebellion, even then, was only beginning to fall away. But with each little step I took toward Him, He came closer to me and gave me more.

When my allowed thirty days' time at Gateway ended, the staff urged me to go right to a halfway house in Boca Raton,

Florida. They said it was one of the best, so when I walked out Gateway's doors, I drove my van all the way there.

The halfway house also used a twelve-step program, but there I had the freedom to come and go during the day, as long as I attended the meetings and counseling sessions. I even went to a church service for the first time since I'd been on my own. I still heard God's voice and got occasional visions, and I tried to understand what He was showing me. Sometimes I'd know instantly, but other times bits and pieces of understanding would come over time.

After only three weeks in Boca Raton, I slipped. Because I had the freedom to go out and still had cravings, I started using crack again. Someone in the halfway house figured it out and told the staff, and I was kicked out. When I left, I drove to Fort Lauderdale, about a half hour away, and checked into a cheap motel. Then I drove around the ghetto areas looking for a place to buy more crack.

I turned onto a block that looked like it had sellers on just about every corner. I pulled over to the curb to decide who I would approach first and just happened to take a glance in my rearview mirror. Across the street behind me was a big stone building with an especially large front door. For some reason, it captured my attention. Suddenly, as if superimposed by something, the door became especially dark in color and I got this sudden strong uneasy, creepy feeling. I didn't understand it, but by then I knew to pay attention to such feelings. I gassed it and drove out of there quickly.

As I took off, I glanced in the mirror again and saw the door to the building fly open and an army of SWAT officers flood onto the street. The dealers scattered in every direction like rats with the police in close pursuit. I realized more than ever now, that creepy feeling was a warning sign for me to leave, and that it was God who was giving me the warnings. It was another of the ways He spoke to me, even when I was doing stupid things. I ended up huddling in the Florida motel room for another two weeks. Still feeling helpless, I binged on crack the entire time.

When Maryanne learned of my departure from the halfway house, she went on a mission looking for me. I finally dared to answer the phone and talk to her about it, and she urged me to come back to Pittsburgh and sent me some money for the trip. I drove back, but it was again to my empty Lovelace Street house and I was still deep in addiction.

By now it was January, and the Pittsburgh temperatures were extremely cold and I still had no utilities on in the house. One night I sat alone in front of my fireplace, high and about to pass out, when I saw a vivid vision of one of my friends burning in the fireplace. It was God's way of showing me that my friend was also in great danger of hell. He was a junkie too. (I learned only many years later that he finally died from an overdose). By now, I was learning that a lot of what God gave me was not only meant for me, but for others as well.

I stayed in the Lovelace Street house another two months, scraping by as best I could. Then Maryanne got after me to go back to Gateway Rehab for another thirty-day stay. I quickly agreed this time.

Rodney, my former counselor and friend, welcomed me back with great care and concern. I went through the program again, getting cleaned up and healthier. But once out, I had nowhere to go but back to my house of death. This time, it was only a day before I started using crack again. When Maryanne found out about it, she came charging after me like a bulldog and got me set up in a Pittsburgh halfway house called McKees Rocks.

The staff there took one look at my long hair and said I'd need to cut if before they would let me in. With no other choice, my waist-length hair was cut short. This made me pretty angry, but I stayed and did the program. I got totally clean again—but only for a few weeks. Not waiting for them to boot me out this time, I packed up my bag and left.

When I got home, I started using heroin again. I felt completely hopeless and desperate, knowing every possible source for getting drug money had all dried up. I had burned out everyone I knew by now, and I could sense the once unseen but spacious perimeter fence God had around me, and my options, closing in on me. Frantic, I began to hatch big ideas.

I decided to rob either a bank or the nearby methadone clinic. Every Monday the methadone clinic received all the heroin addicts' one-hundred-dollar cash payments for weekly supplies, so I looked around the house trying to find one of my old guns. All I could find was a little five-shot Derringer pistol, but it didn't matter. I'd already decided what I was going to do.

I drove my van there and slowly cruised around the clinic to case it out first. Unbelievably, on every street corner was a cop car. One even sat right in front of the clinic. I was so determined but now utterly frustrated. I'd been to the clinic so many times in the past and there had *never* been a cop in sight. So I sat across the street with the engine running and my mind racing as I tried to come up with any possible way around the scenario. That's when I heard God speak audibly right into my van, "You're dumb to try this one!"

"Man!" I raged. "No drugs…no money…can't even rob the place because of all the cops!" I was experiencing really uncomfortable withdrawals, and I also worried that I wouldn't have enough gas in the van to even make it home. I lost it, cussing away and banging my fists on the steering wheel.

My painter's van was so thrashed from not being maintained for years that the brakes had worn down to nothing. I had to drive it slowly and carefully because the only way to stop it was to run it into something like a curb, a hedge, or a pole—while trying to stay unobvious, of course. On the way home from the thwarted clinic grab, I stopped by the house of an old friend who had once been a roadie for me. He understood my situation, and, seeing I was in desperate need, gave me enough money to get some drugs and put some gas in the van. I was grateful. I had made it through another day.

I went through the full circuit of emotions as I drove home. From being so frustrated…to shocked…and then to angry and annoyed, despite hearing God so plainly. I was so utterly upset, I even wanted to cry. The whole unreal situation was just so ludicrous, and I wasn't used to that.

Later, after I got home, calmed down a little, and was reflecting on the day, I knew everything that had happened was too obviously perfect to be only a coincidence. Then I began to realize what lengths this crazy God had gone to in setting things up with half the town's police force strategically placed in just the right place—at just the right time—to stop me from doing something incredibly stupid. And here I was stewing about it all, with God no doubt watching me and staying so obviously silent.

Finally, in resignation, I burst out laughing at the realization of His bold audacity. And it was right then that I distinctly heard God let out a loud, hearty belly laugh into the room, right along with me. There was no doubt anymore. He had totally set me up—and it was surreal!

God has an amazing sense of humor. He was really just showing His great love for me. Still, He relentlessly pursued me, trying to protect me and continuing to call me closer to Him. But I was amazed He was so in control of things. It seemed my life and all I would do should be trivial amusement to Him. In reality, He already knew me and everything I would do—even before I did. He also knew where He would take me. I couldn't get over His confidence about it all. He seemed absolutely determined to get me through—and to my destiny that I didn't yet believe but He could plainly see.

And then the big unseen perimeter fence began to close in even more on me. The set-ups increased and I could see the tide really changing. Things that I easily got away with for the prior forty-six years of my life now turned into repeated close calls. I knew they were more warnings. I could feel the hand of God like an invisible gentle pressure. Again and again, He kept showing me just who He is and that He was still not about to let me go. After all He'd already done for me, I still hadn't totally yielded to Him. I was still driven by my own desires, ideas, and self-will. But none of this stopped Him from continuing His ongoing relationship with me.

The next morning when I got up, I visited a good friend who was in jail. I felt a fresh wind of confidence and wanted to be an encouragement to him. Ironically, I hoped to comfort and inspire him to trust God to help him get on the right path, though I wasn't there yet myself. Amazingly, the right reassuring words came pouring out of me with compassion and care.

While in the jail building, I noticed that the cops there kept staring at me. They watched me as I left, and when I started home, I looked in my rearview mirror to find them following me in their cars. Soon they pulled me over. When they learned I had no insurance on the van, they removed the license plate and told me to leave it on the shoulder of the highway. They then offered to drop me off at the nearest exit.

Great! I though after they left me at the off-ramp. *I'm dumped off on the exit of Route 28, a major highway, and now I have no car, no plates to drive it, no money, and no drugs—because all the crack I have left is back in the van. What am I gonna do now? I can't be seen walking down a major state highway to go back and get it!* (Amazingly, the cops hadn't searched my van.)

I obediently walked down the exit off the highway until the cops pulled away and disappeared. Then I turned around and walked as fast as I could back to my van, weaving in and out of the bushes beside the road trying not to be seen. I made it and drove home through the back streets while finishing off my crack.

Even so, new frustration and worry set in. Getting away with things just wasn't easy anymore.

Part Two

...INTO THE LIGHT

Tim at the historic First Presbyterian Church in Pittsburgh reminiscing when God first tapped him on the shoulder as a young teen and highlighted to him the big, hungry crowds attending Kathryn Kuhlman meetings going on there. ("Still a lot of glory and big angels hanging around this place!")

Tim re-visting (13 years later) the old and long abandoned "house of death"—the Pittsburgh, Lovelace Street house (the house he died in).

Tim at the Pittsburgh Cemetery visiting his parents' graves and thankful for God's intervention in his life pulling him from an early grave and hell.

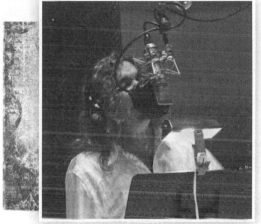

Tim recording "inspired message" voice tracks at Capitol Records, Hollywood, CA

Feelin' the "heavy glory presence" while recording voice tracks at Capitol Records, Hollywood, CA

Tim pauses at "The Miracles" star while on Hollywood Street ministry assignment.

Tim Ehmann
Hollywood Street ministry assignment

Tim on music video shoot for "Heart of Love" single, Big Bear Lake, CA

11

GO GET
TIMMY NOW!

Come to Me, all you who labor and are heavy laden,
and I will give you rest. Take My yoke upon you
and learn from Me, for I am gentle and lowly in heart,
and you will find rest for your souls.
For My yoke is easy and My burden is light.
— MATTHEW 11:28–30 NKJV

Around this time, I got a surprise visit from an old friend, Beau, who lived in Washington, a town not far from Pittsburgh. Beau was an ex-addict who had painted for me on and off for about nine years. He now ran a halfway house in Washington while painting and doing fix-it jobs to help support it. He hadn't seen me in years and happened to be doing a job nearby and needed a painter to help him, so he stopped by to see if I wanted the job.

I was just leaving the house to go and try something stupid again when I saw him sitting in his car on the street. He'd already come up to the porch and looked in the windows, but he'd returned to the car, too scared to knock on the door.

When I walked up to his car window, he took one look at me and bellowed in disbelief, "What are you doing to yourself, man?" He couldn't even look at me. "Look at this place!" he barked, gesturing toward the house with utter disgust on his face. The last time Beau had seen my Lovelace Street house, he was on my painting crew fixing it up with me. It was immaculate back then, and he couldn't believe how it looked now.

We talked for a while, but he had a hard time holding eye contact. Finally, he blurted out, "Come with me—and stay in Washington!"

Without any other options, I agreed and left with Beau.

I slept on his apartment couch for the first three nights and went to work with him days, painting the best I could. After that he arranged to get me an apartment in the twelve-step halfway house complex he ran, but I was required to go to their rehab meetings. By the time I settled into the new apartment, he had me running his painting crews, which included some of the guys in his program. Once again, I got and stayed clean. But after only three weeks, I started slipping away on my lunch breaks to drive to Pittsburgh to cop some crack.

Soon everyone in the drug-free program knew I was back to using. I had just given up. I even stopped going to the mandatory meetings. I didn't believe any of that could help me anymore. Nothing I did through my own "willpower" could stop my long-entrenched habit and intense craving for drugs. However, when Beau found out, he carefully weighed everything out and decided to let me to stay.

One day I quoted a bid to paint a residential house owned by a couple who turned out to be a Christian pastor and his wife. Beau told me I had to bid the job high at fifteen thousand dollars because he had an agreement with the apartment complex owner that he was to give him half of what he made as payment for the rental apartments he used for his program. The quote was ridiculously high, and I thought for sure we weren't going to get the job, but I did as Beau directed.

The couple had already gotten other bids for the job, the lowest being two thousand dollars by a pastor friend who painted on the side. As they discussed the bids with each other, though, God spoke to them, saying, "No. I want you to choose the highest bidder."

They were stunned, saying, "What, God? Really?" Understandably, they struggled with this for a while. But since the couple knew God's voice and were committed to following Him, they hired us.

It was late October, too cold for outside painting in Washington, so that was another "coincidental" aspect of getting this job. As well, I had only myself and one other painter to do the work, so it would take some time.

The pastor's wife, Debbie, would come out to check on our progress, occasionally bringing us hot drinks and staying to chat with me. Then she started inviting me inside for my breaks, providing a warm house and friendly conversation. She seemed curious about my life and asked a lot of thought-evoking questions. Then she'd share about her and her husband's lives, but she'd interject it with talk about God. I learned that they pastored a church in the inner-city area of Washington and ministered to drug addicts and prostitutes in that neighborhood.

After three weeks working there, I told her what I'd been experiencing with God. She got excited, quickly affirming it was "so obvious" that God was dealing extraordinarily with me and acknowledging that it was plainly evident that I had a great call on my life. She and her husband were very kind to me, and we had a great time talking. They encouraged me at a time I truly needed it, and as Debbie talked to me, she was strategically planting seeds in me.

Months later, she shared that soon after we started the work on her house, God spoke to her, saying, "Go get Timmy now!" A little embarrassed, she admitted she happened to be sitting on the toilet at the time, but said that was why she started inviting me inside for breaks. The crazy thing was, we spent so much time talking that it got to where I was mostly at their house to hang out for a month and talk—while getting paid.

The painting job wasn't finished until spring, but nobody seemed concerned about that. We finally agreed that God had set the whole thing up, just to get me even closer to Him through good conversations, caring love, and encouraging friendship without judgment. Debbie and Steve became good friends, and even after the job was done, they often invited me over for dinner. God was also tapping me on the shoulder and showing me a great example of a stable, godly marriage with a family life marked by peace, love, respect, purpose, and joy. After years of turbulence, instability, and craziness, this was foreign but also intrigued me. In fact, it attracted me.

Around this time, November 2002, when I was still doing crack and heroin daily, God tightened the unseen perimeter fence another huge notch. While I was alone in my apartment one night, resting on the floor because I was really high, a flickering started in front of my eyes. It resembled an old black-and-white film playing intensely fast on a screen. I felt like my life again was about to fade out.

When I glanced across the living room, the TV was off, but there in the screen I clearly saw the face of Satan—red and threatening and staring straight at me with a hideous, evil grin. Immediately, I knew what was up. My life was flickering out, and I was terrified.

That evil face stared at me with that horrifying grin for at least a couple of minutes. I began to panic uncontrollably, and my heart raced so fast that I thought it would come out of my chest. I said to myself, *I know how to get out of this one!* That's when I cried out for the very first time in my life, "God! Please help me!"

"Go get a phone book!" He immediately answered.

"What? Go get a…phone book?" My mind raced on overload. But most of the things God said to me made no sense to my natural mind anyway, and I wasn't about to debate with Him now. I got up and scrambled all over the apartment, trying to find a phone book I didn't know I had. Unbelievably, I found one.

When I picked it up, God said, "Look up a church!"

Huh? I thought as I randomly split the book open with my thumbs. It happened to land open right in the section where churches were listed. I looked at the long list through my still-flickering eyes, wondering which one I was supposed to call. I grabbed the phone and dialed the first one on the list, but it rang and rang and there was no answer.

It was late on a Saturday night, and I was so desperate that I couldn't think straight. *Are churches even open on Saturdays—or is it Sundays—let alone late at night?* I didn't know. I couldn't remember, and dread overtook me. Praying desperately, I cried out again, "God, help!"

Randomly, I slammed my finger into the open page and called the church it landed on. The phone rang and rang again, and just as I was about to hang up, someone picked up. A girl's voice told me there was no one there to talk to me as it was after their business hours and added that she wasn't even supposed to answer the phone. But then she paused and suggested I come to their service the next morning and gave me the time. For some reason, before she hung up, she stressed with urgency in her voice, "You go!"

After I hung up, the flickering settled down and my apartment appeared normal again. But I was still uneasy and very nervous. I even started to get sick with worry. It felt like I was being encircled by the "fence," and I knew I was running out of options and time.

That night I couldn't sleep. I lay there in bed thinking through the circumstances of my life up to that point—all the surreal events I'd been constantly protected through, the uninvited but merciful invasion of God into my life, hearing His voice day and night, the perpetual encounters, always being seen and "followed" no matter what I did. Even the invasion of my thoughts. This pursuing God also seemed to have some sort of weird influence on people and circumstances around me. I was being relentlessly chased by this crazy, out-of-control God no matter where I was or what I did!

I weighed my alternatives too. I was still being hunted by the Devil—and I knew he *really* wanted me back in hell. I'd been increasingly sensing and even seeing the looming danger God repeatedly and lovingly warned me about. I knew this Enemy was *very* real, and I could even feel and see his intense, seething anger and hatred toward me at times. I felt like the target of a very personal vendetta—and I knew I didn't want any part of that.

Moreover, I thought about what was holding me back from jumping into God wholeheartedly. The last thing I held onto so stubbornly was the thought that I'd somehow lose "me." But in light of all the truth God so patiently and repeatedly had been teaching and showing me through the relationship He had just started with me, I thought, *What do I really have to lose anyway?* Nothing I did on my own was working. My life was all junk, destruction, and death. It was all the wrong road. But maybe—just maybe—I had everything to gain?

My thoughts flipped back and forth all night as I tried to think everything through. It didn't really matter anymore. I couldn't hide, and I could no longer outrun God no matter what I did. He invaded my life time after time. I couldn't go anywhere to get away from Him. Even going to hell couldn't stop Him from finding and coming after me. This wild and crazy God who I'd never looked or asked for in the first place came at me from every angle now. But mercifully, He gave me enough to allow me to see and know my real choices. I was totally hemmed in.

Emotions flooded me as I came to the stark realization that what I'd been running from—and what relentlessly chased me my entire life—was Love Himself! I cried a lot that night. The reality and truth hit me hard, bringing my clarity to a whole new level.

The next morning I drove to the church for the morning service. When I got there, I sat in the back row by the door. I wasn't used to being in church and kind of hoped no one would notice me. I sat there wondering what I was supposed to do—and what was going to happen next. I was just doing what God had told me to do.

A couple came up to me not long after I sat down, and they introduced themselves as the pastor and his wife. Then their worship music began. As soon as the music was over, the pastor walked up to the front and picked up the mic while everyone waited in silence. He pointed directly at me and announced he had a "word from God" for me. Then he prophesied in front of everyone the words God gave him:

> "My son, I have brought you from the darkness of your past—and put a desire in your heart to seek Me. I have plans for your life that you cannot even imagine yet. I am taking hold of your life! For a season you will experience Me like never before. There's a call on your life. I have saved you for a reason. Apply yourself to seek My face, study My Word. I will use you to redeem people out of the same things I have redeemed you out of. I will lay my hand on you and draw on your family too."

I was stunned. That pastor didn't know anything about me. I'd never met him before that morning.

Something broke in me that day. I could feel the change. The weighty ton of bricks lifted off my back and I could breathe again. I felt different—light, happy. Most of all, I felt pure freedom unlike I'd ever known before. All the bondage suddenly left. My thirty-year-old deep-seated addictions, the cravings, even the desire to get high—just left. *Gone.* God just took it all away, and again, I hadn't even asked Him to! And, incredibly, I had no withdrawal symptoms.

My whole life changed that day. All I now wanted was more of this God and to *really* get to know Him—and to fully respond to and step into the love relationship He had just started with me. I could think of little else besides Him and His outrageous love for me.

The prophesying pastor, Craig, contacted me often to check up on me and invite me out to talk. At one point, we reviewed the day we met, and both of us couldn't help but be struck with wonder. It had obviously been another "God set-up." He had positioned, timed, directed, and used everyone on my behalf. Craig also told me he only gave prophetic words in the mid-week classes he taught. He hadn't prophesied in his Sunday services for the past twenty-five years—until the day I walked in. He said he *had* to that day; God had spoken to him, telling him he needed to do it then and there.

It turned out his daughter Rachel was the girl who had answered the church phone on the Saturday night I called. We all marveled at the "coincidence" that she happened to be at the church office late on a Saturday night, which she never was. She also told me how unusual it was that she picked up the church business phone because she "never does after hours." I again learned that God is not only in control, but that He also uses the unusual and impossible as a signature mark of how He works.

Today, I'm so ever grateful that God didn't leave me alone. He never once gave up on me, and I've repeatedly experienced how He stays faithful to me even when I haven't been faithful to Him. I would have been lost forever in hell's torment if His love hadn't been so tenacious. Even when I didn't care about Him or want to know Him, He kept pouring rivers of His mercy, love, and undeserved favor over me while protecting me as He brought me to know Him. It was that perpetual love that finally broke me, proving irresistible in the end.

God is totally unintimidated by anyone or anything. No "case" is too hard for Him. He's amazingly creative in how He tries to get us. He's the most radical "rebel" of all time, in total revolt against whatever tries to enslave us, rip us off, and destroy us. He's a fanatic on a mission for *you*. No resistance can stop His plans—no indifference, rebellion, or even unbelief in Him. Even death can't stop Him. In fact, I've come to personally know that this "raising the dead" thing is one of His *favorite* specialties.

At this point, it had been two years since God pulled me from hell and started His relationship with me. I finally surrendered and reciprocated, stepping completely into Him as much as I knew how—because now I *wanted* to. I can't even take credit for that. He orchestrated even that desire for Him in me.

It all began with two simple but earnest words: "God, help!" That was all He had so patiently waited for—and things *really* took off from there!

12

ASK GOD!

Therefore, if anyone is in Christ,
he is a new creation;
old things have passed away;
behold, all things have become new.

– 2 CORINTHIANS 5:17

What an incredible, personal God! Now that He'd taken away the last major strongholds that had been destroying and hindering my life, He finally had my full attention. Mostly important, He finally had my heart.

I really wanted to know Him and be fully engaged in our relationship. He had waited a long time for me, and I could feel His excitement, knowing that we could finally "do more things together." He had much more He wanted to show me, and I could no longer help myself. All I wanted was more of Him and his blazing love affair.

I started reading the Bible and couldn't put it down. God put this hunger in me, to "will and desire" for the things of Him (Philippians 2:13). This new desire didn't come from me trying to manufacture it; it was supernaturally deposited in me and seemed to overtake my heart. And all things became new.

It's easy to do what you desire to do. I read the Bible for eight hours a day every day, unable to put it down, because it sparked an all-day back-and-forth conversation opportunity with God. The revelations and discoveries I made while hanging out with Him were actually fun.

I often felt Him poke or nudge me, throwing in added comments here and there as I read. Occasionally, I'd catch glimpses of Jesus looking over my shoulder, personally pointing out what He wanted to emphasize to me. Through it all, He personally imparted more of His deep truths into me.

I could plainly sense and see His great delight in all of it too. He seemed like a giddy kid in a candy shop as I felt His hard-won satisfaction at getting to watch me discover all the treasures He'd been waiting to show me. I thought He had purposely planted some things in that Bible just for me, because I could see how everything spoke directly to me and my life. It blew me away that things He'd been telling and showing me were already written right there in that book—*after the fact*—and it was thousands of years old! The Bible was another tool God used to speak to me, but He uses anything in our everyday lives to teach us about Himself when we're in tune with Him.

The Bible really is a prophetic book of God-breathed words and truth that will always stand the test of time. It is divine revelation from God, and He loves to reveal it to us. The Bible tells God's love story for us from cover to cover. It's a supernatural book of more than just words printed on a page; the words are actually "active and alive" (Hebrews 4:11 NIV). Really, it's no wonder Jesus is referred to as the "Living Word."

Like just an ordinary closed book, we can't understand the Bible or see it as it's meant to be until the Spirit of God personally comes, breathes on us, and opens our spiritual eyes, ears, and understanding to get it. Then it becomes a very personal love letter tailored just to you—because He'll personally reveal Himself to you through it, truth by truth. It's meant to inspire us to come closer to the lover of our soul who wants us to know Him intimately by interacting with us one-on-one. Even so, the relationship with the author Himself is the most important aspect of all. Without that, we have no understanding of it.

God surprised me further with His next amazing act. My sick,

ASK GOD! – 115

ravaged, and terribly abused body quickly healed. Doctors later confirmed that all my organs were restored. Normal color returned to my eyes and skin, my brain fog disappeared, and I gained all my normal weight back. As if that weren't enough, even my scars and track marks completely disappeared—all except for one bump the size of a pencil eraser on the side of one wrist. I believe God left that there as a physical token of remembrance of His great love and all He'd done for me. He had not only protected me through years of stupid and death-defying acts, but He also saved me, delivered me, and now completely healed me. God truly does it all!

Steve and Debbie, the friends God led me to while painting their house, continued to invite me over for dinner. I also became close to Pastor Craig, who had prophesied over me. I was now eager to get moving on all the things God had told and shown me were part of my destiny. I wanted to get to the music part—to get on a stage where He would use me and I could tell the world all He'd done for me. When he showed that to me, He'd laid it out with such detail and certainty, as if it were already done. I knew it was going to happen. But Craig wisely pointed out to me, "Tim, you need to develop your relationship with God more before He sends you out."

Little did I understand the preparation and challenging training years still ahead of me as I walked in the calling toward my longed-for destiny. I now know that we all must take this path before He brings us to our main mission, the destiny He has for us. He walks right there with us through the entire journey, and I've learned the hard way that impatience or trying to make it happen ourselves will never get us there any faster. Though God gives a lot of encouragement, precious gifts, fun with Him, and inciting previews along the way, the relationship alone *always* has to come first, and it's meant to stay that way from beginning to end.

I was glad to have new friends who knew God and clearly heard His voice. They encouraged me to not only continue listening to Him but also to be sure to obey. I'll never forget the best advice Craig ever gave me. I was asking him questions about God, and he said, "Enough! You already have it. You're hearing God's voice well. Don't ask me any more questions. Ask God!"

Of course, I knew he was right. That's how things started when God first came to me. Why would I let go of that and lean on others for information about Him? He was already personally giving me what I needed firsthand—and I was learning that He's always right on.

God *has* to be our first and foremost teacher once we're on this walk. We can't even come to Him unless He draws us close and we hear His voice calling us (John 6:44). Even when we desire to seek Him out and know Him, He's the one who puts that in us. God seeks us out first, and it's throughout our entire lives He calls us, till the last possible moment—and in my case, mercifully— and even then some. We might think that we've found God, but really, it's always Him who finds us. We just finally recognize it's His voice and that it's been Him that's been calling us all along.

Most can't understand this until they've been brought to a place where they finally know it's Him and that their hearts are ready enough to receive it. For some, like me, that was a strategic process, but I'm so glad He didn't give up on me.

Everything God says is trustworthy and accurate. He knows everything unique about us, and He knows just how to get us, motivate us, and lead us along in a way that's perfectly designed for our unique personality. He'll often talk to us like a friend in relationship with us.

We shouldn't let any voice except God's become the primary voice we listen to and obey. We must hear and recognize His voice, and we're meant to follow it as He teaches us "discernment" of it, which is being able to separate His voice from all the others we hear—including our own.

God is always talking to believers and unbelievers alike, and He often repeats Himself. If we spend time with Him and quiet our mind and heart, we can hear Him, though He talks in many ways. Most often it's to our spirit, but we may hear Him speaking right through our heart or into our thoughts, like spontaneous thoughts that seem not our own. They're most often so soft that we may ignore or dismiss them if we're not paying attention.

Learning to know God's voice and separate it from the other voices competing for your attention can be like maneuvering a sixteen-lane highway. It's always your own voice (mind, reason, and thoughts), another person's, the Enemy's, or His. At first it may feel like you're veering all over the sixteen lanes trying to learn which lane is really Him. Through relationship time, paying attention, and reading His Word, the highway will narrow down to eight lanes, then four, then two—until you find the one precision lane that brings completely reliable accuracy. When you obey it, it brings heaven's realm right to earth—and things are done!

Other times, God may prefer to show you things, demonstrating truths through visions or dreams. This can also come through feeling His familiar presence, "impressions," or nudges, or even through physical or emotional feelings. He also may speak to you audibly or say things through "signs in the spirit" as well as "signs in the natural." These "signs" can occur anywhere around you in the natural world or your circumstances. Always watch for them. They're "prophetic signs" that will confirm what He's been saying to you all along.

"My sheep listen to my voice," Jesus says, "but they will never follow a stranger" (John 10:27, 10:5 NIV). When you become His child, your rightful inheritance is the relationship. When you have that, you have everything you need.

Just like with any relationship, the more you spend time with God, the more familiar you become with Him. Most of all, you're meant to have fun with Him along the journey—no matter what stage you're at. Listen, watch, and practice tuning in and discerning His voice so you recognize it more and more, and guard this precious gift with all you have by obeying it. He'll then give you more.

God is interested in every minute detail of your life and wants to be a part of all of you do and are. He loves to "hang out" with you all the time. You shouldn't ignore Him, because it's a great privilege. After all, this is the Most High God of the universe and your creator wanting to spend one-on-one time with you every day. It's like you're His favorite! He's not a friend who will leave or desert you—no matter what—even when you're doing stupid things. And He can do this with each and every one of us individually because He's God.

I know from experience that it thrills God to have our attention and He loves our heartfelt affection for Him. He actually craves it! Walking with and obeying Him, even when we don't understand, is of primary importance to Him. It's all a matter of *trust*, which is the number one thing we can give back to Him to show our love. That's what pleases Him most.

When God speaks, He never lies like humans can (Numbers 23:19; Titus 1:2). He even went so far as to make a promise that those who put their trust in Him will never be ashamed that they did so (Romans 10:11; Isaiah 49:23c). That even goes for the times when we trust what we know He's said even though we may not fully understand it at the time. He's doing a lot more behind the scenes than we can see in the natural realm. Finally, trust that He's *always* looking out for our good just like He says, and in time that will be evidenced in our life.

One day, overcome with newfound emotions of such closeness with Him, I point-blank asked God how I could better show my love and affection for Him. I was shocked by His reply. With a mushy, cozying-up-to-me tone, He replied, "Just schmoose on me, Timmy. Like you would talk sweetly and affectionately to the one you love. I like that."

He made me laugh. I never knew I could talk to God like that. That's part of a close, intimate love relationship. And He allows us to get in as close to Him as we want. We can even ask Him to place in us more desire to do so.

I'm careful to acknowledge and include Him in everything now, because I know He's the best friend I have, like no other.

He'll never leave me or forsake me in all I do and whatever I go through. And He continually shows me He wants to be acknowledged as with me all the time—even in the small stuff. Wanting to practice this more, I started doing just that.

For example, one day God plainly told me to go buy a football jersey. I was puzzled, wondering if I'd really heard Him correctly. "What, God?" I asked. "Did I hear you right? You know I'm not really into sports. What would I want with a football jersey?"

He knew that wasn't something I'd normally choose to buy or even wear. But He didn't respond with further detail at the time. By now I knew that if God told me to do something, no matter how small, I needed to do it. Though I didn't understand and wasn't in the mood to go buy something I didn't want, I needed to trust Him.

I went down to a local store, Gabriel's, and looked around. I scanned the different sample team shirts on the store wall, waiting to get "something" from God that would lead me. My eyes landed on a jersey that somehow stood out from the others, almost like there was a light superimposed on it. Though I didn't hear Him speak, I got this strong feeling that this was my shirt.

It was a white jersey with *New Orleans Saints* in big gold letters. I stood there almost arguing with God in my thoughts, thinking, *What's going on here? Why* this *shirt?* Even so, I purchased the shirt, and a few minutes later as I walked out of the store, God immediately confirmed it: "Now I want you to wear it every day for the next year."

What, God? Why? I thought, puzzled at the strange instructions.

Again, He didn't answer. But I knew I'd heard Him right, and I had also been learning that sometimes His silence speaks volumes too. I needed to do what He said until He gave further instructions. All of this was strategic training by God.

So for the next year I wore that shirt nearly every day till it was almost worn out. I had to give up what I—or anyone else— thought about it. It wasn't until a full year later that He finally showed me why.

I was home one day when I got a strong urge to turn on the TV, which I rarely watched. Right then a breaking news alert came on, showing Hurricane Katrina hitting New Orleans. God immediately brought my attention to my shirt. He'd sent me to buy that New Orleans jersey exactly one year prior to the day New Orleans got hit by this monster hurricane. I was stunned. It was one of the most devastating disasters in US history, with many losing their homes and lives, and I was watching it all as it happened.

I'd worn that shirt faithfully in obedience to God, not really understanding why. I knew He was using it to teach me to listen to whatever He would tell me, whether I understood it or not. He kept telling me to trust and obey Him, even in the small things. He said it was an integral part of the calling He had on my life, so that one day He could trust me with more.

As I thought about what He had been saying with the shirt, I realized He had made me a walking reminder and a visual prophetic act displayed daily to Him and others. He wanted to show the world, and me, that this city and its people were already heavy on His heart and mind a year before it happened.

There's always deep meaning and many layers to things God says, no matter how trivial or unimportant they may seem to us. Even a little thing can speak a lot, and sometimes only over time is everything revealed. It's not always meant for just us. Sometimes it's for others—or even just Him—but we get to be part of what He's doing. And in some way, I know it's powerfully effective. It was not only part of His step-by-step training in properly discerning His voice, but also His sharing with me more revelation of His great, compassionate heart. My job was to simply listen and obey.

After that, I learned to run everything I did by God first and to quit relying on my own understanding. I even gave up my own opinions on things and just resolved myself to let Him teach me how to think and live from scratch.

Then one day, God freaked me out a little when He took me another step farther and told me to put down absolutely *everything*

I did on my own after that—and that I shouldn't even seek a paying job to support myself anymore. He said He wanted me to learn to rely solely on Him. When I finally agreed, He then asked me to spend most of my time alone with Him. He wanted me to get and stay tuned to His voice and heart and fill myself up totally with Him. When I wondered how I would make it with no income, God again assured me that He alone would take care of me.

After that, everything I did—24/7—was with God. He had me on a fast track. I spent my days one-on-one with Him, talking with Him, worshipping, reading His Word, and just hanging out with Him. He totally saturated me with Himself. Soon I could feel His light and glory filling me in waves, so much that the time passed in total bliss with His wonderful Spirit encompassing me wherever I was.

The Bible says, "In Your presence *is* fullness of joy; At your right hand *are* pleasures for evermore" (Psalm 16:11). King David knew it, as did so many more. Once they tasted His amazing presence, they wanted only to stay there with Him and never leave. I knew how they felt. His presence is awesome, invigorating, peaceful, healing, pleasurable, and even fun. God knows what we need and what we like. In a way, He became my new "high," and He totally knew how to bring it. People are always looking to get it through some destructive counterfeit, but as they say, "There ain't no high like the Most High!" And I was going to drink in all I could.

Not long after that, God started sending me out on what He called "personal assignments" with Him every night. He set me up by opening doors to lead me right where He wanted me to go. If I got off-course heading in the wrong direction, He didn't just gently warn me; He'd set up circumstantial roadblocks so I couldn't go that way. Soon I noticed that every time I heard correctly and went wherever He led, He would back me up with His power and miracles.

My friends soon dubbed me the "prophet magnet." Everywhere I went, if there was a prophet of God who heard His voice well, he or she would have a "word from God" for me. These were often more confirmations of what God had already done or shown me in my life. The words came from people who didn't even know me, but they were also always spot-on. It was great encouragement from Him.

One day I visited a ministry where a gifted prophet randomly called me out of the crowd. Someone recorded it for me. He said:

> God, I thank you for shutting the door on the past—all the threads. I saw like this demonic octopus that was trying to keep a grip on you with its little suction cups, but I saw God severing it off, severing it off. And I saw the key of God just closing that door. I saw chains popping and snapping that the Enemy had placed—wrapped around you. I saw how there was a season when you were so rooted and grounded in the ways of the Enemy—in the world system. But the Lord says, "I'm taking you up out of that," and the Lord says, "I'm bringing you into My way of life." And the Lord says, "I'm bringing a full deliverance." I'm bringing a complete turnaround." And the Lord says, "Get ready, oh man of God. You're like Gideon. I'm calling you a man of God. You'll be wild and you'll be radical and you'll be a soul winner for Me. And many will come into My kingdom because of your obedience." And the Lord says, "You're gonna speak to those in high places; key strategic places—even in the world system that'll even be well known." And the Lord says, "You'll draw them because they'll look at your life. They'll hear My voice speak through you." And the Lord says, "Get ready! Because the door now is being closed on the past. You're never to return there. You're never to go there. It is a prison. It is *hell's gates*. You're never to go there!" The Lord says, "Now march forward, for I'm opening up heaven's gates. I'm getting ready to give you more visions and dreams. Oh, some will think you're looney—some will think you're nuts! But I'm going to show you different

things about my throne room," says God. "All you gotta do is just wait on me."

The Lord says, "I'm strumming you." I saw like the fingers of God inside your heart, your spirit, and your soul, like fingers strumming a musical instrument—a stringed instrument. He's synchronizing you. He's harmonizing you. He's tuning you up to the spirit sounds of heaven. Get ready, because your days are not over! You've been in this holding tank cell while I've been bringing change in your life. But the day comes when you're gonna flourish and bear much fruit for My kingdom," says the Lord. "So the gifting I placed in you that was once tarnished, is now being polished for My glory." Thank you, Father!

Then a couple of months later came another confirming word from God through a prophet I'd also never met before. He took one look at me after I walked into the room, got up, took the mic, pointed to me, and said:

Sir, I saw in your hand a guitar. When I looked at you, I saw a guitar. You are a very gifted man with an ability to write music. And you've written some very powerful songs that have done nothing. And I'm here to tell you, the Lord says that as you keep serving Him, there's going to come an hour and a time that He's going to release, finally release the gift. And some of your songs are going to top the charts; natural songs—not "Christian" songs. What do you think about that? Hmm?

You had wrong friends and you lived the wrong life. And the fact that you're here today is only by God's grace—God's grace that you're even alive! Because you did some very stupid things! You risked your life in some areas and God has had to help you, protect you from things— and you are here. Your life has just begun. You have no idea. You've written some amazing songs that will do well, but you're going to write some even more amazing songs. You are like a wine that has gone mature and you have ability now to write songs better than ever before. Your best songs are up ahead of you—and they're going to touch lives. God doesn't want your songs to be "Christian." He wants them to be in the world with a "Christian flavor," so they will top the charts—and touch the world. Do you understand? Big difference!

It is your destiny—it's what you were born for. Yes, it's what you were born for! You yourself have a lot of love in your heart and a lot to give. God says…that He is going to restore. He's going to fix your life. Better than you could have dreamt it could be! It's going to be a testimony, a story that's going to be remarkable enough to be told on national TV in the years that lie up ahead. It's your destiny. It's what's going to happen! But take one step at a time. Don't be in a hurry. God is with you. You may seem like a little painter tucked away in a small town, but you ain't seen nothin' yet, honey! That's what I'm talkin' about!

13

YOU JUST GOTTA BELIEVE!

He is not a God of the dead but of the living.
– LUKE 20:38B

Craig, my pastor friend, invited me to go out with him on some of his pastoral ministry outings because he wanted to show me "the kingdom of God at work in the world." He first took me to a wedding he was officiating, and I went along to help with the sound system and observe.

My life had been so caught up in wildness that I'd never been to a wedding before, not even my own despite how I was now forty-six years old. God pointed this out to me, and I asked Him if I would ever get married and if I could start dating again. He responded, "Not now, Timmy. We have too much to do. But later you will. You will even get married, but it will happen right before I bring you to your destiny I showed you."

For the first time in my life, I really wanted to meet and marry the right woman—one who also knew God. It became a new yearning inside me, but I had to put it on the back burner because I knew He was right.

In the rock 'n' roll entertainment industry, I'd slept with many women, often a different one every night. But God put a great grace on my life now, and I wasn't even attracted to that kind of lifestyle anymore. Besides, God now let me see in the spirit what I would be getting into if I tried to return to that life, and I wanted no part of it.

There's a spiritual principle that works like the natural principle of "whomever you sleep with, you can get what they've got." Sex is more than just a joining together of flesh as "one"; it's also a joining of whatever spirit(s) are on or in those people. You may not realize it right afterward, but one day you may notice the manifestation of what you've possibly unknowingly joined yourself with. It could be what's attached to the other person's life, such as a spirit of lust, greed, anger, anxiety, fear, or even things like sickness, lack, or poverty. Things you wouldn't think were related to anything you did, may oppress your life. By then, you won't know how they got there. And once there, only God has the power to free you or protect you from these things. He's the *only one* with the true authority and power to make them leave.

The Enemy and his dark spirits are always looking for further "rights" to us. We automatically give him those rights every time we engage in the things God lovingly warns us to stay away from (because He doesn't want us in this kind of bondage). This can also happen whether we're doing it purposely or ignorantly.

Because I'd fallen in love with God and spent so much time with Him, He also helped me in this by keeping me wisely distracted. As well, I respected Him and had so much fun with Him. This was another great miracle He was doing in my life, because abstinence had been such an impossibility for me before. And thankfully, God had a measure of miraculous protection from physical disease on my life throughout my former years as well.

The wedding I attended with Craig was beautiful. I watched it with newfound awe and placed its memory on a back shelf of my heart. Later, Craig took me to see a popular Christian healing minister. He was a heavyset guy, filled with the Holy Spirit, who would sit in a chair at the front of the room. People would walk up to him, and he'd say something over them. They'd come away healed of all kinds of problems, diseases, and ailments. I was intrigued.

A new training period began when God told me He wanted to show me how different kinds of ministries operated. "Most of all," He said, "I want to show you whether they really know Me or not."

So I'd go when and where He told me to go. He also warned me that I was to stay tuned into Him only, and that I was to leave if He told me to do so.

For a while I was led to volunteer as a prayer counselor for a TV station called Cornerstone TV, a Pittsburgh ministry program that people could call in to if they had prayer needs. With a whole bank of telephone operators working there, it amazed me that all the calls that came to my phone were people wanting help with the *exact* problems God had set me free from. God's heart and His spirit of wisdom came through as He gave me the words to say and prophesy into each one's specific situation. Many of those words clearly hit home, because people would comment how precise the counsel or prayers were and how much they helped them.

God knows each and every person. I certainly didn't, but when I stayed in tune with Him, He'd tell or show me exactly what to say or do. That brings a true touch of God on a person, with His power and miracles to back it up. It has to be all Him—not our opinions or words born of our soul realm, but those straight from His Spirit because He's omniscient. He knows each individual's situation and needs, and when we learn to tune in to Him, He uses us for others' good. It's awesome to be a part of what He'll do through us, but we can never take the credit for it. That only belongs to Him.

Not long after this, Pastor Craig offered me a ministry position as the teen worship leader at his church, giving me free reign to run it. I asked God what He wanted me to do, and He answered, "Go for it." After I started working with the teens and their bands, I gave them free guitar lessons and invited them to my home an extra evening each week to teach them to play. I really enjoyed mentoring them. They were there to play the rock 'n' roll vibe to worship songs, but I used the time to teach them to tune in to God and write and play the spontaneous, inspired songs He would give them.

Not long after this, God led me to open a coffee shop in the town of Washington. I named it City Child Services, after one of my former bands. A place for people to hang out and listen to music for free, we had live worship bands of all genres, including rock, punk, and metal. People came for the good music, but they also got the "good message." I held weekly meetings there where I or some of the pastors I knew taught about God. Sometimes hundreds of people would come.

The shop had a little bedroom in the back, which I moved into. One afternoon while I lay resting in that room, an angel appeared at the foot of my bed. He stood there holding what looked like an unlit BIC lighter in his hand. Tears rolled down his cheeks, and he sadly kept looking between the lighter and me, over and over. After a couple of minutes, he disappeared. I pondered this visit for a while before God gave me understanding of it. I knew He was encouraging me to get even more lit up with His light.

Pastor Steve, Debbie's husband, was a great bass player, so I put together a band with him. We played at my coffee shop and also in the Pittsburgh nightclubs a few nights a week. We played mostly hard rock music, and God told me to prophesy through the music as He gave me the words. Through those songs, I would also tell everyone who would listen about what God did for me.

Steve and I loved to hang out and talk with the people who came, and then we also started going to the streets. When we stepped out, God would just draw to us the people He wanted to touch. Soon we started visiting Narcotics Anonymous (NA) meetings, three-quarter houses for addicts, and regular hospitals. Sometimes we'd go to see people in their homes because they were too sick, high, and strung out to leave. God wanted to meet people wherever they were. We reached out to them with His love and encouragement, meeting their needs the best we could and bringing the light of God's kingdom into these familiar dark and hopeless places. I loved how the laughter and joy of heaven would hit everyone and God would back us up with His great miracles.

People high or drunk would get instantly sober, delivered right there from their addictions and other demonic strongholds. God healed their bodies too. We saw them transform right before our eyes. Many subsequently opened their hearts to God because He so dramatically demonstrated His outright love for them despite their situations. That's the way God rolls.

God also sent me to the crack houses in Pittsburgh, even to some of the same places where I used to deal, get high, and sometimes stay. These places were typically filthy and ravaged, and people were always partying, strung out on the floor, or dealing. Even so, He'd show up there too. Surprisingly, being back in my old environment—playing the music around all the drugs, booze, and women—none of it even appealed to me anymore. I went to these places solely because God sent me and I was on His mission. His covering was over me, and none of it affected me anymore, even though I was right in the middle of it.

I began writing and recording new songs during this time, but these were songs that God gave me. I didn't want to play anything I thought up on my own. What came from just me didn't carry God's power, nor would it produce something that would count for eternity. He had me record songs that blatantly spoke to those still caught in drugs, sex, and worldly lifestyles, and the message, I knew, hit home and called them to Him and His ways like they needed to hear. Since the words I was given had His power on them, they made all the difference in the world.

My albums *Love Letters* and *Prophesy* were recorded then. God gave me the instrumental parts first, not providing the words until I stepped up to the mic. I had to just trust He would provide His words at the right time, just like He said. That's how He began using me whenever I stepped on a stage after that. The words from Him would flow, and I'd sing or say whatever He said or showed me.

A lot of people commented that they were really touched by some of those songs. Others would be instantly healed by the power of God just by listening. I never laid hands on or touched any of them. Even I was astounded. In fact, God's miracles, healings, signs, and wonders broke out everywhere. When the precision accuracy of heaven would come, things were just done. Many lives would never be the same.

Steve and Debbie began holding weekly meetings in their house for anyone who wanted to come for good live worship music, encouragement, teaching, and prayer. Many rehabs, drug counseling centers, halfway houses, and government housing buildings existed in the inner-city area where they ministered, and the meetings filled up with drug dealers, addicts, and prostitutes who were enthusiastically welcomed. For them, having "something different to do" was the draw.

Steve led with his acoustic guitar, playing sweet worship music for two to three hours, and God would honor it with His presence. Many people would join in the worship songs. Meetings got so big at times that there was standing room only in the house. They had a chair in their living room that we dubbed the "miracle chair." We noticed that whoever sat in that particular chair got healed—every time. It was wild! We kept that chair a secret between Debbie, Steve, and I because we loved to wait and watch it happen.

One day a Peruvian drug dealer came to the house. His spine was badly curved from scoliosis, and he walked slightly bent over and was always in a lot of pain. He hadn't been able to stand up straight for most of his adult life. When he came in looking for a place to sit, he happened to choose the miracle chair. I got excited, but God said to me, "Don't even get up. Just pray toward him silently." Debbie was standing quietly and praying under her breath behind him, while Steve kept playing his guitar and worshipping.

After a while, the guy got an odd look on his face and kept squirming around, even trying to feel around on his back. We didn't say a word, and then he puzzledly commented that his spine felt different and that his back felt warm and like it was moving. Over the course of an hour, he was completely healed. When he finally stood, his back was perfectly straight and he couldn't stop marveling how all of his pain had just left. The next time I saw him, he was out on the street. He told me he was now an "ex-Peruvian drug dealer" after being blown away by the powerful touch and love of God.

Others were healed in those meetings too. Their ailments ranged from simple headaches to all kinds of diseases, even cancer. One man was sent to me by a friend one day, and he told me he was a pastor. He had great concern for an uncle who was gay and dying of AIDS. The uncle was in the ICU of a nearby hospital and didn't have much time left. The pastor was really down because he had been unsuccessfully doing all he knew to reach his uncle, a very bitter man most of his life. The pastor believed he was yet unsaved and asked me if I'd go see him.

I asked God what He wanted me to do, and He confirmed, "Yes, go." So I took my son, Tee, with me and we went to the hospital.

Because the man was in the ICU, only close family members and formal clergy could visit him. I didn't have any type of identification as clergy, and I certainly didn't look like a conventional minister. Though I was concerned about how we would get in to see him, God had already arranged it.

When we got off the elevator at the ICU entrance, the doors to the unit were wide open and the nurse's station was empty. We walked right in and down the hallway, easily finding his room. The dying man was hooked up to tubes and machines, and he looked terrible—extremely thin and frail, with a distinct death pall to his skin. The moment we stepped in his door, I felt the most amazing atmosphere of heaven in the room. God was already there. The man stirred, but he couldn't open his eyes.

I thought of what I had rehearsed in my head to say to him, but the words I had rehearsed instantly failed me. I took the man's hand, and words that weren't even mine poured out. "God sent me," I softly told him, "and this is your day of salvation." His eyes still closed, tears ran down his cheeks. I looked over at Tee, who stood there wide eyes, speechless. Deep compassion overtook me as more words bubbled out of me, telling him how much God loved him and wanted to save him today. Then I heard God tell me, "I want him with Me."

Hesitantly but obeying, I repeated to him what God had just revealed. The tears flowed like rivers down his face. I put my hands on his head and prayed for him, asking God on his behalf to forgive all his sins and enter his heart. The man couldn't speak anymore—it was too late for that—but he nodded in agreement with every word. We weren't there but five minutes while God just did His thing and then we left. Salvation came to that precious man that day as he received the free gift of life that God had already paid for on his behalf and had yearned for him to receive his whole life.

Tee had been unusually quiet, so later I asked him what was going on with him in that room. He told me he had seen angels filling the entire room, and when he was about to speak, God strongly told him, "Don't say a word. This is a holy moment."

God has His angels always around us, encouraging, watching, and waiting for the very moment a person is ready to receive Him. Then all of heaven celebrates over each person who comes in, because it's the biggest joy to God's heart (Luke 15:7, 10). God has been calling and chasing after people their whole life, just waiting for that day. As well, we need to recognize the time of our visitation and calling too, because we might not have another chance (Luke 19:44; 2 Corinthians 6:2).

Two days later, I received a report from the man who put me in touch with that pastor. He said he had died two days after we left and that his whole family, who visited him daily, kept saying that they couldn't understand why he looked so happy in his last days. But the pastor and I knew. Christ came into the man that day, and he smiled all the way home.

I've had the awesome privilege of being used by God to lead others to Him right at death's door. One of those was my old friend Allen, who I had regularly gotten high with when I was sixteen. He was one of the friends I was with when everything in my view turned upside down as God tried to warn me that I was on the wrong road. We were both now in our forties, and I'd received word that he was dying of terminal cancer in a hospice. I looked him up and went to see him. He still didn't believe in God, but it was a precious, defining moment come full circle for both of us. God showed up, and He was ready in that moment. Tears flowed uncontrollably down my old friend's face, and it was the day he stepped into the waiting heart of God and His kingdom of heaven. He died three days later.

Sometimes God decides He wants to take someone home rather than heal them. This was hard for me at first, having seen Him do such amazing miracles of healing. However, I've learned to stay sensitive to what God says and wills. Sometimes I think it's because He so wants people with Him or because He knows it's His best opportunity to get them and protect them from not being able to handle what's ahead. Where we're going to spend eternity is all that really matters to God, and with Him we're more alive than ever.

Though Dad got to see the amazing turnaround God had done in my life, Mom suddenly died just prior to when God saved me. She and Dad had never stopped praying for me, and God knew I harbored great sadness and disappointment that she didn't get to see the results of their many intercessions for me. But God was about to give me yet another unasked-for gift, and in His unbelievable love and mercy, He showed me He hadn't let my parents or me down.

One day I was invited to play with a band consisting of worship leaders from various churches who got together for a college-age outreach event. The concert was held at a large two-story church in Pittsburgh and "happened to" fall on Mother's Day of 2003. I was playing lead guitar, and we were rock-'n'-rollin' it up heavy for the college crowd there that night. I had just stepped forward on the platform to really wail the solo lead part on my guitar when I felt this wind come out of nowhere and blow through my long hair. But there weren't any fans on or open doors in the place.

I looked around at the other musicians on the stage, and no one else was experiencing this wind. It blew my hair right off my face. That's when I noticed a bright light—the familiar heavenly light—streaming in through one of the church's many upper stained glass windows. In the window I plainly saw Mom with Jesus standing right behind her, His hands on her shoulders. Both were dressed in white robes, and Mom looked down at me with an amazing smile, watching me play with great joy and contentment on her face. Jesus had a knowing smile of satisfaction on His face too. Then, within about four minutes, they faded away.

Words can't express what God did for Mom and me that day. He's the God of the living, not of the dead. It was a great Mother's Day gift for both of us as the Lord allowed her to look down from a window of heaven and see for herself that all of her prayers hadn't gone unanswered.

You just gotta believe! The prayers of mothers and fathers are so precious and powerful to God. As a Father of so many wayward kids Himself, He understands *exactly* how a parent feels. Parents need to give their children to God by continuing to hold them up in prayer, trusting Him to do what only He can do, no matter what. Those prayers go before His throne and He hears them. They don't expire, staying before Him and working even after the one who prayed is gone. Souls are even more precious to God than they are to us, and He's always looking for those who will ask and believe Him enough by standing in the gap in prayer for their children. His promise of "the effective, fervent prayer of a righteous man avails much" speaks volumes (James 5:16).

Our trust is like precious gems to God. It's in the waiting that people sometimes grow weary or want to give up. I believe that waiting is the hardest part of faith for people. We get too easily hurt and offended at God when it looks to us like things aren't going right or it seems like help is taking too long. But God can do anything, and I guarantee His wisdom is best. We have to trust that He is working out all the necessary things in His way and timing, letting His perimeter fence of love do its work. Look what my parents went through with me. Sometimes when we think all is lost, God knows better. My story shows firsthand that "it ain't over till it's over—(and sometimes) and then some." We need to cover and pray our kids through their trials and keep trusting God, even when we don't see things happening the way we want.

Another time, I had just dozed off when I had a special encounter with the Lord. Jesus came, picked me up, and started flying me all around the earth, high up at cloud level with Him. I could feel myself traveling through the air at super speeds, with Him rising and dipping. I felt like Superman.

As we soared high in the sky, I looked down and all I could see were skeletons all over the earth. I knew they represented spiritually dead people. After showing me this, He then took me higher and higher and up into heaven, but we were still hanging in the air. With a large sheet of what looked like clear Cellophane, He wrapped my whole body. Then He pulled out another sheet and wrapped another layer around me. He did this three times. I could still move because it was like I was wrapped in a big three-layered bubble. We were both laughing while He did this, but He never said a word. After He was done, He brought me back and put me in my bed. I couldn't see the bubble around me anymore, but I could still feel it securely surrounding me for the rest of the night. He left me to think on what He was saying with this fun, unexpected trip.

Scripture I had read instantly came to my mind: "Having believed, you were sealed with the Holy Spirit of promise" (Ephesians 1:13). He was demonstrating to me that I was totally safe and protected, sealed up in Him. Wrapping me up three times, I believe, represented the covering of the Father, Son, and Holy Spirit. He was letting me know that despite where I am or where He sends me, no matter how dangerous it may seem, He's got me.

I love the encouragement God always gives. It's another way He keeps showing how much He loves me.

14

GOD'S TRAINING PROGRAM

He is the God of the impossible—
and if it doesn't look impossible, it's probably not Him!

– Tim Ehmann

With the "God of the impossible," there's no end to what He can do. One thing I know for sure, we haven't begun to see or hear the half of what God has planned for this world. I can feel it. God and all of heaven is excited for it. Now and then He gives me glimpses of things He has planned ahead.

Despite all the bad things going on in our world, when darkness starts to rise, that's when God especially loves to pour out His light to overcome it and encourage us through. God loves to show off! Wrecking hell, which is trying to destroy His kids, is His highest priority, and He and His angels enjoy further humiliating the Enemy and taking back what's rightfully His. He wants us to do that *with* Him.

It often takes conflicts and trouble before people pay attention God's way. God's dynamic perimeter fence of pure love needs time for its work to finally bring our attention to recognizing and hearing Him. God's always at work setting things up for just the right opportunity to show this world just who He is. The time is now here, though, and He won't even ask for people's stubborn permission first anymore!

My life and what He's done with me is a good example of that and what He's doing these days. I know I was born for such a time as this, and I'm excited about it. I've never had more fun in my life than I've had with God in His kingdom. I have the greatest, most powerful friend and the best bodyguards, and I still get to be a "rebel." My rebellion is just pointed in the right direction now.

One day God challenged me I could have as much as I could believe Him for, so the limits would only be set by me—not Him. He is an unlimited God. Sometimes this may be harder than you think, though, because God will require you to get out of your own comfort box and abandon every former limit you've been holding on to and learn to ask and believe Him for totally unlimited things. Everything God was doing with me was designed to teach me to rely on Him for more and more. This trusting and believing thing is the basis to receiving anything from Him, and He wants to give us more than we can imagine—if we can only get our own limits off ourselves.

It's all part of "God's training program." It's necessary boot camp for anyone on this walk. Scripture tell us, "It's impossible to please God apart from faith. And why? Because anyone who wants to approach God must believe both that he exists *and* that he cares enough to respond to those who seek Him" (Hebrews 11:6 MSG). Always remember, one of the signature marks of God is that He is the God of the impossible—and if it doesn't look impossible, it's probably not Him! (Luke 1:37, 18:27; Matthew 17:20).

God began giving me more levels of Him as I walked through His strategic training. He started increasingly letting me see more of Him, His light, the angels, and the heavenly realm. It's great encouragement to me, and He knows nothing excites and refreshes me more. I think one of the reasons He lets me see so much of Himself and His kingdom at work, is because it counteracts all the dark stuff I encounter as He shares with me the truth of what's going on behind the scenes.

Often He shows me specific things that hold certain people or places in bondage. Sometimes they look like chains, bars, or ropes wrapped around people's legs, necks, arms, or bodies. I also sometimes see hideous demons sitting on someone's shoulder, head, or back, around them, or even in them. They're ugly, evil creatures that manifest in various appearances. At times they look like snakes, dragons, monkeys, creepy monsters, or other dark beings.

He also shows me certain colors or mists superimposed on or in people or things, and He's taught me what each one symbolizes. For instance, when I saw someone with black lips, He was revealing to me that the person was a God mocker. Then He began showing me certain sicknesses inside people.

I've often felt troubled by all God has me see. It can be distressing and spiritually depressing at times. So many people are walking around in various bondages of the Enemy. Every day that I walk past people, I see souls that are going through life like zombies; it kind of feels like the Twilight Zone all around me. With the spiritual veil pulled back, I plainly see the cruel, ugly, barbaric underworld of Satan's kingdom in operation around me. I hate seeing it. But God shares it with me because He hates it too. He wants people who will partner with Him to do something about it using His given authority over it. God wants people in real freedom—healed, whole, filled with His Spirit, and operating in His kingdom of light.

God also shows me those who belong to Him, with His familiar light inside them. Other times, that light is only on or around people; this tells me God is close around them and up to something in their lives.

Then it became much wilder. Not only would I "know" all sorts of things about people, but I also started hearing their thoughts. I'd pick up what they were thinking, even what they were thinking about me, without them saying a word. I even knew their secret sins. Often I'd know experiences that happened in their lives, good or bad, current or past, and sometimes God would show me what would come in their future.

God's Spirit was strong in me, and over time it grew even stronger. Sometimes He'd show me so much that it was almost more than I could take. But for some reason, I guess He thought I was ready for it. He showed and shared with me things as only He could see and know them. This "seeing" weighed heavily on me, never really going away. I couldn't bear any of it without God with me. He taught, upheld, and encouraged me through it all. He had to.

God is the source of all knowledge, wisdom, truth, and power, and He dwells in the believer by His Holy Spirit (John 14:17; 15:26; Romans 8:11). Therefore, all of Him—including His mind, eyes, ears, even His heart—dwells in the believer by His Spirit. When the supreme seer, knower, and discerner of all things comes to live inside you, He can impart what He sees and knows right to and through you at any given moment, in any given measure, as He wills (Isaiah 11:2–3; 1 Corinthians 12:1–11; Isaiah 11:2–3). This is normal life for those who walk in the real-deal relationship with Him. But we have to be in alignment with God and lit up in His light, because He's the only trustworthy source for moving in gifts like these in truth and accuracy; otherwise it's polluted. I've since learned the level of relationship we have with Him equals the level of what He'll share with us. My training in the discernment realm was exploding, though, and it came almost faster than I could process it.

I volunteered my time everywhere I went. God told me upfront that He didn't want me to take a dime as payment for the ministry work He sent me to do. He also strictly said to take no government or social assistance. He kept reminding me that I was to rely on Him and not to worry. He wanted me to learn total trust in Him to keep me pure and ready so I would be reliable in whatever He wanted to do with me.

When springtime rolled around again, I asked God about possibly going to work at my painting job again. He told me to start taking jobs and allowed me to make some money. The season started out great and I got a few big commercial jobs right away.

The business built quickly and things were going great. I'd made about twenty thousand dollars, and was hyped up and looking forward to more work, when He told me, "Now stop working. You're done for the rest of the year."

I was stunned. Things were going so well that I could have easily made much more. But He wanted me to spend the rest of the year in one-on-one time with Him and continue to go on assignments as He would lead. He added that I was to trust Him alone to take care of me for the rest of the year. I knew it was a test. He wanted to see if I'd obey. What else could I do? I was all in and it was all about following Him.

When the next year's painting season came around, He told me I could start working again, but this time He said to stop after I'd made only about ten thousand dollars. This continued yearly, and by the third year He told me to quit working after making only three thousand dollars. God did take good care of me, though, and I was getting totally saturated in Him. I was being led on a progressive path of learning to listen, unquestioningly obey, and completely trust Him. He was also growing me more as I passed those vital tests of the heart.

God kept pointing out that I shouldn't worry about everyday things. He told me if I obeyed and kept putting Him and His kingdom before anything I might have wanted, He'd always take care of me. When He spoke to me about all this, He did it using a Bible verse I read one day. He said this was to be my specific calling from Him:

> You therefore, my son, be strong in the grace that is in Christ Jesus. And the things that you have heard from me among many witnesses, commit these to faithful men who will be able to teach others also. You therefore must endure hardship as a good soldier of Jesus Christ. No one engaged in warfare entangles himself with the affairs of this life, that he may please him who enlisted him as a

soldier. And also if anyone competes in athletics, he is not crowned unless he competes according to the rules. The hardworking farmer must be first to partake of the crops. Consider what I say, and may the Lord give you understanding in all things. (2 Timothy 2:1–7)

I was learning this walk is always a test of our heart—and what we love most. How much are we in love with God and entering into this great love affair invitation? Learning to love Him more than anything else that calls for our heart. In fact, our whole life is really just a bunch of tests, to see where our hearts are and who or what we're going to love more. It's all simply about the heart. That's what really matters with God.

I realized He had taken care of me my whole life, even through my crazy, stupid years. It was even His great love that allowed the invisible perimeter fence to close in, taking away my wide-open space. In the natural, things looked pretty bad to me, but it was really Him closing down all other options so He could lead me through the only door He left open—to Him, and to *real* life. I had a roof over my head, food to eat, clothes to wear, a car, and even a cell phone. But I have to admit, sometimes it was a little hard on me. I'd get a little anxious, sweating it out because He seemed to purposely wait till the last possible moment before He'd supply what I needed. But then it would come in the most miraculous ways. This too was something God used to stretch my trust so I could go even farther.

Later, God led me to lead another youth group at a church in Monessen, Pennsylvania. The church eagerly searched me out after hearing about my work with Craig's youth group. Soon after, I started receiving offers from other churches that wanted me to work with their bigger and more well-known ministries. One of them liked me so much that they approached me with an outright offer for a permanent youth pastor position with a fifty-thousand-dollar annual salary.

That excited me, and while I considered the offer, another one came my way. This one was an offer to travel with a circuit minister and his team around the country, also for a fifty-thousand-dollar yearly salary but with all my expenses paid. They wanted me to assist their ministry by sharing my story about what God did in my life, but I knew they were also interested in using my God-given gifts.

Temptation really set in. Being noticed and requested by large, established ministries seemed exciting to me. I reasoned that these offers looked and sounded good. I'd get to minister either way, and it was something I'd love doing. Besides, I rationalized, it was all "good work for God." The churches offered a chance for good pay I could live on and some "recognition," and I was also getting some pats on the back. That felt good. I even tried to conclude that I had now passed enough "trust tests" and that maybe the offers were some sort of graduation time and reward from God.

But right when I had just decided to take one of the offers, God interrupted my thoughts with a blatant question: "What are you doing? Are you going to sell the gift I gave you?"

I was totally caught off-guard—and speechless. In fact, I hadn't really asked God, which had been the first and most important lesson I'd ever learned. I'd been enticed and blinded. While the offers had looked like they were from Him, they really had nothing to do with what He was saying to me. That's a dangerous place to be for someone on this walk. I realized this was another major test and a detour that would have cost me precious time on the wrong path; it just came in a different package this time.

Since I've known Him, there's only been a few times God has asked me, "What are you doing?" I took note that it was similar to the phrase he used with the prophet Elijah when he got off track and was hiding in a cave, something God didn't lead him to do (1 Kings 19:9). It's a phrase that stops me dead in my tracks, and I kind of feel like I've been taken to the woodshed, though God's always said it in great love. I've learned that hearing that question is the biggest warning I get from Him, telling me that I'm getting off-track.

With the offers, I squirmed uncomfortably more than I should have though. Something about them got a hold of my heart, because I was way more bothered about letting go of them than I should have been. I desired "easy street," and I've learned that God doesn't always point out easy street as the path we're supposed to take. In reality, He was showing me that I still hadn't surrendered another part of my heart to Him and that I was walking out of tune with what He was saying. In the end, I knew those positions would have been a self-made detour that would only lengthen the accelerated track God already had me on. So I politely declined the traveling ministry and offers for pay, but I did volunteer some time helping out with the youth group at the other church for a while.

We all have to pass the heart tests. Otherwise God may shelve us right where we're at and stop using us until we get it. It can stunt our growth in Him, keeping us at a certain level where we can't go forward until we finally get back on the right path.

Consider the story of the Israelites in the book of Exodus, after they came out of four hundred years of slavery in Egypt. It's another great story of God starting the love relationship with people, but en masse and with a big bang of mighty deliverance that launched them miraculously out of their life of bondage. God called them out and started the relationship—a lot like He did with me. Their adventurous training walk of learning to trust Him also began immediately.

They too were given miraculous previews of who He is and what He would do for them. They were offered an accelerated track to get to the "Promised Land" found through relationship with Him. But they kept getting stuck at lower levels because so many couldn't pass the heart tests. Just like them, we can get delayed and stuck while going around and around the same mountain for "forty years" while God's waiting for us to get it.

God loves to take us up the levels; in fact, He's more excited for us to accomplish them than we are. The training process, the journey, to get us there is more important to Him than the end goal. By the time the end goal—our destiny—arrives, the most important hard work has already been accomplished in us.

God's not in a hurry like we are. He already knows how long it's going to take to get us there, and with great patience and love He encourages us to follow Him every step of the way. He already knows the times we're going to blow it, and all that matters is that we recognize where we got off-track, admit it, and start going forward on the right path. He doesn't hold it against us, and He never stops the relationship or leaves us when we fall—even when we're in stubborn rebellion. Instead, every time I fail or get caught up in stubbornness, He's my biggest fan, cheering for me to get me back up and keep going. It's not about "twelve steps," which never did anything for me, eternal or otherwise. It's always just "one step"—right into Him. He takes care of the rest.

"Repentance" is the most beautiful word in the Bible. It's not about condemnation, harsh guilt trips, shame, or judgment. That's not your Father God's voice. Repentance has everything to do with His great love and mercy cheering us on with open invitation to just step right back into Him and keep running the race with Him. He's always right there waiting for us with pure joy and love, ready to keep moving forward with us. And once we step back into Him, we can go on as if nothing interrupted the relationship. He's so beyond over it that He doesn't even mention or remember it. He's just excited to have us continuing forward with Him so we get to do more fun and adventurous things together.

If God has destined you with a high calling and big assignments, the training period He'll take you through will be lengthier and more difficult, as evidenced by examples such as King David, Joseph, and Daniel. But when they passed their extremely trying heart tests, God brought them to wonderful destinies that greatly impacted the world. God wants to train you so you'll make all your mistakes "backstage" as you learn to love and trust Him enough to explicitly obey no matter what. Then He'll put you up on front stage in your greatest mission, which may also be to the world.

This is a great responsibility, being Christ's representatives to masses, because so many are affected by everything you are, say, and do. It's not just for protection of His name and honor; it's also because He so loves you that He doesn't want to lose you. You are the most important thing to God, not your ministry or whatever "work" you do for Him. None of that matters to Him as much as the love-affair relationship He has with you. God wants your heart to be thoroughly tried and tested so it is sold-out to Him. Then He knows He can trust you with the "more" He's so eager to give. Should recognition, fame, or money come your way, from high-profile ministry with abundant breakouts of His power and miracles being released through you, He doesn't want to lose you through subtle compromise, temptations, pride, weakness, or giving up and walking away from Him.

Those with front-line or high-office callings to the masses need our prayers. Many of these people have already walked years and years of an unbelievably difficult preparation-training walk that cost them absolutely everything. They're always a much bigger target of the Enemy; he works overtime trying to take them out early because they reach so many.

Just like the accounts of the great prophets of old, God sometimes allows us to go through a process of total crushing of self, often with loss of all in this world until we count it as nothing compared to the greater riches of a fully sold-out love relationship with Him. It's the walk of the total breaking of our heart so that only God's heart can live completely in us. It's the walk of continual and great faith that brings great reward.

However, once "processed" through this unseemly harsh method in the natural, birthed truly from the overwhelming love of God, He can then confidently trust these people with so much more and use them greatly for His kingdom on earth—without losing them. If they stay faithful through it all, He will more than make it up to them several times over.

In reality, though, all believers have their own frontline ministry they're called to wherever they are. It doesn't matter how big or small the frontline is—even if it's to only one person. If we're faithful wherever He puts us, God's reward comes when we simply obey. Kathryn Kuhlman, a well-known front-stage healing minister of God, often said, "I die a thousand deaths before I even walk out on this platform," and "It will cost you everything!" I was only beginning to understand how right she was.

While I was finally discerning and passing more of the heart tests, I was about to learn that God sometimes takes us back for review on some of those tests. He wants to make sure we're strong in certain areas before He can take us forward to higher levels in Him. Not long after turning down the bigger ministry offers for pay, another test was to come my way, but this was one of those tests of review. I had no idea what I was in for.

I was home in my Washington apartment one afternoon, giving a weekly guitar lesson to the church teen youth group. Things had been going great. I'd been spending a lot of time with God, and I was feeling strong and confident in Him. I thought I was doing well on my walk, and I was busy with regular volunteer ministry at a few small churches. God had been using me greatly, but for some reason, I felt uncomfortable and strangely restless this entire day.

While teaching the teens guitar, I'd also mentor them, and the prophecy gift would flow out of me accurate and strong during these sessions. Everyone would get encouraged. We enjoyed hanging out together and having fun, and the kids seemed to love how I was kind of different and showed them that knowing God was fun. By this point, it had been a year since God had taken the drug addictions and desires away from me. I was not only clean, but I also hadn't given drugs a thought.

Finally, I said goodbye to the last of the kids on that cold but perfectly clear afternoon. Out of the blue, the restlessness I'd been feeling that entire day turned into an old, familiar nagging thought. In fact, it really began to eat at me. I kept brushing it aside, repeatedly trying to refuse it entrance into my head, until it became so strong that I could barely handle it. I made a sudden, really stupid decision, saying to myself, *I'm going to use again.* But the moment I had concluded that thought in my mind, the distinct voice of God replied, "No, you're not. I'm not going to let you!"

The urge continued on intensely strong though. I couldn't shake it no matter how hard I tried. I actually began arguing with God—and even tried to ignore Him. I got up off the couch and paced my emptied apartment for a while, then went to check out my windows, again noting the clear afternoon. I shot another glance at my van parked out on the street.

After a few hours of more back-and-forth, I simply couldn't take it anymore! I grabbed my keys and started to head determinedly out the front door. But no sooner had I stepped outside, a blizzard started. It came out of nowhere! I stood there in disbelief, looking up at the sky and watching it fall fast and heavy. Even so, I still weighed my options, reasoning that if I hurried, I could go cop some crack and be back before my old van couldn't drive on the roads anymore.

With willful determination to end the old foreboding restlessness the only way I'd ever known how, I decided to go for it. I spun to shut and lock the door, but when I turned back around, the snow was now coming down in an absolute deluge. I couldn't even see my van parked just ten yards away. The snow piled up thicker and thicker on the ground, and I stood there, keys in hand, looking up at the sky and wondering with desperation, *How can this be happening to me?* There was no way I would make it anywhere fast—but I also suspected exactly what was up. I couldn't help but have a frustrated but guarded chuckle about it.

The ground and street disappeared under about eight inches of snow within the hour. It would have been impossible to drive anywhere until the streets were plowed. Still pretty upset, I went back inside, flung my keys on the table, and slumped onto the couch, pouting like an angry, stubborn child. My feelings were even hurt. That's when God suddenly retorted loudly into the room, "I told you so!"

I couldn't believe it! Sitting there thinking on the whole outlandish scenario, I could barely get my mind around the crazy lengths God had gone to again, just to stop me from the momentary madness that somehow snuck in and got a hold of me. Still feeling hurt about being outdone, I blurted out, "I can't believe you would do this to me!" But really, it was all so unbelievably comical. It was the perfect storm, and I had been perfectly one-upped. I couldn't help but burst out laughing hysterically about it all. It was right then that I heard a big, hearty belly laugh break out audibly in the room along with mine; God obviously enjoyed what He'd done too.

Then, as our mutual laughter resounded in the room together, a thick, weighty cloud of His wonderful presence dropped down over me and the tangible joy of heaven filled the room. Overflowing peace rolled into me like waves—and the uninvited urge completely left. A new lesson was ingrained in me: If the Enemy can't take you out when you're down in the ditch, he'll try to take you out when you're soaring like an eagle in God. This is when you least expect it. Another great lesson.

I'm so glad God had such a strong grip on me and caught me before I fell. He taught me more about properly discerning the tests, staying in tune with Him, and trusting and relying on Him for everything. And He still wasn't about to let me go.

You see, the dark side can also see the special gifts and destinies God places in you from your mother's womb. The timing of your birth is not a mistake. It was carefully planned and is timed for the special place and time God wants you and your unique gifts and destinies to come into this world—no matter the circumstances of your birth. These things are plainly seen by the spiritual realm first. I can often see these giftings and destinies on people when God shows them to me.

The dark side's aim is to either take you out early or keep you and those gifts working for evil. The Enemy operates first through lies, deception, and/or trying to keep you ignorant or in unbelief of the truth of the identity God gave you. His aim is to steal, kill, and destroy everything dear to God's heart and keep all potential threats away from his own dark kingdom and its expansion. Believers who know their true God-given identity and are filled with God's Holy Spirit are a terrifying threat to the Enemy and his kingdom of darkness.

That's why there are so many abortions. Abortion stops God-given destinies with special giftings short, before they're born, discovered, lit up in God's light, and used in His precision power and effectiveness. As well, if the Enemy can't take you out via an "outside job" (others or circumstances around you), he'll resort to an "inside job" (suicide, drugs, alcohol, or other self-incapacitations). These things can be carried out slowly or quickly, and all are accomplished when you're operating based in unbelief, fear, despair, hopelessness, lies, deception, ignorance, pride, etc.

Look back on your life or the lives of others. Consider people who have a lot of struggles, near misses, or unfortunate happenings that don't seem to make any sense. These are often the very ones with high callings and giftings. Our prisons and streets are full of them. Many are actually special chosen gems in God's eyes. The world, their Enemy-targeted families, and they themselves may see them as "losers," cursed, or even unlovable, but God only wants them to know and believe their true and powerful identities and destinies. He wants to get them lit up and going in Him.

Many can relate to this. If the Enemy can keep you beaten down in unbelief and ignorance or trusting in vain, empty things in life—even religion, which is anything but a real-deal relationship with God—he doesn't worry much about you. He already has you under control and on his side because you're rendered powerless, even though you may not know it. In fact, he can also use you to spread unbelief and ignorance to others.

Knowing and believing the truth about your amazing worth to God, your true identity, and God's resident power within you as a believer sets you free from lying mind-sets and propels you into freedom, with the great power and effectiveness God planned for you. You become an overcomer with Jesus, over this world as well as anything the Enemy can throw at you. When you're finally walking in the real love relationship with your creator, you also operate toward your amazing purpose—and that will get you to your God-given destiny.

15

IT'S YOUR TIME!

And I'm going to send you places
where no one else can go.

– GOD

As the end of 2004 neared, God incited me again one day with a fun, excited tone to His voice. "Let's just hang out, Timmy!" Now when the almighty God of the universe and the creator of everything calls you out personally for some one-on one time with Him, it's never something to take lightly. It's the most precious opportunity of your life. It's your time!

God calls many for this, but few heed the special call. Therefore, few get chosen for some great opportunities. I knew this invitation was far from ordinary, and I was determined I wasn't going to miss it. When I said yes to God, I was serious, although there were some important things He needed to discuss with me first.

One of the primary things He asked of me was that I put aside the things that kept us from being closer. He told me it was time to lay down my guitar for a while, even though I'd been playing for thirty-five years. Then He told me to stop watching TV because there was too much satanic influence on it. Garbage in, garbage out. It clutters your ability with its inherent influence of "other voices," keeping you from clearly tuning in and hearing God's voice, which is totally opposite the world's.

Finally, He asked me to do something incredibly difficult.

He told me to throw away all the music, recordings, tapes, CDs, photos, and videos of my old-life music career, including my personal music memorabilia. This included a lot of my released and unreleased music and videos of certain bands. Thirty-five years of hard work and memories. But this time His words were much more than a request; they were a direct command. I have to say, I hesitated more than a bit on this last instruction. Though I'd been asking for more of Him, I found myself uncomfortably deliberating it. I had come to another test of my heart.

What did I really want more? I knew God was showing me that there were still things holding my heart from Him and all He wanted to give me. But I didn't want to admit that to myself. I also knew that without obedience to this, I'd never get the "more" of Him I'd repeatedly asked for.

Finally, I reluctantly filled up bags with all my stuff, asking Him if I could keep a few of the very last items. He said I could because they were basically "uncontroversial" items. Then with a heavy heart, I made three trips to the Dumpster behind the building I was living in and threw all the bags into it. Talk about tough. It felt like a big emotional funeral. Each load I took seemed heavier than the last. I wanted to cry as I saw all the memories, songs, and past friends' pictures and performances disappear with resounding thuds into the depths of the Dumpster.

On my third trip, the man who had been sleeping in cardboard boxes beside the Dumpster stirred. I had woken him up with all the commotion, and he pulled himself up and asked what I was doing. He tried to strike up a conversation with me, and though I wasn't in any mood to talk, he kept questioning me. It was then I learned he was a former banker who'd lost his job, then his home. He was totally down and out because he was addicted to crack and it had stolen everything from him. This turned into a divine setup, and God pointed out to me one of His other great purposes in having me get rid of my stuff.

The poor man was dirty and thin, and the more he talked, the more I realized the depths of his depression and hopelessness. It was all too familiar, reminding me of where I'd been not so long before. While he talked, I heard God's words from when He saved me echoing again in my mind: *Timmy, I saved you. Now you go and save my children.*

I knew what was up. God was tapping me on the shoulder and showing me what was on His mind and heart. Then more of God's first words to me repeated in my mind: *And I am going to send you places where no one else can go.* God was trying to show me one of the hidden gems so dear to His heart. He wasn't wasting any time. Here He was, already releasing some of those "new things" He had promised me, at the very moment I was obeying Him and throwing my old stuff out—even though my whole heart wasn't in it.

The stranger and I connected as God flooded my heart with His compassion upon the remembrance of all He'd done for me. Then He gave me the precision words that struck home, encouraging the man like no one else could have because I had experienced both sides of this fence—and I knew the only real answer. God had strategically prepared, set up, and placed me there at that exact moment, in that exact place, to release His empowering words of life to this man who desperately needed to hear them.

Incidentally, this led to a friendship where I kept in touch with the man in an ongoing mentoring relationship that God orchestrated. He quickly got on the road to knowing God and also experienced His freedom from addiction and hopelessness. He ended up later marrying the sister of a pastor friend of mine and doing quite well.

As well, when I walked away from that Dumpster and all that I'd once held so dear, I felt a new determination and freedom because God was showing me that I was on the right path. I thought back to when He had promised me that whenever I obeyed, He would bless me and move me up the levels with Him. In reality, I was so weakened that day, even to the point of feeling physically ill about obeying His last request, that I barely made it through. *This was a really tough one,* I thought. But then the realization hit me that while I was concerned about my "treasures," God was concerned only about *real* treasures—and He reminded me that one of His greatest treasures was *me*.

I had just passed a big heart test to determine what I loved most and would be loyal to. He wanted to get all of my worthless rubble out of the way so He could replace it with His priceless pearls. After it was done, I was wrecked and in awe as I felt God's pleasure with me. A renewed gratefulness flooded my heart. Emotionally exhausted and wiping tears from my eyes, I learned another lesson: that in order for us to get the best out of where God wants to take us, we sometimes have to be willing to walk through deep difficulty that most will never venture through. God was trying to get me past my own limits to make me ready for much more.

Prior to this time, I'd been given a pretty advanced level of spiritual seeing and discernment gifting by God, but what came after this last test at the Dumpster went way over the top. God opened up new levels and realms of Himself that were beyond my wildest imagination. I experienced Him so deeply that I plainly saw Him 24/7. This wonderful period continued for five years.

By this time, God had me going on the road a lot, driving everywhere through the states of Pennsylvania, New York, West Virginia, Maryland, and Ohio on assignments. The drives were sometimes long and wearying because I'd often cover seemingly endless stretches of barren highway. Because of my long days doing assignments, I did most of my driving late into the night. Though I was tired and surrounded by darkness, those were also the times when God would totally pump me up and revive me with great encouragement. I knew He was always with me, and He was plainly showing me that by letting me see heaven's backing all around me.

On those drives, I'd often see thousands of His angels lined up shoulder to shoulder on either side of the road like guardrails. When I came upon them, I'd first see bright white shafts of light, but as I got closer, I'd see their whole forms. They were each about twelve-feet tall, had beautiful white wings, and were wearing shining white gowns of light. They would smile and wave to me as I passed. God was not only encouraging me; He was also showing me how He was specially protecting me along the way. "Yeah!" I'd shout, and it totally refreshed me so I could drive on with renewed strength.

True to His word, Jesus and I were literally hanging out like best friends all the time now. Sometimes the room would open up and I'd see Him with the backdrop of heaven around Him as He watched me. This would happen on those long drives too, and I'd see Him up in the sky, standing on a cloud as he looked down on me. Often He would remain visible to me for the whole trip.

Then, wherever I was staying, He'd physically walk into the room. He usually came in and sat down on a chair or on the end of my bed. Sometimes He'd plop down on the couch and lay back, relaxing with his legs crossed and his arms casually outstretched on the back pillows. We'd talk just like old friends do.

There were also times when He would pick me up and hold me on His lap. His body, though looking as physical as you or I, would go right through and under mine and He'd put His arms tenderly around me. Love exuded out of Him, and the peace and safety of His embrace often put me in tears. It reminded me of when He first came and saved me, pulling me up in those same wonderful arms of protection and comfort. I'd rest my head on His shoulder or His chest and just sit quietly in His arms, listening to His heartbeat as He rocked me or rubbed my shoulders. It felt just like an earthly father comforting and reassuring his child.

In the morning, He would often wake me in interesting ways. I'd be gently coming out of a long night's sleep, and Jesus would already be physically in the room. He'd be pacing the floor like He couldn't wait for the moment I'd wake up. A few times He startled me by having his face right in mine when I opened my eyes. He'd press his nose into mine with these wide-open, comical eyes and a big grin and greet me in a loud, silly voice, "Whaaa…tsuuup!" as He playfully screwed His head side to side. He loved to ambush me like this, and we'd both start the day off in laughter. I'd get excited all over again, looking forward to another day with Him and wondering what we were going do next. He'd start out the day with, "What do you want to do today?" Then I'd answer, "I don't know. What do *you* want to do today?" And He'd immediately shoot back, "I don't know. What do *you* want to do today?" We'd ask this silly question back and forth, laughing, until one of us eventually gave up and changed the subject.

Sometimes He'd tickle me awake. Other times I would wake up to see him majestically enthroned in a cloud in my room, just contentedly looking at me. One thing I know, Jesus loves to play and joke around, telling silly jokes. He loves to laugh and is the greatest comedian I've ever met. He always comes up with much funnier things than I could ever think up—and there's great lessons in each and every one of them too. And He loves to play games with me.

For example, one day I was at a nice hotel waiting for the start of an event He'd sent me to. I stood around in a big open hallway of floor-to-ceiling windows, looking out over a beautiful golf course with palm trees and lakes right outside in front of me, but I was getting bored waiting. I even complained a little to Jesus about how bored I was because nothing seemed to be happening yet. He responded, "Okay. Let's play count the angels."

Just then I saw angels appear all over on the golf course. They ran around, trying to hide behind the bushes, rocks, and little grass knolls—even behind or up in the trees. Like kids in a lively game of hide 'n' seek, they'd peek their heads out and then hide again as soon as I saw them, or they'd run back and forth between the trees trying to dodge being counted. The angels were getting a big kick out of playing this game with us, and their antics soon became gut-wrenching hilarious. People passing me in the hallway couldn't understand why I was looking out the windows and laughing my head off. I have to say it brightened my mood quickly. God knows just how to do that with me.

Another time, I was home resting on my bed on a not-so-good day. I was in a sullen mood, and God sent a few special angels into my room. They actually started doing slap-stick comedy routines at the foot of my bed! It was kind of like watching a mix of Chevy Chase and Three Stooges antics as they knocked each other around, fake-tripped, and stumbled into each other with these hilarious looks on their faces. I couldn't help but be totally lifted up, and the sadness quickly passed. More than that, it always touches me the lengths God will go to for me in our relationship. He cares deeply about every one of us and every aspect of our lives.

Because of my love relationship with Him and the deep respect I've grown to have for my wonderful God and Friend, at times I become literally overwhelmed just at the thought of Him. There were times like these when I'd blurt out to Him, "You're beautiful!" He would answer me, "No. You're beautiful!" Then I'd respond with a stronger, "No. *You're* beautiful!" And here we'd go again, trying to emphasize it more than the other each time, until one of us finally gave up.

God is so awesome. I love Him, and He loves me. It's like He can't help Himself, and it's been that way since the day I met Him. Sometimes, when we're not doing anything but kicking back and enjoying each other's company, His wonderful presence alone says it all. He knows how much I like it.

A lot of times, He opens up panoramic-scene visions, like ultra-high-def movies being played right in front of me, and illustrates in living color something He wants to share with me. Other times, moving 3D-like figures or objects appear before me as He just demonstrates what He wants to say.

God showed me many visions as He talked with me on those unhindered hours on the road too. He'd take me into a vision and I'd watch it like a show. Don't ask me how I kept my eyes on the road; I don't know how to explain it. It was like being in two realms at once. I just trusted He had control of the situation. Sometimes the vivid 3D visions came like eight different visions all at once. All of it had deep meaning as He shared with me precious portions of His heart, His truth, and things as He knows them.

God also speaks through signs seen not only in the spiritual realm but also here in the natural world. It's all the same to Him. Like a punctuation mark, these signs often confirm things He's already been saying. God's signs can also be a confirmation that we're either on the right or wrong path. He'll also endorse our words or actions when they're in alignment with His, by backing us up with His spectacular signs, wonders, or miracles. It's just God doing His thing, with and through His children. It's heaven's realm coming right to the earth and His will being done—the way He always meant things to be.

God's signs leave us amazed at how in control He really is, because things couldn't possibly all line up as they do at that precise moment without Him setting it all up. The ways God gives signs in the natural can be something meaningful just to us or to others as well. They are always exhaustively creative and sometimes astonishingly funny, and at times they're repetitive or sequenced. This is because He wants to teach us not only to listen, but to "watch to hear" His voice in the many ways He speaks, both in the spirit and in the natural.

One of the signs in the natural that He often gives to me has to do with airplanes. He knows I have a thing for airplanes. They symbolize the travel and new places He said He would send me to when he told me about my destiny. He encourages me like a father to a son, with something like, "Fly high to your destiny, son," or "Keep in the spirit, son, soaring like the eagles." Every time that happens, when I look up, without fail, an airplane is flying overhead.

When God lives so close inside, we need to be aware of the things He says to us. He often comments to me about occurrences during my day. Things like, "Hey, did you see that?" or "That was pretty funny, huh?" Sometimes it's "You like that, huh?" or "I'm going to show you some more of that. Yeah!" Sometimes after I've asked Him a dumb question, He'll answer with a hilarious, "Duhhh!" (I have to confess, I get that more often than I'd like to admit.)

Before God sent me out to all the places that required a lot of driving, He instructed me to buy another car to be used exclusively for ministry trips. All I was doing was full-time ministry assignments He'd send me on. It was a total faith walk because He never allowed me to take any pay for ministry. I didn't have much money, but God was really tight with me on this. He wanted me totally free to send and obey, trusting only Him.

I went to look around a car lot, and when I finally found one I liked with what money I had, God confirmed, "That's the one." It was a dark green '95 Camaro that already had one hundred thousand miles on it, and I bought it for thirty-five hundred dollars. It wasn't a nice high-end sports car, but I liked the fact that it was at least a sports car and a little bit "me." I was glad God had approved this particular car, but what I didn't realize was that He was planning to teach me something through that car. When I drove off with it, He affectionately called it "our ministry car."

When God says go, you go. I left the details all to Him. I went everywhere in that Camaro and put another one hundred thousand plus miles on it over the years. However, it didn't take long before I had renamed it the "miracle car." Amazing things happened with that car—things that were nothing short of everyday miracles.

When I bought it, everything on it was original. Nothing had ever been replaced. Every time I got in that car, I thanked God for it, and I said a blessing over it before my trips. It operated pretty well for the first couple of years, but soon after that things started going wrong with it. God had me living lean while learning the trust-walk with Him, and I didn't have the funds to get it fixed or even to maintain it. The brakes were badly worn and the shocks were totally shot, so it floored me when it still passed inspection each year. I had to trust that despite the obvious, God had everything under control. Then after two years of driving it everywhere, one day it wouldn't start. When I'd turn the key, there wasn't even a sound. It was totally dead.

"God, you said this was 'our' ministry car," I reminded Him, trying not to sound too whiny. "You told me to buy it, and you told me to go wherever you send me. You know where I am with finances to fix it." I was actually reminding myself more than Him. Then I pulled it together and prayed over the car. I just blessed it up and tried the key again. Without fail, the car started right up. But this was the way I had to start that car for the following three years. I had to *totally* depend on Him.

There were also certain periods when I went on long trips but didn't have money to put gas in the car. When I knew there were long stretches of desolate country without much civilization and no gas stations, I'd watch the gas gauge as I drove and it would stay pegged on whatever line it started on for the entire trip. Other times, the gauge would be pointed on empty but it never ran out of gas. I always got wherever I needed to go.

Sometimes God would change things up a bit by sending a stranger who would stuff money in my hand to bless me and I'd go buy some gas. I never asked anyone for it. God would just send them. I'd thank them, but most of all I thanked God for His wonderful, faithful supply. He always knew what I needed. Possibly, these "people" were even some of His angels in disguise.

I never put new oil in the "miracle car" until about eight years after I bought it. That's when I finally took it in to a garage to have them look it over and check the battery. The garage guys couldn't believe what they saw. The battery was original, and it was so old that it had corroded into the engine compartment and fused with the metal all around it. They used a meter to check it for a charge while laughing about it just to humor me, and it was of course totally dead. It was also completely dry as I'd never put any water in it either. We concluded that the battery had to have been dead for at least the past two and a half to three years. They just shook their heads in disbelief. They couldn't understand how I had even gotten it to them, let alone been driving it like that all those years.

Then they began a routine maintenance check on the car and put it up on a lift. They were shocked when they found that both the engine and the transmission mounts were completely missing. Nothing was holding either one in place. As their inspection moved on, they also discovered that nothing held the rear end of the car's body to the chassis. All the bolts and connectors were worn down or missing and so were other normal back-end parts. They looked at me dumbfounded. All I could do was chuckle and matter-of-factly reply, "It's a miracle car."

That statement went right over their heads. By the way they flashed kooky looks and rolled their eyes, they thought I was just kidding. They couldn't stop laughing and shaking their heads through the whole service process. I ended up getting their fifteen-dollar oil change deal and waiting another year before I put a new battery in the car.

God assigned that car for our ministry, so He took care of it just like He took care of me. When God is in you and you're in Him, you know what He thinks and feels. When I'd bless the car up and acknowledge Him, I could expressly feel He was pleased to supply whatever was needed because I was willing to do whatever He asked. Never underestimate the power of relationship, prayer, and thanks in agreement with God's will for you.

16

GOD AND HEAVEN ARE FUN!

Do not fear, little flock,
for it is your Father's good pleasure to give you the kingdom.

– LUKE 12:32

God and heaven are fun! In heaven there are no rules and regulations. Everything simply operates by the overpowering spirit of love, and that brings pure, vibrant life and freedom in everything there. There are still many times when God takes me up to heaven with Him. This is something that's part of our inheritance, now, as His children and as "citizens of heaven" already seated with Him in heavenly places (Philippians 3:20; Ephesians 2:6; Luke 10:20). God is the source of everything, and all of heaven, even all of eternity, is sourced from and resides in Him. Yet heaven is a very real, tangible place, a "world" all its own, and you'll definitely know it when you're there.

One day that God took me up to heaven with Him was very special for me. One moment I was on earth and the next I was standing on a gleaming golden-brick pathway with silver bricks lining its edges. Vivid green grass sprawled in gently sloping meadows dotted with trees and flowers all around me. Absolutely everything, even the air there, pulsated with life. It was paradise.

Jesus stood next to me, inviting me to stroll the path ahead with Him. He held pink cotton candy on a stick, and when I looked at my hand I was holding cotton candy too. We casually strolled the path together, walking and talking and eating. His mood was light, carefree, and fun, and I was totally at ease with Him as we enjoyed each other's company. People strolled by in the opposite direction on a path adjacent to ours, leaving an area that we were walking toward, while others strolled along the path ahead of us. Everyone looked so happy.

Soon we came to a beautiful arched entryway made of a mix of materials—some kind of white metal, ancient-looking wood, and expert masonry work. As we walked through it, we entered a huge amusement park. There were all sorts of rides on either side of us, with people, children, and families everywhere. People screamed with laughter on some of the rides, enjoying themselves immensely. The rides resembled some familiar ones like the Scrambler, Ferris wheel, and even race cars, but they had supernatural elements to them. People eagerly waited their turn to get on while others got off.

We walked past a large group of trees where people picnicked and played underneath them. After some time Jesus led me down a side path that led to a different area in the amusement park. We came to a giant roller coaster—the biggest ride I could see in the park—and there was no line because its access was roped off and no one was around. Jesus pointed at the coaster with a big smile and said, "Look, Timmy. This is a new ride I made just for you—and it's never been ridden before."

Wow, I thought as I gazed at it in wonder, *Jesus knows I love roller coasters!* The bigger and crazier, the better, and this one looked massive. I stared at it, amazed He would do something like this just for me. But the next thing I knew, I was back on earth. I guess it just wasn't time for me to enjoy it yet.

Yes, God even thought of fun and entertainment when He created heaven. When you delight in the Lord, He gives you the desires of your heart—and then some (Psalm 37:4). There is no good thing He withholds from those who walk uprightly (Psalm 84:11).

Heaven is amazing. It's full of wonderful, exciting things to do. God shares everything with His kids freely, and no one could possibly be bored there. Jesus loves to party, laugh, and have fun. That's why He made His home an amazing place where people get to enjoy it with Him forever.

Purity, perfection, and life reverberate in everything there: the grass, trees, flowers, soil, mountains, sky, and rivers. Even the rocks and buildings are alive. While heaven can be busy at times, the whole realm of heaven is an atmosphere of tranquility, peace, and God's glory abounding in everything and everyone there.

Heaven looks a lot like the earth with nature, buildings, and cities. After all, the earth was God's idea, and a lot of what we see down here is just a shadow of what's in heaven. There are beautiful country areas, and the cities have unimaginable homes and huge mansions made uniquely for each and every person. God is preparing your place to your unique liking and special God-given gifts, which you will continue to use there. Everyone is busy about the business God gave them to do or enjoying themselves in heaven's immense beauty.

A lot of people's ideas and inventions on earth began as inspirations dropped from heaven, whether they realize it or not. God releases certain inventions at the set time He wants them created on earth and offers them as "ideas" that come from heaven to certain people. Though, regrettably, many don't understand or acknowledge they're from Him and others get perverted or used for the wrong purposes here.

Of course, you will recognize other people, family and friends that make it there, and they will recognize you. If family members have gone on before you to heaven, you can be sure they're up there cheering you on to run your race well down here. Angels and God's other created spirit beings—even animals—live and mix with redeemed people and the heavenly host in heaven.

Many colors there are indescribable because they aren't found here on earth, and they too are vivid and living. God's illuminating glory and life is in everything there—from every molecule of dirt to every droplet of water. Sickness, lack, death, and decay are not found in heaven because it's a place of total life. Even people vibrate with life, and they look much better there than they do here. People are youthful, strong, and whole, illuminating with the glory of heaven coming out of them too.

There seems to always be symphonies of praise and worship songs rising and falling throughout different areas in heaven. The music itself is alive, and it goes right through you. Everything and everyone there praises God nonstop, sounding out His glory in one way or another. There is so much planned for us there that we couldn't imagine it in our wildest dreams. It's a place specially prepared by God that no one wants to miss.

Yes, when you belong to Him, God reveals ahead of time some of the things He has already given and prepared for His children. Only He can reveal it to you by His Spirit. You qualify the moment you become His, and it can be revealed to you now.

But as it is written:
"Eye has not seen, nor ear heard,
Nor have entered into the heart of man
The things which God has prepared for those who love Him."
But God has revealed them to us through His Spirit. For the Spirit searches all things, yes, the deep things of God. For what man knows the things of a man except the spirit of the man which is in him? Even so no one knows the things of God except the Spirit of God. Now we have received, not the spirit of the world, but the Spirit who is from God, that we might know the things that have been freely given to us by God. (1 Corinthians 2:9–12, emphasis mine)

The secret things belong to the LORD our God, *but those things which are revealed belong to us and our children forever.* (Deuteronomy 29:29, emphasis mine)

Each time God takes me to heaven, I see something new there, and through it He shows me deep truths and other aspects of Himself—from His awesome, majestic throne and the crystal glass-like sea, to the river of life and waterfalls, the mountains, and the libraries full of books and scrolls. Heaven is huge. I know I've only seen small glimpses of all that's there. Heaven seems endless because God is always creating new things there, and we are even invited to partner with Him in what He's presently doing.

Heaven is beautiful beyond description. Many of the streets and paths are paved in gold so pure that it's transparent, and there's precious gemstones everywhere, countless as sand, and they, as everything else, are pulsating and alive. The purity and life in everything is unlike anything you think is alive here on earth.

In heaven, nothing compares to the place of God's amazing throne room. I've been there more times than I can count. There are times when I see Jesus enthroned in majesty from wherever I am on earth, but other times I'm instantly in heaven with Him. I can reach out, touch, and feel everything because I'm there.

Often, Jesus takes me up the steps to His throne hand-in-hand. Sometimes, He sits on His big, ornate golden chair that reminds me of a medieval throne, and it's glorious. He often pulls me up onto His lap and lets me hang out there with Him. The throne's platform area is large, open, and circular, and you can see it from any angle. I can only describe it from the mere glimpses I catch each time I go there. Often it's so bright, illuminating with such glory and power, that I can't see everything yet. My eyes are simply overcome with its brightness.

The atmosphere of the throne room is filled with such holy awe, majesty, and wonder, and powerful electricity reverberates through it. It all overtakes me. A brilliant, colorful rainbow fills the place, seemingly enveloping me. It actually emanates from there out into all of heaven.

Before reaching the steps to the throne's platform, I've encountered a landing area that at times I see a wide crystal river running beneath, coming from His throne. I only catch glimpses of it now and then, when I can see through the floor. Sometimes I can see the earth below the crystal clear, flowing river. It reminds me of God's Word where He says, "Heaven is my throne, and earth *is* my footstool" (Isaiah 66:1). Everything is plainly seen and open before God.

At times I've seen the twenty-four elders referenced in the book of Revelation all around His throne on this lower platform. Sometimes they're prostrate, worshipping God on their faces in front of their own beautiful throne chairs. Often, I'll notice the living creatures described in the book of Ezekiel and Revelation (Ezekiel 10:9–12; Revelation 4:6). But I see them not only in heaven, but sometimes also on the earth. They are big, magnificent four-faced winged beings, full of eyes that have large wheels underneath them full of eyes too. Often, I see the big wheels alone on earth at times. These living creatures carry the thick throne-room-glory presence of God wherever they are, and I've found they each have personalities of their own. They can actually be quite funny at times.

There are all kinds of rooms just off the throne room area. Once I was permitted, only by special invitation by the Lord, into one of them. An angel escorted me through a big ancient-looking wooden double door. Inside was a very private, quiet affair going on. Jesus stood there behind a chair in the middle of the room, facing away from me. In the chair was my future wife, and He was rubbing the back of her shoulders, comforting her with such tender love.

When I entered, I was allowed to sit on the floor in the very back of the room to quietly observe. Jesus was dressed in a beautiful white gown that looked like it was made of brilliant diamonds, and He glanced back at me with a look that said, "I've allowed you in to watch, but you can't interrupt." No one else was allowed in that inner chamber room, and the angel stayed at the door like a sentry to be sure no one else came in. My heart was struck with wonder as I watched Him impart great affection, love, and comfort to her. When He finished, He placed a long, flowing robe of many colors over her shoulders. It billowed in drapes of deep, luxurious folds onto the floor. I sat in awe at the scene before me. I was so honored and appreciative that He allowed me in to see this wonderful, intimate moment.

One day, Jesus let me look into another of the rooms off the throne room area. We walked down some steps, through the doors, and He took me to a big table. On it was what at first looked like a large model of a stadium. But as I got closer, I realized it wasn't just a model. It was real. He was showing me a stadium in the world that we were looking down on. He just gave me a knowing smile, and I knew He was encouraging me about the places He had said He was going to send me.

I've had the great honor of being taken to see my mansion waiting in heaven too. Jesus told us He was going to prepare these places for us, for when we come to live with Him (John 14:2–3). I was allowed to see the inside of mine, though I don't remember seeing its outside. It was huge, possibly three or four stories tall from what I could tell, and I just knew it had some sort of basement too. The huge foyer had tall ceilings, and when I walked into this large entryway, it took a long time just to walk through it to the wide hall that led to the other rooms. Those rooms are also large, with floor-to-ceiling windows that revealed a garden just out the back that stretched for acres. Amid colorful flowers and perfectly manicured plants and trees were fountains and birds, and it had a peaceful stream running through it.

So far, I've seen what I'd call a living room, which had a big, long white couch in it. Streaks ran through the leather-like fabric of the couch and the whole room seemed to vibrate with these streaks. When I got to the dining room, it had a huge, grand white dining table with large white kingly chairs. It seemed a couple of thousand people could be seated there. Of course, the kitchen was incredible as well—ultra-modern is the only way I could describe it and large enough for preparations for a huge crowd of guests.

The bottom floor had a sweeping ivorylike staircase that led to the upper floors, but there was a golden elevator on this level too. I walked up the stairs to see more, but I could only go halfway. For some reason, I couldn't continue any higher. I suppose that's because it's not completed—just as God hasn't completed what He's doing with me here on earth yet either.

Many of the neighborhoods in heaven are tree-lined suburban-looking areas, but I've also seen what looked like big country resorts surrounded by green meadows that seemed to stretch to forever. I've also been shown what I was told were the streets of the prophets. I was escorted there once by an angel, and I saw some street signs there. One street was called "Prophet Lane," and the street that intersected into it was called "Prophet Way." Both have huge, stately mansions on them, and some resembled medieval-style castles made of light.

While there, I saw many of the prophets and apostles at different times: Moses, Noah, Abraham, Elijah, Ezekiel, and Jeremiah, as well as King David, John, Peter, Paul, and more. Only Paul spoke to me. Whenever he'd see me, he'd stretch out his arm pointing his finger straight at me and say, "Go!" I knew what he meant. I'm still running the race for God's kingdom that Paul talked about in the Bible, and I know I'm not done yet (1 Corinthians 9:24–27; Philippians 3:13–14; Hebrews 12:1).

One of my favorite places in heaven is a mountain on the edge of a blue- and emerald-hued sea. While standing near its peak, beside and slightly below me is the face of a wide-mouthed waterfall, possibly a quarter-mile wide, that cascades majestically down. Its waters are crystal clear mixed with colors of blue, green, and gold that fall into that sea that stretches off into the distance as far as I can see. Though the waterfall puts out tons of water that crash down, it's totally quiet. I love it there. I can't help but stay for a while and reflect on the great beauty and peace. Sometimes Jesus is there with me as we quietly hang out and enjoy it together; other times I'm there alone.

There's another mountain I also visit when I'm taken there. This one has an outcropping ledge near its peak that I sit on, taking in the spectacular view. I'm always surrounded by song-birds singing beautiful worship songs to the Lord. Their songs are unlike any worship I've heard on earth. We haven't yet captured heaven's sounds and ability of worship here. It's so strikingly superior, and I look forward to when we'll worship like that.

Above me and all around on this mountaintop are what look like pine and oak trees, and it's carpeted in certain places with wildflowers of all colors. It has tidy natural paths with etched-in-the-soil borders going around and up the mountain. Below, a wide swath of the crystal sea reaches way out in the distance where I know the heavenly city and God's throne is. On one side of the huge sea, its waters meet a golden-sand beach that glistens and sparkles. Way off in the distance are more beautiful mountains set in ranges with shimmering shades of burnished and glistening amber, copper, and gold.

On the other side of the sea, gently rolling brilliant-green meadows spread as far as I can see. And yes, they actually move, gently swaying and rolling, because they're alive too. Sometimes, I see people walking around those meadows or on the beach, enjoying the beauty of this area.

God has many different types of angels. I've seen them in heaven as well as on earth. They're awesomely strong and powerful beings, with some chiseled and fierce looking, like warrior angels, while others look more like humans, but with perfect beauty. One of the angels I saw standing on earth had huge feet that spanned miles apart, and I could see only up to his waist before the rest of him disappeared somewhere high above the clouds. Others are so big that I can see only part of their faces spanning across the earth's horizon. Some have wings, while others don't (or I just can't see them), and they range in color from shining bright white to gold to every color of the rainbow. Heaven is full of colors, so I know God loves color in all His creations. I like the "drippy" angels. They drip what looks like different-color oils that streak down their garments like light. I believe they're imparting something they carry from heaven.

God has many other beings and creatures, such as those living creatures and the cherubim and seraphim too, who look like torches of blazing fire. I get real whacked up feeling the heavy glory power emanating from them. I've seen specific spirits of God too. Spirits are different from angels. They can appear in human form sometimes, though they're not human. The spirit of wisdom often appears like a beautiful female being of white light with blonde hair, but then I've seen the same spirit of wisdom appear in the shape of a white graduation cap on a man's head too. God was showing me that particular man was highly gifted with the spirit of wisdom, though he wasn't yet using this great gift for God's kingdom yet. He was still a crack addict but a naturally gifted entrepreneur, brilliant in making money and full of successful business dealings and ideas. Should God get a hold of him one day, I know he'll be used greatly in this gifting for Him.

Because God and heaven exist outside time as we know it, He can take us anywhere by His Spirit. He can show us many things as they happen in the past, present, and future—even from before the world began or far into the future—because He can take us right there. I've see Noah when he was standing by the ark with all the animals coming toward it. I've also experienced different scenes of the crucifixion of Jesus. The horror of that crushed me as I stood by Mary and John, so sullen and in such grief and shock watching Him hanging there, beaten, bloodied, and suffering before His death for us. Sometimes, when they're nailing Him to the cross, the sound of the nails being pounded into his hands and feet resounds at decibel levels as loud as an arena concert. It's not a vision or dream. I know I'm actually there, and I can see, feel, hear, smell, and experience everything firsthand. Despite all I've seen, though, I know very little about heaven and God, let alone anything. He's let me take only the first steps toward what He considers important for me to know for now. The rest may require all of eternity.

There were many times that God gave me some of His heavenly gemstones as personal gifts. Sometimes He'd place them right on my hand, like putting a ring on my finger. Interestingly, it was always on my left hand. I knew He was confirming to me that I was His "beloved" and that He would be faithful and committed to me forever. I saw them in the spirit, but I knew they were real and mine—now and forever. In reality, only things in the spiritual realm are eternal, while things in this natural world are temporary (2 Corinthians 4:18).

Once, there were twelve specific precious stones that He showed me over a period of a year, a different one each month. I'd see them come into the room and suspend in the air in front of me, sometimes for the whole day. They were big and at least as wide as I am. These stones were literally alive, not like any gemstones on earth. They were pulsating, brilliant, and always completely vibrating with life. They were amazing to behold.

The twelfth one He showed me was a brilliant purple color, the "amethyst." I confidently joked with God on this one, acting like a school kid jumping up and down in his seat with his hand up. "Yeah, I know what this one is!" I said. "It's the twelfth stone of the heavenly foundation in Revelation."

God chuckled back, pleased that I got it. "Yes, it is!"

That's because as He showed them to me over the months, I had finally realized what He was doing, but not until that twelfth one. Just weeks prior, He had caught me up into heaven and I found myself observing the foundations under the heavenly city. There were twelve different levels of foundations, one on top of the other, and each tier was made from a different and absolutely giant precious gemstone. I was stunned to see these were the same gemstones He had shown me so far. I was more surprised when I realized He'd been showing them to me in the same order as I saw them laid in the foundations in heaven.

These foundations are mentioned by the apostle John as he described the heavenly city in the book of Revelation:

> The foundations of the wall of the city were adorned with all kinds of precious stones: the first foundation was jasper, the second sapphire, the third chalcedony, the fourth emerald, the fifth sardonyx, the sixth sardius, the seventh chrysolite, the eighth beryl, the ninth topaz, the tenth chrysoprase, the eleventh jacinth, and the twelfth amethyst. (Revelation 21:19–20)

I know that when God gives us gifts, they're often not only for us but also meant for others. There is always an impartation of a part of God that's in His gifts, and it carries something that's meant for release through us to the world.

God also gives me crowns. They usually symbolize a reward from Him. Sometimes I see Jesus in the room walking toward me and then placing the crown on my head. Other times, just His hands come down with a new, beautiful crown He wants to give me. Each one is different and unique, but the bases are usually made of gold and they're different shapes and sizes. He's even given me crowns that appear to be from another era and have what looks like some sort of tambourine skin on the inside.

God gives gifts to His children in many ways, though we may not always be aware of them. I believe some of those crowns are crowns of salvation or crowns of righteousness. Others are like memorial rewards for passing tests of hardship in our walk with Him. I know there are also beautiful crowns won for partnering with Him to lead souls to Him.

Almost daily I see God's oil too. It started when He'd come into my room and pour a cupful right on my head. I loved it so much that I asked Him for more. Then He began bringing big buckets. I can smell it, taste it, and feel it as He pours it on my head and it drips down my shoulders and body.

The bucket usually looks like an old wooden bucket, held

together with metal strapping. I know this is an anointing oil of some kind, and it smells like various scents of incense, refreshing and peaceful. The oils come in different colors too: golden, white, and various colors of light. It makes me feel heavenly, like I'm being transformed into the actual body of Christ (meaning I'm not aware of my flesh body anymore; it feels like only a spiritual body).

He gives the oil as His gift to walk in every day, but it also seems to be stored up in me. I know there's a day coming when He's really going to use all the great anointing He's been giving me. I believe it's for the greater things He wants me to do here in the future. One of Jesus' names is the "Anointed One," and oil is also symbolic of the Holy Spirit. He anoints His kids just because they're His and also for special tasks He's preparing them for.

Definitions of "anointed" include: to be made sacred or consecrated. To be set apart and dedicated to serve God. To be endowed with enabling gifts and grace. To be divinely designated, inaugurated, or chosen and empowered for some purpose.

I'm still so blown away at how much Jesus loves me. He's always telling and showing me, in new and creative ways, that I'm special to Him. He must know it's something I need to hear a lot. Even when He's doing this, He loves to have fun with me. He gets a kick out of amusing me because He likes to keep me smiling and happy. That's why He lets me see Him pouring buckets and buckets of oil on me all the time.

For about the last two years, He has exaggerated the procedure with great, hilarious drama. He shows up with a tanker truck full of heavenly oil with Him. An angel drives it, and Jesus stands there with the big hose, directing the flow of it back and forth all over me. It feels like a river of heaven that flows over me, and I get whacked up with this wonderful glory-drunk feeling so full of His thick, heavenly presence.

God enjoys showing me that I'm cherished by Him and close to His heart. The love He continually shows me never stops, even when I've gotten off-track and done stupid things while learning my walk with Him. He never leaves me, and it's through the never-ending love relationship that He seeks to draw me back into alignment with Him. It's truly a love that's always outta control and knows no bounds.

About eleven years ago, God began showing me a large book. It was thick and had a scarlet cover. As I looked at it, I was given a "knowing" in my spirit that this was the Book of Life. This book is spoken about in the Bible (Philippians 4:3; Revelation 3:5, 13:8, 17:8, 20:12, 20:15, 21:27, 22:19). Only the names of people who are His are written in it. He opened it for me one day, and there were pages with rows and rows of names written there. He even let me see my name.

After that He also showed me a big black book. I knew this was a book of records about people's works, actions, deeds, and thoughts. God has some very important books He keeps. Our entire lives, every single thought and action, even the motives of our hearts, are recorded and an open book to Him.

Nearly every day for years, He's shown me these scrolls, books, and other writings. They look ancient, and most often appear right in front of me. Sometimes He takes me into huge, multi-roomed libraries in heaven that have shelves stacked to overflowing. One book room has ladders that slide along connected to the shelves; others rooms have high ceilings and tables with many scrolls on them. There are millions of them. They come in all different shapes and sizes, and no two look the same. The scrolls are interesting because each one, so unique, has a different type of roller. Some are very detailed and ornate.

I was allowed to look inside some of the books and scrolls, but I couldn't read them. The words were blocked from my vision because they were so bright with light. Then on occasion, when He'd show me them again, I would start to see the writing but I couldn't make it out. The words were all gibberish to me.

Lately I'm getting glimpses of words and short sentences I can read, but sometimes God has deliberately drawn lines through words so I can't see them. There are simply some things not meant for us to know yet, and some things are meant to be shared with us alone. Recently I was able to plainly see a few words, but I'm still waiting for God to give me understanding of them. Beautifully hand written, the first line read "To Judea," and a couple of lines down it read "Wisdom Excels." Everything else was crossed out.

I can't wait to see more of God's writings, because He's beginning to give me more in this realm. That's all I'm allowed to say on this for now.

17

THEY DON'T
KNOW ME

It's all about the light inside you.
Is it really God's light?

— TIM EHMANN

I had just received word that Dad had been taken to the hospital. He collapsed in his house from a brain aneurism. When I rushed to the hospital to see him, I was relieved that he was still conscious and we could talk. I was so grateful we'd had the opportunity to rekindle our relationship over the three years since God had gotten a hold of me. A lot of forgiveness and love had been expressed during that time, and Dad got to see what God had begun in my life. It made him so happy.

While I was in the hospital room with him, I searched for the mind of God and what He was planning to do. But He told me it was Dad's time and He would soon take him home with Him. Those next thirty days became a very special time in my life as I visited him every day. We had some wonderful talks that were priceless for both of us. When he died, I was in the room with family. I witnessed his spirit leave his body and float to the ceiling and up toward heaven. I knew He was safely in the arms of God.

Just after this important chapter in my life closed, God moved me to a new level of His training. It surprised me when He basically told me to just shut up. As I sat on my couch at home, He explained His purpose to me. "Timmy," He said, "words that come from just you carry no weight or power in them. They're mostly empty, idle words that come from your flesh or soul realm. They don't carry My power or glory, and they don't really produce anything good. I want you to keep your mouth shut and not say anything unless they're words that I give you to say."

At first, I felt like He was putting me on a pretty short leash. It immediately reminded me of when I was growing up and Mom used to say to me, "If you don't have anything nice to say, don't say anything at all."

But this exercise God required of me was one of the most important lessons I've learned from Him. I no longer jumped to say the first thing that popped into my head. It taught me three important things:

1) Wait
2) Listen for or "ask God" first
3) Speak only what God is saying—if at all

For the next five years, I went through this "silent period." Some days I spoke only five words the entire day, and other days I said nothing at all. This was pretty hard at first, but over time it became much easier. Obeying God in this practice led me to be used by Him in some of the most amazing miracles I've ever seen. This lesson has stayed with me to this day, though sometimes, to be honest, He takes me back for review on it. It's priceless training from Him, with great reward.

When He first asked for my silence, I thought back to His first words to me the day I met Him: *Son, I've called you to be a voice for me since the day you were born.* It took me a couple of years before I even began to understand what He meant by this. He was talking about being a trusted voice for Him, and I knew it was a high calling that carried a lot of responsibility and accountability with it.

I soon learned I knew little of the process, training, and journey God would require of me ahead, while He began to train me in the first baby steps of this. If He had shown me all of what it would require upfront, I probably would have balked and run. But God is wise in how He trains us up and leads us. He's fully invested in helping, equipping, and seeing us through, and He'll take us through it step by step and level by level, encouraging *and* rewarding us all along the way.

Learning to guard my every word was one of God's leadings to hone me to better accuracy so I could operate solely in what came from Him. He wanted to make me more trustworthy, effective, and usable by Him. We don't realize how powerful our words can be, especially when God's added power is on them. Like a powerful lethal weapon, our tongues can even be downright dangerous! We all know how our words already have a level of "power" or influence on them, and they can bring either life or death (Proverbs 18:21). It takes the help of God's Holy Spirit to train and keep our tongues. We simply cannot adequately control our tongue all on our own, as God says (James 3:8). Though one word from God, delivered with precision accuracy with His power on it, can totally change things, even atmospheres, including greatly encouraging or changing a person's life.

I took my silence training pretty seriously, though, and once I began putting the effort forth to practice it, God wasted no time rewarding each little step I took and didn't wait until I mastered it.

It was then that He sent me on an assignment to Fredericktown, a small town about two miles from where I lived. He told me to attend the services of a popular church there because He wanted to show me how He was going to use me when I waited, listened to Him, and obeyed. He also said He wanted to show me how some churches operated.

He gave me a lot of visions while I was there, and since I wasn't allowed to talk, I just stood in the back of the church and observed. He plainly showed me ribbons of yellow caution tape wrapped around some of the church leaders there. I wondered what He meant by this, but knew I needed to wait, keep my discerner "antennae" up, and stay in tune for whatever He would say.

Over time attending the service as a quiet observer, I noticed a couple of excellent Bible teachers with a lot of knowledge and wisdom regarding doctrinal and historical biblical knowledge. But then God showed me a contrast in operation there too. Some church teachers excelled in a more natural area of knowledge and wisdom about God, while the prophetic people operated more by the spiritual, revelatory side of God. Both have value, but they need each other. It soon became evident that these people were very resistant to each other, and subsequently, little of God's Spirit was allowed to move there, except in back-room meetings attended by those hungry enough for it. Consequently, I could feel God's heart was grieved because He wasn't able to move in the freedom He so desired to bring into that church.

One day, God told me to start attending the back-room gatherings held on Sunday and Wednesday evenings. I stood quietly in the back of the room, watching and waiting on Him. God finally instructed me, "I'm going to show you things, you're going to speak them, and I'm going to make them happen." So I waited, and as I looked around the room, my attention was drawn to a woman in a chair in the front row. In the spirit, I saw a picture of a big lizard on her back. God nudged me and said, "Go talk to her."

Carefully, I approached and asked to speak with her. I started by telling her as sensitively as I could what God had shown me, wondering how she would take it and what else I was supposed to say. I was kind of nervous because He hadn't given me anything else yet. Right after I finished my starting line, though, His words came to me: "God says He knows you've been going through a long dry period, but you've been very faithful to Him, and He says He is going to honor you for it." She appreciatively received the word, and I went to the back of the room and sat down.

At the next meeting, she came running up to me, full of excitement. She admitted she indeed had been going through a dry time and financially had been "hanging by a thread," though she prayed about it all the time. But she said she had just received an unexpected thirty-two-thousand-dollar check that showed up "out of the blue." Her faith was totally renewed (frankly, so was mine). So I just waited for more, watched God strategically work, and listened for what else He would say.

At another meeting, as I scanned the room, God pointed out a lady sitting with a big Bible on her lap. As I looked at her Bible, it changed into a gun. So I went to tell her what God had just showed me and delivered the message that immediately came: "God says you use the Word of God like it's a gun and you always hit your mark right on—and it pleases Him." I learned that she was known as a diligent prayer warrior and accurate intercessor, and her prayers were always acknowledged by others as very effective. She was totally enthused that God would encourage her heart through a total stranger.

This is all part of "prophesying," which often works with other gifts of the Spirit. It's hearing what God is saying and delivering it exactly as and where He wants us to. It's important to only say what He is saying and not add our own words or take away from His. That only waters it down or changes what God is really saying.

Sometimes He may give further interpretation of something He may show, but we need to ask Him whether we're supposed to deliver it to the person or not. He'll give us more if He can trust us to deliver the initial small amounts as He directs. Sometimes it may be only one word that will be very meaningful to the person. If God's saying it, it will always be right on, effective, and powerful. He may also want us to do something else after delivering a word to someone, like give them a "word of wisdom" (1 Corinthians 12:8), which may be God's specific direction on what to do with the first information, or He may lead us to pray for the person's healing, freedom, or salvation.

One day as I walked down a crowded city sidewalk while out on street ministry, God pointed out a stranger walking toward me. "Go say 'spaghetti' to that man," He told me.

"What?" I nervously asked, shuddering as I slowed and the man quickly approached.

"Do it!" He commanded.

But I was struggling because it seemed so way out there. I worried about being looked at as a weirdo or maybe even getting punched. I could feel the hand of God pressing on me stronger and stronger, though, and there was no way I could escape my sudden uneasy feeling about resisting.

While I kept squirming and deliberating, I hesitated, and the man passed right by me. Feeling so uncomfortable, I stopped, not really wanting to do it but knowing God expected it of me if I really wanted to be used by Him. I turned around, caught up with him, and blurted out, "Spaghetti!"

The man stopped in his tracks and looked at me like I'd just slapped him in the face. Then he began to just bawl like a baby. Tears flowed in streams as he let loose whatever it was that word meant to him. I never asked. I just turned around and walked away.

Who knows what God was up to in that man's life. I imagined something critical in his heart, like wanting to kill himself and challenging God to prove to him He was real by picking some random word he demanded God have someone say to him before the day was done—or else. Whatever the word's meaning, I'd done what God told me to do and the rest was up to Him.

Walking with God is always a thrilling adventure, and I love being used by Him and getting a front-row seat to watch some of the outrageous things He does. To see this stuff, we have to be willing to get out of our comfort zone. Not only does it totally bless and awe the other person about God, but it blows me away each time too.

Another day while at one of the back-room church meetings, God pointed out a woman with crutches and a Velcro support brace on her leg. She had broken her foot and couldn't walk on it because she was in so much pain. This time He told me, "Go up to her and just put your hand on her shoulder. Don't say a word." I did as He said.

She jolted in her chair and shouted, "I just felt something like electricity going down my leg!" She stood up and started walking on her foot with no limp and no pain. God had healed her instantly, just like that.

Eventually, I was approached by one of the church leaders and asked to assist in leading the teen worship group. Before long, we had a bunch of new worship bands started. Some were really good. I taught them how to set up their stages and equipment, play their instruments better, and write new songs. Soon they were taking their gigs outside the church and playing worship songs at coffee houses and small rock 'n' roll venues.

At God's direction, I attended the church services and back-room meetings for about a year. I mostly helped out, serving and taking part outwardly while God showed and taught me things inwardly. True to his instruction, I never shared them unless He told me to.

One day in the morning church service, God pointed out two women who regularly attended the back-room gatherings and were known as mighty prayer intercessors. He plainly showed me a specific gift of prophecy on both of them; that is, they were called by Him to be prophets in a prophetic office, not just to prophecy now and then (which anyone who hears His voice can do). It was their specific calling.

I took notice when God showed me, but I waited to see if He wanted me to do anything with the information. Right as the church service concluded, He told me to go and tell them what He'd shown me. One woman looked at me dumbfounded, but the other understood. God already had her in training for it.

God wanted to stir them up and encourage them a little. He told me to tell them three specific things that would come up later in the evening meeting—things they would be asked to pray for. He gave me specific names, particular details, and way-out-there, never-heard-of-before situations that would come up as unusual prayer requests. Sure enough, as God said, that's exactly what happened in the evening meeting, right down to the smallest detail. I knew why God was doing this. His eye was on them, and He was calling and encouraging them to start walking confidently in their callings and toward their destinies.

God continued giving me His three prayer details for them every week for the entire year I was there to encourage them. Though a lot of the people were hungry for such prophecy, it soon became obvious that the church leadership didn't trust or want anything to do with the prophetic things of the Spirit of God. After some time, two of the pastors approached me about it and actually threatened me. That's when God told me He wanted me to speak with the lead pastor.

Our meeting began with the pastor questioning me on whose authority I had to speak about God and demanded proof that I really heard His voice. God told me to begin by telling him three specific things from Him. These were detailed incidents that happened in the man's life that no one other than him and God could have known. So I repeated to him what God had just showed me.

The pastor got all shook up but finally acknowledged they were all true. Then as we talked more, he opened up a little, and I thought I could deliver the rest of what God was telling me to say. But the moment I mentioned the word "prophets" and that God still uses them today, He didn't want anything to do with it. *Oh no, God!* I thought. *What do you want me to do now?* He replied, "You're done here now. You've done what I told you to do, and it's time to get ready to leave this place."

The pastor quickly ended the meeting, and as I was on my way out the door, God spoke to me again, saying, "Before you leave, I want you to go and anoint with oil one of the two women who I've called to be a prophet for Me. This is to be a sign to her from Me that I have fully commissioned and anointed her for her calling."

The next time I saw her was at the last meeting I attended there. I told her what God said and asked her to step aside with me for a moment, then quickly anointed her with oil while speaking over her God's beautiful commissioning words that He gave me.

She gratefully received it, and it was one of those holy moments, but in no time, a group of church elders and leaders who were now watching me like a hawk approached. "Who gave you the authority to anoint people?" they demanded.

I could only answer, "Uh…God did."

At first they didn't know what to say, but then they started arguing and trying to get me to quarrel with them, attacking me verbally.

God didn't give me anything else to say, so I just stood there trying hard to keep my mouth shut. It was really getting hairy though. I thought they might grab me and throw me off a cliff if there were one nearby. I knew the door God Himself wanted so much to open in that church was being held closed tight by the leadership.

While the men continued to angrily jab at me verbally, God showed me two big black spirits standing next to each of them. Then chains began to appear around them, and hovering right above them was a dark spirit of witchcraft. The Pharisees of Jesus' time came to mind. God was showing me some of the same spirits and things He Himself commonly encountered when the religious leaders of His day wouldn't receive what He was saying. "They're not rejecting you, Timmy," He said in a soft, comforting voice. "They're rejecting Me." It made my heart ache for God.

Later, He pointed out Scripture as back-up encouragement and a reminder:

He who hears you hears Me, he who rejects you rejects Me, and he who rejects Me rejects Him who sent Me. (Luke 10:16)

I had met some great people at this church, as well as some astoundingly good Bible teachers who were gifted at getting people grounded in God's Word. But it amazed me that no one in leadership there really heard the voice of God; that is, no one but the young prophet woman He was strategically training and setting up in their midst. I knew now why God so wanted to encourage her. She would have a big job if He intended to keep her there for long. I didn't understand how people acting as spiritual leaders of God's people couldn't hear the voice of God for themselves. In fact, the more I thought about it, the more it scared me.

Knowing *about* God isn't the same as *knowing* God. Knowing His Word—the Bible—is a great fundamental tool, but we need to hear His voice to know and walk in vital relationship with Him. Salvation is meant to be a personal two-way relationship with God. It's our talking to Him and Him talking to us. His sheep should hear and know His voice, just like He says (John 10:27). It's the most basic aspect of knowing Him—and it's especially vital when you're leading others.

For a while, Jesus kept showing me a giant clear glass dome. It looked kind of like a rounded-top glass frying pan lid. He held it by its big handle and kept putting it down on areas of the earth over certain cities or sometimes certain people. Often the dome covered the entire horizon. When He did this, He would say, "They don't know me."

I thought He was talking about the people and wondered about it all. But as He kept showing me this scene and repeating this same phrase over and over for about six months, I became somewhat disturbed by it. Finally, I asked Him, "Who doesn't know You?" He replied, "The church. Duh!" It was then I was given understanding that the clear dome was His mercy coming down and covering them, waiting until the day when they might come to *really* know Him.

God yearns for many who think they know Him to quit relying on religion, rituals, traditions, middle men, and feel-good stuff they're fed once a week. That has nothing to do with a real personal relationship with Him. God wants to be let out of the box He's been put in by many people and church systems. He wants them to truly know Him! Their very souls depend on it.

Some people leave their weekly Sunday service feeling picked-up and happy because they heard a great feel-good message. While it may have fed and strengthened their souls, nothing changes in their spirits or lives. They walk out just as chained up and spiritually dead as when they walked in. We need more than our souls and minds built up and strengthened; these are what are usually in direct opposition to the things of God's Spirit (Galatians 5:17). Instead, we need our spirits made alive, nourished, and strengthened by the precise and powerful impartation that comes only from hearing directly from Him. It comes from His Spirit to our spirit. Then with our spirit in line with His, and the life-giving fresh revelation He brings daily, we allow our souls—our minds and will—to line up with that.

God put a desire to mentor in my heart soon after I began to know Him. He had me releasing to others the things I'd learned directly from Him. I saw many gifted ones who had no idea about their true identities or destinies in God, but He would plainly show them to me and He wanted me to encourage those whom I could. God spoke to me about this several times, and one day He specifically showed this to me as I was reading 2 Timothy.

"Pass on what you learn from me," He said. "Devote your time on the ones who can teach others. Always look for the ones who are trainable and can teach others and spend your time on them." He then earnestly added, "Timmy, save my children. Bring me my babes. I'm just looking for the ones to send. You just get them home to me and I'll train them."

That's been a big part of my calling from Him since then. I can't stop feeling God's heart yearning for His children to know Him. So many are wandering, not realizing that they're already destined to be His. Many, like I was, may not understand that they're already hearing His voice. They don't have anyone to tell them, "Yeah, that's Him! Get up and go with it!" They don't realize they have a great calling on their life and how easy it is to believe it, step into Him, and start walking in it. They don't know the great identities they've already been given by God. And they haven't yet believed how trustworthy, faithful, and in love with them He is, and how He wants to sweep them into the freedom and fun of His kingdom.

I'm humbled by the privilege God's given me to mentor hundreds of people over the years. I've seen Him do amazing things in people's lives when I watch Him do it His way. He's always teaching me more even while I'm teaching them.

Through a lot of my beginning training years, God sent me into different church ministries to help, but He's always told me to learn only from Him. I call these beginning years my "church period." I met a lot of great people, and I honor them and a lot that I learned there, but God told me early on that I wouldn't stay there long because He wanted to use me for His ministry to the world—to those not even looking or asking for Him, just like it was with me.

The Bible says, "For God so loved the *world*, that He gave His only begotten Son, that whoever believes in Him should not perish but have everlasting life" (John 3:16, emphasis mine). It doesn't say, "For God so loved the *church*," as some in the church think. God speaks to the saved and the unsaved alike. He loves everyone the same. He sent His Son to die for the *world* that it might be saved.

Jesus spent more of His time among the broken, poor, forgotten, and wretched—the thieves and prostitutes—than He did in the churches of His day. In fact, He said many of these people will get into heaven *before* some of the church people will (Matthew 21:31). His true church is made up of people who are truly His, not the ones who are just trusting in practicing a religion or relying on an ordination only by man or some organization. In God's kingdom, there's none of that. His people are those who know Him personally and hear, recognize, and obey His voice. These are the ones who are walking in a true love relationship with Him, and God Himself is the one who personally calls, anoints, and ordains them.

I've found more often that the unchurched tend to receive the things of God, His message, and His miracles much more readily than many in religious circles do. I really believe my assignment is much easier than that of those He assigns to the churches. Theirs is a tough calling, but also a very high calling from God. I get less beat up on assignments with God out in the world, and yet that's a very sad commentary on what some call "God's church."

Religion says that before you can do anything in God, you have to first study the Bible after getting saved, before stepping out. Christ says the instant you receive Him, "You're a new creation. Now get up and go!" When He steps into you and you step into Him, you can go straight into "third heaven" operations where everything you receive and are taught comes directly from Him—and it's pure, powerful, and accurate.

I think it's appropriate to define here what is commonly referred to as the first-, second-, and third-heaven realms, which is terminology that some readers may be unfamiliar with. We need to know what "realm" we're operating in and from. We all operate from at least one of them at any given time. A definition will also give a basic foundation to understand spiritual realities.

The "three heavens" illustration is a fairly popular model used to attempt to explain the basic differences in the natural and spiritual realms, though it is by no means perfect; in God there are many realms (even realms within realms) and they're all made and owned by Him. While putting spiritual realities in human terms is difficult, the three heavens illustration suffices only as a general model in this attempt. I'll do my best to explain it here, including both a basic definition (A) and a prophetic (meaning God-taught) definition (B).

First Heaven

A) The natural physical material realm, such as the earth, skies, and universe visible to the natural senses. Also refers to the natural physical body and natural senses of sight, sound, smell, touch, and taste, and the natural soul (mind, will, and emotions). Also referred to as the "natural man," "flesh," or "carnal" state.

B) A person operating only here is fully in the carnal or flesh state (natural mind logic, earthly reasoning and ways, natural senses). Death is in operation here, as is total spiritual darkness or "walking death." No interest in spiritual things. Lost.

Second Heaven

A) The spiritual realm that exists all around the natural, physical (first-heaven) realm, but is mainly hidden to the natural man/senses alone. God's holy angels and host pass through in transfer between the third heaven and the first heaven. However, it is also the realm where evil spirits, demons, principalities, and powers reside, have access, and operate from (see Ephesians 2:2, 6:12; Revelation 12:9; Luke 10:18).

B) Spiritual acuity for some people here. Spiritual senses of sight, sound, smell, touch, taste, and a "knowing" perception for some who operate in this realm. Both light and dark spirits are at work here; therefore, it's a mixed realm. The soul realm of man (mind/will/emotions) can operate here also. However, this realm is not pure, accurate, or 100 percent trustworthy. False "light," perverted/twisted "truth," deception, and counterfeit/mock imitation spiritual experiences can operate here. True salvation is indefinite for people who function/operate only in or "up to" this realm, including people who believe they're saved but are not. "Spiritual mediums," "channellers," "fortune tellers," and the like operate in/from this realm, as well as some so-called (blinded/deceived) "prophets."

Third Heaven

A) "Heaven" or real heaven, the "highest heaven," or the "kingdom of God." The spiritual realm and dwelling place of Almighty God, where He, His heavenly host, and redeemed people in true relationship with Him dwell. It is "far above" the first and second heavens yet totally encompasses and can come into/through all three realms because all realms were made by and belong to God.

B) The 100-percent-accurate realm. Genuine light, truth, and eternal life are here. Salvation is assured. God abides in this realm, and this realm abides in God. His kingdom, presence, glory, power, revelation—even His voice—are sourced from here. When God abides in the believer through His Holy Spirit, it follows that God and the realm of His kingdom of heaven abides within the believer. To have complete accuracy in spiritual things, the believer must operate *in* and *from* this realm *in* God, and that's found only through relationship with Him. I prefer to call it the "party place" because it is totally pure, holy, awesome, and perfect—with total freedom and fun here.

Bottom line, it's all about the light inside you. Is it really God's light?

Religion and just plain "spirituality" will try to keep us in the first- and second-heaven realms, where there's no true flow of heavenly revelation or real power of God's Spirit. The Enemy loves this because it keeps us as no real threat to him and his kingdom of darkness; we're powerless against him. It's another form of false light. Likewise, the information and experiences received solely through the first- and/or second- heaven realms are like blindness compared to the complete accuracy received through third-heaven operations. (We need third-heaven operations to properly discern, direct, and guard our way and life.)

Because the spiritual realm indeed exists, supernatural beings (angels and demons, holy spirits and evil spirits) and events from both the second- and third-heaven realms can manifest in the natural realm. So how do we know the difference?

God warns us not to put our trust in any supernatural being or encounter without testing its source first. If we receive a visitation from an angel, supernatural being, or popularly called "spirit guide" or the like, it's vitally important to have God's discernment to know if the spirit being (people included) or its message is really from Him. We're warned by God ahead of time that even Satan and his deceitful servants often masquerade as God's servants and as "angels of light." Why does He warn us about this? Because they're real—and it happens! We need discernment and to know how to test the spirits, because if it is God's doing, we don't want to discount or miss Him either. (For further information on "testing the spirits," see 1 John 4:1; 2 Corinthians 11:14–15; Galatians 1:8; Matthew 24:24; and 1 John 4:2–4.)

The person who truly meets God (solely a third-heaven event) can in one minute know more than someone sitting in a church pew for thirty years. It's because encountering Him personally is the real deal! Being one with Him in the love relationship is all that matters. We need to know how to tune in to and discern His voice and learn everything firsthand from Him. He wants people to know for themselves who He really is, not who He may be mischaracterized to be.

Only God can personally show and teach us this, and He's eager to do so. Those already walking in this can offer mentoring and encouragement to others, but ultimately it's all about mentoring people to Him—to the hearing, discerning and obeying of His voice, having one-on-one with Him—and not the mentoring of just human beliefs and ways.

First, nurture your two-way relationship with Him. Learn to practice discerning His voice, then He'll teach you more. The real prophetic ability comes when you know Father God's heart and what He's seeing, thinking, feeling, etc., because you'll know His genuine voice. He'll release in and through you His righteousness, purity, goodness, will, and desires. He'll then pour His love through your heart to others. It's not your heart alone but His heart operating in and through you in precision accuracy and power. It's all for the purpose of being in unhindered relationship with Him and walking in your true calling toward your destiny—and you also get to set other captives free with Him.

Demons are after power. The kingdom of God is about love. Love is where the real power comes through! People have varying motives for power. It doesn't matter if it's through New Age religion, witchcraft, Satanism, or plain old worldly success, wealth, fame, or even church leadership. It's all apart from God when people are drawn to it only after the "power" without the true real-deal relationship.

For some, this power search can include seeking entrance into popular "Christian power schools" to learn how to become a "prophet with power" under the banner of a church name. If you're after the power without the relationship with purity and holiness operating through God's spirit of love, it's all the same—it's corrupt. These things are spirit. Ask yourself, "What spirit am I operating in?" Love is a spirit—the Spirit of God.

God loves New Agers, witches, and Satanists the same as He loves all people. He's yearning and calling for everyone to know Him and His love for them, no matter what they've done or been involved in. He receives anyone who calls on His name and will deliver them from the power of darkness and all the oppression, lies, bondage, chains, and claims the Enemy has ever had to them. We all can know the genuine and greatest power—the power that only comes from the author and source of all creation, love and life Himself.

A friend of mine who owned a recording studio once gave my phone number to one of his customers. The man was a musician who had heard about me and wanted to talk with me. When he called, He asked if I could help out his wife. She had already heard and recognized God's voice to her and believed in Him, but she wanted to be baptized. She felt God was leading her to it. Her husband said she was frustrated because she tried to get baptized the only way she knew how, by going to a church, but she had been turned down by three different pastors because she was still a drug addict and living a promiscuous lifestyle. But she knew she heard and was being drawn by God, and she wanted His help.

When the pastors met with her, all they saw was the way she dressed and her rough look and demeanor. She wore revealing clothes with a miniskirt and spike heels, and had tattoos all over. They took one look at her and turned her away, saying they wouldn't do it.

Her husband, already a believer, stuck with her through a tumultuous marriage marked by her addictions and sleeping around on him. He loved her, and he recognized the great desire that had sparked in his wife's heart as she received the obvious draw of God on her life. He knew she'd been asking Him to help her. Now she wanted to be baptized because she felt led that this was an important step God wanted her to take as an outward sign that she believed in Him. She didn't know anything else at this point or even how to get free from all that had a stranglehold on her life.

After hearing the husband out, I took a moment to ask God what He wanted. He answered, "Invite them out, and you do it." So I agreed to meet with them. The next weekend they drove one hundred miles from where they lived just to meet with me.

My son, Tee, and I met them by the river at a beautiful park in Pittsburgh's South Side. We got there early and spent time praying the place up and tuning in to what God wanted to do before they arrived. He orchestrated the whole thing. When they showed up, Tee took the husband aside to minister to him while I spoke with his wife at the picnic tables. She came dressed in her miniskirt and heels and was chain-smoking cigarettes while we talked. I could tell she was a hard-core drug addict, but I also knew God didn't care about any of that at the time.

As we talked, she shared with me about her life and her addiction to crystal meth and crack. She then told me she also had a problem with hearing "bad voices in her head." I knew what was up. I could also plainly see it, but none of it could stop what God was about to do. We talked for a while, and when I finally asked her about her bottom-line belief in the Lord Jesus Christ, she said that she really believed in Him and wanted to know Him more.

That was it.

I walked her down to the river and was ready to take her into the water to baptize her when God stopped me. "Wait!" He said, sounding even more excited than I was. "First I want you to baptize her in My Spirit." So standing there on the grass right at the river's edge, I asked God for the baptism of His Holy Spirit on her, which is a baptism of power that God does personally, just like at Pentecost (Acts 1:5, 2:1–18, Matthew 3:11; Mark 1:8; Luke 3:16; John 1:33)

Bam! Instantly she was hit so heavily by the power of God that her knees gave out and she fell backward on the grass while I blew back the other way, almost falling down myself. (This was something pretty rare for me when I prayed for others.) It felt kind of like a supernatural electricity bolt hit us. When she stood up, I saw this dark "thing" lift off of her and leave. Suddenly, she shouted that the voices that had been constantly speaking in her head left her.

God said to me, "Now tell her I've called her to be a prophet, a healer, and one who can see the third heaven. Then baptize her in the water." So I repeated to her what God had told me. The realization of it all overwhelmed me with awe as I literally saw before me what He had said. Indeed, here before me was a special, gifted one with such a great and high calling on her life. He had been just waiting for her to be launched into it. She was another of God's amazing hidden gems, in a rejected-by-the-world package but personally handpicked by God to shine His light to the world.

She still didn't understand or know it. She was yet to learn, believe, and step into her true identity. But I plainly saw her as a little Kathryn Kuhlman, starting on her journey with God toward her destiny.

I baptized her in the river, miniskirt and all. When she came up out of the water, a physical gleaming light beam came from somewhere across the river and landed only on her like a spotlight. Everyone in the park could see it, and people who were walking by with their dogs stopped to look, point, and comment on it. God had broken in and done His thing. Later, she told me that even the drug addictions left her at that moment. She didn't desire drugs anymore and didn't suffer any withdrawals. Jesus just came and took it all away.

Before we parted that day, I explained what had happened to her and about the great calling God had on her life. I assured her the presence and power of God that resided in her would help her and keep her along her way as she stayed walking in close relationship with Him. I made sure she knew God's Holy Spirit would be her primary and greatest teacher and encouraged her to stay tuned in and let Him teach her to discern His voice. I also offered to keep up with her and her husband by phone so I could encourage and mentor them along the way.

When the woman called me the next day, I reminded her of the three things God said about her and how they were already as good as done in her life. He had anointed and gifted her, and I encouraged her to freely give out what she had freely received. I gave her some Scriptures about healing the sick and raising the dead like Jesus and His disciples did, and encouraged her to get going.

For the next three days, she called me daily with exciting reports. Everywhere she went, people were healed. Curious, I asked her what method she was using. She responded, "I don't know. I don't even really know how to pray yet. So I just put my arms around them and this deep compassion comes over me and I start to cry and say, 'Jesus heals you.' And it's done." Soon she even began going into hospitals to release God's healing to the sick. Amazing reports kept coming in, and I marveled again at the goodness of God and how He just does amazing things with His kids.

I had the pleasure of encouraging and mentoring this couple every day by phone for the next year and a half. God had me pour into them everything I knew and whatever else He gave me to say. With a foundation of learning their identities in Him and hearing the voice of the greatest teacher of all within, they had everything they needed to take off from there. I knew they were in God's very capable hands for the rest.

God gave me an amazing crumb from heaven through this couple. As I wondered about it all, He broke into my thoughts and said, "Timmy, that's nothing. This is only a preview of what I'm about to do in unparalleled numbers with people all over the world." He meant that it's where He just shows up and does it all. "Just lead them to Me, Timmy," He reminded me, "and I'll take care of all the rest."

I don't know why I was in such awe. This was really no different from the way He'd called and commissioned me. God has a great and simple plan. He reveals Himself to individuals when they hear and recognize His voice. They believe and freely receive Him, and He steps into them and they're saved. Then they can freely give Him out to others. No twelve steps, and no required programs or special man-approved affiliations. No requirement to study the Bible first or take a new-believer's class before you can go. It's just one step, when God steps into you and you step into Him.

It really struck me that this precious woman was passed up by some churches. They didn't want anything to do with her because they saw her only as a drug addict and an adulteress—but God saw His special hidden gem. The truth is, we've all been adulterers against God in one way or another. Anytime we don't listen to or walk away from Him, we're committing spiritual adultery, and I think we've all done it at one time or another. God refers to this rebellious natural human nature hundreds of times in His Word, in both the Old and New Testaments. He's the supreme lover of our souls and we are His "beloved." He longs for us to be in close companionship with Him, and it hurts Him greatly to be apart from us.

This woman had never read a Bible or been to a church service before. Now she was hearing His voice, filled with His Spirit, anointed for miracles, and walking in her calling the day after He touched her. The drug addictions were gone, she no longer had desires to sleep around, and her life totally changed because she instantly became a total new creation, empowered by God's Holy Spirit. He truly is the God who does it all.

Salvation comes from God's grace and goodness. No one finds God. God finds us. God's mercy always triumphs over judgment. We need to stop judging by seeing things only through our natural eyes. "Things are not always what they seem" is a bona fide true statement with the things of God. Remember, God's goodness leads us to salvation—not judgment, shame, or guilt trips. That's not God's heart. That's not His voice. No matter how messed up and steeped in sin anyone is in, God only feels immense love for them and sees all the potential He put in them. Real salvation brings a total deliverance and new creation. And yes, God has to do it all for it to be real.

It's the personal revelation that flows directly from God to you that's important—what He shows and teaches you personally (not following formats, formulas, or programs). This is vital to being in true relationship with Him. Tune in to Him and let Him teach you personally. It's a two-way relationship, with Him talking to you and you talking to Him. It's all about the relationship—and let it be a relationship of love!

It wasn't until much later that I encouraged this couple to get involved in a church pastored by a trusted friend of mine. I knew he mentored others in the same way I did. But after what they had been through, they were reluctant to go. They argued that they were already walking in and experiencing the real thing, so why would they want to risk stepping into something that could potentially be fake? They had a good point. Church is not necessarily where the Lord really is. You have to know God's voice and let Him train you in discernment of it.

They were having the time of their lives walking in personal relationship with Him and were growing exponentially. Some churches might have hindered, detoured, or even held them back from this and how they were taking off with Him. In fact, some of the churches probably would have been too boring for them anyway, just as the drugs and extramarital sex had become after what they were now experiencing. They were already walking in the real deal.

It bothers me that the terms "Christian" and "church" often denote fakeness to so many people these days. There are also not as many true Christians as some think there are. Jesus said, "Narrow *is* the gate and difficult *is* the way which leads to life, and there are few who find it." (Matthew 7:14). Simply walking in morality isn't going to bring salvation. Morals are just good works of our own, unaccepted by God and with no saving grace in them. Knowing the Bible or knowing only *about* God won't get you into heaven. These things can even be idols—things we put all our practices and trust into, thinking they'll save us because they look and sound good. But beware of idols, little children. Behind every idol, there's a demon (1 John 5:21).

Some churches have become too much of a commercial business. Others are all about control whereby people can be kept in bondage to mesmerizing formalities, Spirit-compromising systems, or a growth rate in God allowed only somewhere under the leader's level. It may look and feel good to the natural mind and soul, but God is not allowed to do what He wants through the real deal of His Spirit.

Talking about God is okay. Reading His word and using Bible studies is okay. But the Holy Spirit God gave to live in and lead

His people is often resisted, ignored, quelled, or even kicked out, relegated to sitting on the sidelines or out the back door of His own so-called "church." Nowhere does God say today, "Build Me a temple!" God says, "Heaven is my throne and earth is my footstool. What kind of house could you build for me?" (Isaiah 66:1; Acts 7:49). The house God has chosen to dwell in is right smack on the *inside* of His own people.

> Do you not know that you are the temple of God, and that the Spirit of God dwells in you? (1 Corinthians 3:16)

> "The kingdom of God does not come with observation; nor will they say, 'See here!' or 'See there!' For indeed, the kingdom of God is within you." (Luke 17:20b–21)

The real kingdom is about miracles. Everything God does is a miracle from start to finish. It's all the work of His Spirit, not man's, and it comes from the supernatural realm of God. That includes every time you hear Him talking to you—it comes from God's realm, and we can be receivers *and* conduits of those miracles to others.

Finding and raising up new believers who hear and follow God's voice, while staying protected and free, is what God wants. If a church is a gathering place of people who truly know Him and hear His voice or are being encouraged and equipped in this, then that's God's heart. I'm glad there are more and more churches that are finally encouraging and equipping people in this—and there are some great ones. But still, none of this should ever replace God's first place teaching within you at all times.

One day, when I was spending one-on-one time with God at home, I was praying, worshipping, and having a great time hanging out and conversing with Him. After a couple of hours, I decided to shift gears and walked over to pick up my Bible, thinking I'd get a little reading time in. But a few minutes later, as I fully put my attention into reading, God said to me, "What are you doing? Put the book down. I'm talking to you."

It shocked me. I sheepishly put the Bible down and we laughed about it. When God's loud laugh came into the room, it sounded like a big Echoplex with a joyful choir of thousands of angels singing with Him all around me. He knew I got it, and it's a lesson I'll never forget.

> You have your heads in your Bibles constantly because you think you'll find eternal life there. But you miss the forest for the trees. These Scriptures are all about me! And here I am, standing right before you, and you aren't willing to receive from me the life you say you want. (John 5:39–40 MSG)

What I learned that day is vital for all of us. God desires, more than anything, personal, interactive now-time with us. Reading His Word is good and necessary and will help ground you in the recognition of His voice and ways, but reading the Bible *about* the author alone can't ever replace relationship and interaction *with* the author. Especially when He's currently talking with you. The Bible is God's love letter written to us and an ongoing integral foundational read that God often uses to confirm what He's saying or to peel back layers of deeper truths and revelation of Himself. But, it's not right to ignore Him, choosing to go read *about* Him when He's right there already speaking and interacting directly with you.

God has much more to say to us presently and personally, and He wants to impart Himself and His truths right in His personal love language with you. He *is* the love letter, and He's constantly writing new and ongoing chapters of His beautiful story right inside and through you for the world to see. These stories don't all get written in books on earth like the Bible, but they are written in heaven. I'm sure our books are already there, somewhere in one of God's many big libraries.

The apostle Paul wrote about this deep truth too:

> You are our epistle written in our hearts, known and read by all men; clearly you are an epistle of Christ, ministered

by us, written not with ink but by the Spirit of the living God, not on tablets of stone but on tablets of flesh, that is, of the heart. (2 Corinthians 3:2–3)

What you get personally from God is unteachable by man. Precious gifts. This is how things happen when you're walking in relationship with Him and being led by His Spirit. You get and stay full of His light—and then the unity of heaven happens. His light is not obtained through simply spending time with teachings, listening to good sermons, or reading the Bible. It's won through personal one-on-one intimacy time with the author, listening to His voice, and walking in the ongoing love relationship with Him.

Christ's anointing abides in the believer to teach the truth about Him and His ways. His Holy Spirit reveals it step by step through relationship. God's revelation is pure, uncontaminated by a single lie, and tailored to each person's unique personality to help bring understanding, which He also gives. It's that personal revelation given through a clean and clear channel directly with heaven that matters, not all the teaching you get from man.

But the anointing which you have received from Him abides in you, and you do not need that anyone teach you; but as the same anointing teaches you concerning all things, and is true, and is not a lie, and just as it has taught you, you will abide in Him. (1 John 2:27)

Seeing what God sees, hearing what God says, and knowing what God knows is of utmost importance to me—so I can release what He wants released in the unity of heaven. When I'm lined up in the unity of heaven, no matter how crazy or impossible it may seem in the natural to my own reason or flesh, I can release it. It's completely accurate and powerful. It's done! It becomes God's heart in me; it's no longer just my heart, and I get heaven's backing. Second-heaven or soul-realm stuff tries to distract us onto another path and keep us away from this. But we *need* to get this.

When He sends us out there, it needs to happen with precision accuracy. Otherwise, it's just coming from us and God's not in it.

Remember, it's also about the light in you. Is it really God's light? Pure light is God's light. Of ourselves, we can't produce true light or anything that counts for eternity; we were made to be dependent on God. God wants to fill us full of His light so we can accurately find our way.

Always check yourself and be sure that the light in you is not false light or some powerless counterfeit of darkness. When you're in His Spirit, this light comes from Him. It goes right through us and back up to Him—and also out to others.

> Therefore, my brothers and sisters, make every effort to confirm your calling and election. For if you do these things, you will never stumble, and you will receive a rich welcome into the eternal kingdom of our Lord and Savior Jesus Christ. (2 Pet. 1:10–11 NIV)

> Then Jesus spoke to them again, saying, "I am the light of the world. He who follows Me shall not walk in darkness, but have the light of life." (John 8:12)

> Let your light so shine before men, that they may see your good works and glorify your Father in heaven. (Matthew 5:16)

18

THE FAITH WALK

Timmy, if your life can't write a book just as good
as any of my prophets or apostles,
what makes you think you're even saved?

– God

God really incited me one day when He stated matter-of-factly, "Son, if you obey Me and trust Me enough, you can do the same things that my prophet Elijah did." This stirred me with excitement, but at the same time I felt the limits of my own mind struggling to fathom it. God, seeing my dilemma, then challenged me with a profound question: "Timmy, if your life can't write a book just as good as any of my prophets or apostles, what makes you think you're even saved?"

Wow, I thought, astonished by what He was saying. He was talking about people who were sold out to Him, people who let God fill them and were led in everything by His Spirit. Their faith resulted in lives that powerfully rocked the world.

When we truly give God our everything, in return He gives us all of Himself. Trusting Him enough to step into Him fully is an exchange where we give Him all our dead, worthless rubble and He gives us all His pure, abundant life. What a great exchange. When this happens, we can't help but be a living, walking glory-bomb for Him.

Scripture verses God had previously pointed out to me flooded through my mind throughout that day as God reminded

me and confirmed what He would do in my life if I truly loved
and trusted Him with all my heart.

> For whoever desires to save his life will lose it, but who-
> ever loses his life for My sake will find it. (Matthew 16:25)

> For as many as are led by the Spirit of God, these are sons
> of God. (Romans 8:14)

> No one having put his hand to the plow, and looking
> back, is fit for the kingdom of God. (Luke 9:62)

> Now the just shall live by faith;
> But if anyone draws back,
> my soul has no pleasure in him.
> (Hebrews 10:38)

God kept showing me what being fully *in* Him meant. It's
an all-or-nothing deal where He calls us deeper and deeper into
the love relationship with Him. I already knew everything behind
me—my past, everything I worked for in my own reason and
power—was worthless in the light of eternity. My life, works, and
aspirations produced nothing but death in the end. While this
fact may seem more obvious in my life because of the way I lived,
none of us can do anything worthwhile apart from Him. None of
it counts for eternity (Isaiah 64:6). We need to let Him lead and
do it all through us, just like Jesus said:

> I am the vine, you are the branches. He who abides in Me,
> and I in him, bears much fruit; for without Me you can
> do nothing. (John 15:5)

Truly, though, God is now my *entire* life. There's nothing
behind me that's worth going back to when compared with what I
have now. I was a walking dead man and entirely lost even before
I died. I was raised to real life only because of Him, and I know I
can never go back to my old life or I'll end up where I was. I now

understand there's nothing good or life producing in what I do apart from Him.

So what's holding me back from all *of Him?* I thought. *And why can't I be like Elijah? Why can't my life write a book as good as Elijah's, Paul's, or John's or any of the Bible prophets? In fact, why can't my life's book play out and read even better than theirs did?* That's exactly what God was challenging me to do. Jesus said those who believe would do greater works than He did when He walked the earth (John 14:12), and His were pretty awesome.

When God lives in and through us, He's the one who does it all. He'll use anyone. We're qualified as soon as we become His. He just wants to know if we're willing to let Him do all He wants to do in and through us, and He encourages us forward to it.

God's Spirit dwells in us in His fullness, not in just a piece of Him. That's the same spirit and power that made everything, seen and unseen, the whole universe, and you and me. The same power that raised Jesus—even me—from the dead, and He gets the credit and glory for it all.

I deliberated, *If He's really in me—and I'm really in Him—and we've become 'one,' just as He said, what's holding me back?* Really, God was provoking me through these back-and-forth thoughts and questions. I already had seen so many of His great miracles. In fact, my whole life had been one long, ongoing, spectacular string of them. Yet nagging unbelief kept creeping into my mind and threatened to hold me back. His challenge included seemingly insurmountable levels of Him that I couldn't imagine at the time.

Then I was reminded of a few more things He'd pointed out in His Word:

If you can believe, all things are possible to him who believes. (Mark 9:23)

Did I not say to you that if you would believe you would see the glory of God? (John 11:40)

For assuredly, I say to you, if you have faith as a mustard seed, you will say to this mountain, 'Move from here to there,' and it will move; and nothing will be impossible for you. (Matthew 17:20b)

But without faith it is impossible to please Him, for he who comes to God must believe that he is, and that he is a rewarder of those who diligently seek him. (Hebrews 11:6)

Even as Abraham believed God, and it was accounted to him for righteousness. (Galatians 3:6 KJV)

For whatsoever is not of faith is sin. (Romans 14:23b KJV)

Something inside me leapt as His living reminders flooded into my mind like an instant download. I blurted out like a kid, "Yeah, God. I'm on!" Not long after that, He began to reward that child-like trust.

I'm glad God doesn't wait until we perfect our trust before He pours out His amazing wonders and miracles on or through us. He's a loving Father, and He knows He's raising up little children in the things of Him—things we can't possibly know or experience without Him teaching or showing us. He leads us with gentleness and love that spurs us to believe Him for more and more, while giving encouragement and lots of previews along the way. The previews never cease to put me in awe of Him. It's like a carrot on a stick, and He knows just how to provoke me to believe Him for more.

At this time, I had just arrived at the new assignment God sent me on, in Brooklyn, New York. Bushwick Community was a rough neighborhood known for its gang violence, crime, drugs, and poverty. Here, I was to gain more experience and training in street ministry, which allowed access to people who were involved in much of the stuff I'd lived through. I'd had a "chance" meeting with the exceptional ministry's founder about a year and a half prior, and he'd urged me to come help with the challenging inner-city ministry He pioneered. God had impressed the ministry on my heart back when we met, and He was now telling me to go.

The founder had many volunteers and ministers there, learning and ministering in the rough neighborhoods. He also ran an intense internship program, and God wanted to use it to teach me new things. When I arrived in Brooklyn and checked in with his staff, I asked where they wanted me to help.

The ministry had obtained a large abandoned hospital building and used it as temporary housing for some who helped in the ministry, though it was planned to one day be refurbished into one of their main ministry buildings. All of us were given an empty hospital room, and we set them up with old hospital bed mattresses that we found strewn throughout the old building. We also each received fifty dollars a week to buy our own food and necessities. I was grateful for place to stay, but my first job was cleaning up the dead rats and cockroaches and dog poop throughout the building. Starting at 6 a.m. every morning, I'd spend four to five hours cleaning before I went out with the teams to do ministry. The job lasted for six months straight, and I had to swallow any pride I had left. I absolutely hate bugs and dead things, but God held me to it, expecting me to stay faithful and humble.

We had a bus and truck ministry that regularly went into the surrounding neighborhoods. Teams used entertainment through drama, acting, singing, and puppet shows to creatively bring the gospel message to the kids of the inner-city ghetto while also reaching out to meet their other needs.

Teams went out in vans and box trucks that had a side that flipped down to make an instant stage. The trucks would pull up over to curbs in strategic areas of the streets, and the vans would drop off the interns to do their assignments. Some groups also went to the city's parks and set up areas to evangelize and speak to people over bullhorns.

In the afternoons, I went out with the van teams to minister in ghetto areas all over Manhattan, Harlem, and the Bronx. We were dropped off in teams of two near big high-rise projects one of my team members was a sweet young redheaded girl had grown up in a small Midwestern town. She was only eighte and had never seen a big city before.

On one of the days, she and I were dropped off on a street in the Bronx. Right after the van drove away, gun shots rang out and two men were shot dead right across the street. A couple of big guys came up to us on the sidewalk, and one of them grabbed me by the front of my shirt and started shaking me violently. "What are you doing here?" he demanded in my face as his friend cursed and threatened us as well. The girl stood resolutely still and confident, not even seeming concerned.

Then just as soon as it started, they stopped and walked off, though still cursing us out and heckling us all the way. They knew why we were there. Still a little shook up, I asked, "Aren't you afraid you're going to die here?"

She gave a confident grin and said, "I know God sent me here and He'll protect me."

Wow, I thought. Her strong faith, unlike mine at that moment, reassured me. *Yeah,* I had to remind myself, still a bit frazzled and alarmed at my momentary lack of faith. *It's exactly why I'm here too. We* are *sent—and we're gonna be all right.*

We headed toward our destination, praying the whole way as we passed a park filled with drug dealers and hardened gang members hanging out and playing basketball. Being white, we really stood out, and guys called us names and cursed at us while packing and brandishing guns or knives most everywhere we went. We had been given a list of project apartment numbers, and our assignment was to minister to the people and families, find out their needs, pray for and encourage them, and speak words of hope that God gave us to impart into them.

Other times, we were sent out in teams of two to ride the New York subway trains. One person would stand with a bullhorn at the front of the car to give testimony while the other

...mewhere in the back of the crowded seats to pray. We saw
...hol and drug addictions disappear as we ministered in these
...ces, and people would get sober or come back to their right
...inds instantly. God was really on the move.

The final couple of months of my six-month stay in New
York ended with me helping a group of the ministry's young pastors, teen leaders, and interns plant a new church project on the
Lower East Side of Manhattan. I got to minister about prophecy
and the love-affair relationship with God to these bold street war-
riors, but it troubled me that these things were foreign to some of
them. The thought of them ministering in dangerous areas without hearing and knowing the voice of God scared me. But God
showed me the covering of His mercy and grace there using my
previous dome lid covering vision, promising that He covers, cares
for, and protects people even while He's still wooing them into
that deeper place with Him.

One day as I stood on the sidewalk with a group of ministry
leaders and other interns, we started discussing the subject of God's
kingdom on earth, what it looks like, and how God backs up His
children with signs, wonders, and miracles. I shared with them the
principle of how God had challenged me, about how if I would obey
and trust Him enough, He said I could do the same things as Elijah. Surprisingly, few in the group believed that God still does such
things like these today. They actually laughed at me about it. One
of the young interns became visibly upset with me and taunted, "If
you can be like the prophet Elijah, then…make it rain!"

I was on the spot. But then I remembered Elijah's story when
he met with the same type of taunting challenge (1 Kings 18:17–
39; James 5:17–18). I hesitated a moment, with all eyes on me
after I'd boldly opened my big mouth. There was no way out, but
God had me right where He wanted me. The only thing that got
me through was the sudden realization that it wasn't me on the
spot; it was God. After all, He had brought it up and incited me
in the first place. But I knew well enough that I'd better ask Him

first. So in my heart I quickly did. He responded, "Yeah, do it!"
I looked up at the sky and simply said, "Okay, God. Make it rain."

Within seconds it began to rain, and not just a light rain. It drenched us!

The group's eyes widened and their mouths dropped open. They couldn't believe what they were seeing. I couldn't help myself. I laughed and laughed. Really, though, I was also trying to hide my own shock. They had nothing more to say. "God, you're really cool," I told Him.

Later, when I was alone in my hospital room resting on my old mattress on the dirty floor, I was overcome thinking about what God did that day in front of everyone. I started crying like a baby. "I love you, Papa-Yahweh!" I blurted out, feeling a new unbridled affection for Him. A long, deep sigh released audibly into the room with a sweet tone of satisfaction.

"Mmm…say that again!" He cooed back.

"Papa-Yahweh!" I shouted with a laugh.

"I like that!" He said. And I could feel His pleasure and amusement at the affectionate nickname I'd called Him. What a privilege it is to be a friend with God!

During my last month on the assignment in New York, God said He wanted me to go out on my own in the afternoons and walk the streets of Manhattan. He also wanted me to ride the subways alone while praying and prophesying what He instructed over the city and the people. Sometimes I would do this late into the night.

I never mapped out the city. I just picked a street and started walking. Then I'd ride the subway and get off at another street I felt led to walk. Along those streets God showed me different spiritual atmospheres and issues He wanted me to pray about and release His various words and blessings over. It took me twenty-eight days, but it wasn't until the end of this assignment that I finally got of a map of the city. I was amazed as I looked it over. I'd covered every single street in the city. That was another great moment when I deeply felt the awe of God and how I could

.pend on Him by paying attention to the leading of His nudg-ngs and voice.

I also had an interesting encounter when I was walking Man-hattan's busy 5th Avenue. The streets were normally bustling at noontime, but when I turned onto 5th Avenue, it was completely empty. No people out walking, no moving cars. It was eerily silent and totally surreal. As I walked the deserted sidewalk, I looked up ahead of me and about three blocks away, a lone witch stood by the curb staring me down. She wore typical witch garb, with a long black dress and a black pointed hat. With her arms at her sides and her feet planted open, like in an old western shoot-out showdown, she glared at me with a menacing expression. I took note, but casually walked toward her praying whatever God gave me to say. A few minutes later, she just walked away and the street began filling up with people and cars again.

God sent me out on more and more assignments after that. He wanted me to go to certain places just to walk the area and release whatever He wanted to release. I knew it was because He was preparing to do great things in these places. He is after the world and determined it will know Him.

When I returned to Pittsburgh, God sent me on another remarkable assignment—though it was something I never expected. He told me to rent a place at a sprawling working horse farm in the countryside, amid beautiful green rolling hills, cor-rals, barns, and outbuildings. A busy entourage of customers and guests came and went daily. My place was a two-bedroom loft apartment situated above one of the horse barns. Though it was small, the open country atmosphere was lovely and inspiring. I wondered why God sent me here and what He was up to.

Right after I finished getting my few things moved in, I strongly sensed something was wrong. The atmosphere was "off," and I started to feel that familiar creepy warning sign. I asked God, "What's going on here?" Just then, a big witch flew right up to my window and peered inside. This one also wore the long

black dress and black pointed hat. God was showing me the s
operating here—and the main one—was witchcraft.

As I questioned why He'd sent me here, He assured me that F
had me exactly where I was supposed to be. He said He was preparing to teach me more about how the spiritual Enemy operates,
and, more than that, He wanted to reaffirm how He protected me
as promised. He had assigned to me two big angels, and they were
with me wherever I went (not only could I sense their heavenly
presence, but I also plainly felt and saw them at times).

I settled into the new apartment and started my days as I had
before, by staying alone with God and getting in tune with Him.
The inside of my little place would fill up with the atmosphere
of heaven and so would I. At times, it would get so strong that I
could even see what looked like white light emanating from my
body. It was so bright I couldn't even see my own flesh, and it was
a great comfort and confirmation because I knew I was walking
full of God's light and with what God had me doing. There was
no better place to be.

I often ran into the people who came and went at the farm.
Before long I noticed a group of women—close friends—who
came to hang out at the farm a lot. They'd strike up conversations
with me, and though they were very friendly, I sensed a coldness
in their hearts. When they came, they'd go into the main house
for meetings. Soon I learned this wasn't just an ordinary horse
farm; it was also a central gathering place for a New Age witches'
coven, and they called the farm their "church." I couldn't get over
why God had sent me to live here, but it didn't bother me much.
He said there was much He wanted to show and teach me here.

Casual conversations with the people at the farm always
seemed to turn to spiritual subjects and their New Age point of
view. This started long talks, and I would listen and wait for what
God wanted to say in response. He told me to pay close attention to the spirit of what they were saying and their hearts rather
than just their words. This was because they spoke in terms that

...ded very parallel to God's truth, but in reality were com-...tely different in spirit and meaning. They even claimed to ...onor "Jesus," but I knew they believed in *another* Jesus—a whole ...different spirit.

Their beliefs embraced ideas from many different religions mixed with science and humanism, which deifies self as god, over God. It's a combination of beliefs with admirable-sounding tenets of love, peace, and charity that look good and make it appealing to many, but I knew it was actually a doctrine of demons—and a counterfeit to all that is God's truth. New Age is simply recycled idolatry.

The apostle Paul warned:

> For if he who comes preaches *another Jesus* whom we have not preached, or if you receive *a different spirit* which you have not received, *or a different gospel* which you have not accepted—you may well put up with it! (2 Corinthians 11:4, emphasis mine)

The best way to tell a counterfeit is by knowing the genuine so well you can easily spot it. A counterfeit of anything is always made to look as close to the genuine as possible, and that's the Enemy's first tactic. Those who don't really know God and His word are easily deceived. People purposely seeking and operating in second-heaven-sourced spiritual experiences and spiritual "powers" may think they're encountering the true Most High God, but instead they're engaging with dark spirits that try to appear as spirits of God, His truth, and His light.

God told me to continue staying in tune with Him, walk in His love toward the people He really loved at the farm, and to answer them only with what He gave me to say. Even so, they soon tried to recruit me. And then it didn't take long for them to realize what I was about. I became their target, but this didn't worry me much either. After all, I knew that God had planned it all for His purposes and that He was with me.

One day as I stood on my balcony overlooking the farm and its

surrounding beauty, a group of about ten of the women meeti
there came over to ask what I was doing. I knew what they were u
to and really wasn't in the mood for more of their recruiting efforts.
I laughingly half-joked, "Learning about spiritual warfare. In fact, I
feel like doing some." They immediately screamed and ran.

The woman who was the leader of the coven farm knew I was
a believer, and she obviously recognized my God-given calling,
because one day she commented she could "see" a prophetic gifting on me. This intrigued her all the more, and she did her best
to try to convince me to join them. But God was using my time
there to allow these people, so precious to Him, the opportunity
to see Him and be called through His love. He wanted to show
them the truth and the difference.

Near the end of my stay there, the leader tried one last
approach, with all the friendliness and attraction she could muster.
She outright offered me what she thought was a tempting propo-
sition of a position as a New Age priest in her church. Moreover,
she told me she would buy me a big church building to use as my
own with offers of money, fame, and, most of all, the "powers" she
talked about. But the power she was operating in had nothing to
do with the *real* power of Almighty God!

I easily recognized this test; it looked much like the former
ones I'd received when I was offered a position with the Christian
ministries, though now in yet another package. The witches also
were eager to bring me on board because they wanted to use the
gifts God had given me in exchange for what was really offers of
notoriety and money. It was just presenting itself in a different
package this time.

As I pointed out earlier, both sides—light and dark—have the
ability to see into the spiritual realm. Many are born with this
spiritual gift from God already operating. The Devil often tar-
gets these people when they're young, hoping to steer them to use
those gifts for his side or to hurt or frighten them or those around
them about the gifts in order to shut them down.

For the most part, the church at large has been way behind and often confused—even fearful—on this subject. Sometimes it even ascribes these spiritual gifts to the realm of darkness. These God-gifted individuals get intimidated, mislabeled, or shunned, so they leave the church only to get sucked in by the all-too-ready welcome invitations of the Enemy's camp. His followers gladly take them in, encouraging them to use their gifts in New Age, spiritualism, witchcraft, Satanism, or whatever label we want to put on the dark side. Those individuals and their inherent God-given gifts simply need to be lit up in God's light and tuned in to the proper channel. There are only two channels: the channel of God and the channel of hell.

I plainly knew this woman operated on a level of "seeing" too. However, people accessing spiritual realms outside the genuine Jesus Christ can only see and operate up to a second-heaven level. They can't see into or even get into the third-heaven realm, also known as *real* heaven or the realm of Almighty God. It's the *only* place of complete accuracy, truth, and light—and where the real power comes from! It's also the only place and source of eternal life.

The gifted seer, upon receiving the real Jesus Christ, can have that gift cleansed and purified, lit up and switched over by God to His revelation and truth. It is then backed up by the precision training of His Holy Spirit and can be used powerfully and effectively through Him.

When we are in Jesus Christ, the only "way" and "door" to heaven and eternal life, we inherit open invitation, authority, and bold access into the third-heaven realm—not only later in the afterlife, but *now*, because God says we instantly become "citizens of heaven" the moment we receive and step into Him. (John 10:1–5, 14:6; Matthew 10:7–9; Ephesian 2:4–6; Philippians 3:20a).

19

THE HOLLYWOOD ASSIGNMENT

For everyone to whom much is given,
from him much will be required;
and to whom much has been committed,
of him they will ask the more.

– LUKE 12:48B

In early 2009, I decided to put my rental house in Vestaburg, Pennsylvania, up for sale. I had my eye on a big two-story house in the city district of downtown Fredericktown. I really wanted that place, thinking I could set it up for a street mentoring ministry downstairs while living upstairs. I'd come into a small inheritance when my father died, and I'd been saving up most of the rent payments I received from the young widowed mother who rented the Vestaburg house. She was really struggling, raising two teenage boys alone, but she worked hard and always made the payments.

As soon as I put the house up for sale, great offers came in. While I tried to decide which one to take, God broke into my thoughts as clear as I'd ever heard Him, "Give your house away to that mother." It caught me by surprise, because I was counting on doing something I thought God had been leading me to do (though I neglected to ask Him about it). I determined I would "pray on it" for a while, but I was really stalling. He knew—and I knew—I'd heard Him clearly.

house was the last substantial material thing I owned, and
't want to just give it away. It seemed the more I kept pray-
it through, hoping He'd somehow change His mind, the more
od stayed silent. I must admit, I hesitated nervously for a few
months, but I could feel God waiting to see what I was going to
do. I was upon yet another test of review—and this was a *really*
big one.

I wish I could say that my heart was fully in it and bursting
with the love of God as it should have been, but this was another
time when it was really hard to do what He asked. I was having
a stubborn, self-imposed pity party. God knows my moods well,
but He also knows how to work with them. While I was digging
my heels in, hoping it would go away or ridiculously thinking He
might "forget," God was once again revealing to me something
that I still hadn't fully yielded to Him.

He wasn't sending me anywhere at the time, and nothing new
seemed to be happening. God just stayed patiently waiting and
deafeningly silent, yet I could feel an increasingly uncomfortable pressure on me. I knew what was up. I was getting off-track
again—and I was the only one who could break the apparent
stalemate. Eventually, I became so uncomfortable that I couldn't
take it anymore. I *had* to obey.

With no other good way out, I went to see the woman. I nearly
choked out the words as I offered her the house as a gift while smiling and trying to hide my discomfort. She couldn't believe it, of
course, and actually resisted for a while. She didn't understand why
I'd do this, claiming it was too much to accept for free. I had to
insist, though, practically pushing the free house on her just to get
it over with. I wanted the turmoil and sick, uneasy feeling behind
me. After a few weeks of repeatedly approaching her about it, she
finally agreed. I signed over the papers and the deal was done. She
was one happy woman, and I knew God was pleased with me.

I had passed another test, but I admit, it was by the skin of
my teeth. Afterward, I felt wiped out. That alone was a telling

flag about conditions still hiding in the deep recesses of my hea̶ But God knew it was time to dig deeper into the masterpiece H̶ once told me He was making. I was learning that those new levels sometimes come feeling like a double-edged sword even though He celebrated and rewarded each step I took.

I had let go of the last valuable (by worldly standards) thing I owned. My friends and family couldn't believe it, and I couldn't begin to make them understand. It was a transaction between God and me. I had to trust Him, believing that He always had my best interests in mind. So I waited, wondering what God had for me next.

A couple of weeks after I gave the house away, I got my new directions: "I want you to move to Hollywood." I started to feel a little anxious. "Hollywood?" I said. "God, why Hollywood? You know how much trouble I got in the last time I was there. Why are you sending me back there?"

Hollywood was completely across the country from Pittsburgh. I'd be leaving familiar territory, family, and good friends I'd made here on the East Coast. I felt like God was pulling a fast one on me, and I was surprised—but He apparently believed I was ready. He'd been training me for almost eleven years now, and I was passing the tests (though not always quickly). I realized maybe this was one of those bigger assignments He'd years before said He was preparing me for.

My mind flooded with thoughts of the '80s—living, playing, and hanging out with just about everyone who was someone in the famous town of rock 'n' roll. I already had an idea of what I was in for. Drugs, clubs, women, partying, and all sorts of deals went on 24/7 in Hollywood. As well, it was a center of a lot of pretense and deception that He had led me away from. Every dark spiritual force, temptation, and former draw on me was there, and they were much more heightened in that strategic place. I was being brought back full circle, though this time it was in Him and I was much stronger. I decided that if I could survive in Hollywood, I could survive anywhere.

With the type of calling God had on me, I knew that when he said, "Go!" you mustn't question. You just go. Abraham and Paul were trained this way and so was the prophet Jonah (the hard way). I never knew how long I'd be somewhere when He sent me, but this time, I didn't know if I would ever come back. Then, for the second time in my walk with Him, God told me that it was time to further lighten my load.

Each time God had me move, I had reluctantly parted with more of my stuff. Now He said He wanted me to be prepared to move quickly. I knew what was up, and I was coming to realize the cost of "to whom much is given, much from him will be required" (Luke 12:48b). God was further purifying my heart and our relationship, along with tactically preparing me. I would need it for what was ahead.

I gave away the rest of my furniture, the painting equipment that I had in storage, and the last of a few special items I loved. I threw out the rest, keeping only what I could fit in my Camaro. I was thankful that my son, Tee, wanted to ride out with me for company on the long cross-country trek. I stuffed as much as I could get into a big suitcase and found room for my only guitar, a bass, and my amp. Then Tee showed up with two over-packed suitcases that we barely wedged in. We were packed full, and the old miracle car's compromised back end hung so low that it groaned under the weight.

On May 15, 2010, with everything behind me gone and only five hundred dollars left to my name, we headed out on our adventure to Hollywood. I could only wonder what God was up to and what He had in store ahead.

The trip was long and at times harrowing in that old car. By the time we reached Ohio, I had to tell Tee to throw out one of his two heavy suitcases. We argued about it for one hundred miles, but I didn't have any other option. With all the weight in the back seat, the frame of the old car rubbed on the back tires with every little bump in the road. I didn't think we would make it, and then

I hit a point when it no longer mattered anymore. I veered off the next exit, pulled up to the first Dumpster I could find, and ordered him to throw it in.

After that, he was fuming mad. We didn't talk much for the rest of the day. I knew how he felt, but things like this were just part of the deal when on missions with God. The car ran much smoother afterward, and in my mind that settled the matter. It was another hard lesson for my twenty-six-year-old son, but I knew God would make it up to him.

Coming down Highway 70 from the Rocky Mountains through Denver was the ride of a lifetime. Long stretches of steep, winding mountain roads had dangerous sheer cliffs—and my car's brakes were close to shot. A few of the turns were pretty hairy. We held on tight and thanked God as we watched Him clear the road ahead of us at just the right times. People seemed to move their cars out of the way even before they saw us coming. We anxiously careened down the steep road and kept praying.

Outside Denver, we came to a rest stop as it neared evening. I just had to pull over. Beautiful mountains rose right off the side of the road, and God was refreshing me after the traumatic ride. He opened my eyes to see the mountains covered with hundreds of His beautiful angels. They were all over the mountaintops just hanging out. Big ones—like twenty to fifty feet tall and dressed in shining bright light. Some had wings I could see, but others didn't. I wanted to stay there all night watching them with the awe of God overwhelming me. His wonderful reassurance of how much He was with me excited and encouraged me.

The next day, we reached Las Vegas, Nevada, and stayed over-night. God encouraged me again in one of my many dreams that night. "I've got your back!" I heard Him say loud and clear. I was reminded once again that none of this trip was my idea; He'd told me to go. Though worry and even a little fear of the unknown pestered me, I was sent by God and therefore knew I had His pro-tection and heaven's backing for the entire trip.

The last leg of the trip brought us into Los Angeles County, and it was obvious we were getting close because traffic got much heavier. I couldn't help but reflect on the reality of the last time I was in Hollywood—how I had then served a different god, rock 'n' roll. Twenty years later, I was entering this town again, now to serve my new God, the King of Kings.

After I pulled off the 101 Freeway onto Sunset Boulevard, we began driving the streets of Hollywood. The old familiar night-clubs and hangouts still dotted the way. Amazingly, not much had changed. I wondered when God would give me His next directions and tell me how I would make it when my money ran out and what would come next. Right at that moment, He said, "Don't worry, Timmy. I will never let you go without a roof over your head while you're here." His words flooded me with peace and comfort.

We searched for the cheapest hotel closest to the heart of Hollywood. Tired and exhausted, we picked one of the first low-rent motels and shelled out a week's rent in cash for a room. We needed time to get our bearings in town, and I also knew we needed time to get in tune with God, watching and waiting for His next directions.

But right away, Tee and I found we were in for more than we realized. On our first night in the cheap motel, we discovered the beds were infested with bed bugs. I don't mean little ones. The indifferent motel manager wouldn't refund our cash, so we were stuck for the long haul. After a couple of days, Tee walked to a store to buy a cheap twin-size air mattress, and we placed it on the floor as far away from the beds as we could get it.

Before long, I joined him on the narrow mattress that continually lost air. There we were, father and son, each clinging through the night to the farthest edges of that small plastic island, trying to keep some sort of manly dignity. We couldn't even use the sheets or blankets.

Despite our best efforts, by the third day we were covered with red, itchy welts. It was a new and different spiritual enemy

territory, but that didn't matter. The time had come to get back i.
serious tune with God. We pressed in and spent most of our time
in prayer. When I woke up the next morning, God said, "Today,
start walking the boulevards of Hollywood. I want you to pray
and prophesy over this city as I lead you."

I recognized God intended this to be an "air force" assignment
from the start. He always sends in His prophets and intercessors—those who will tune in to Him—first so they can pray and
decree His will into it. The military uses similar strategy when at
war. The air patrol and bombers are usually sent in to assess and
clear the way, then the foot soldiers begin their specific missions.
When we're walking full of God's light and aligned with heaven,
it sends in powerful spiritual "bombs" meant to immobilize and
pull down the dark enemy strongholds. Armies of His angels are
released to help clear out and prepare the area for the manifestation of God's will, presence, and miracles to flow.

I walked the main boulevards for hours a day, silently praying, discerning, watching, and listening for everything God would
show me and tell me to do. The sidewalks were always busy, full of
tourists, businesspeople, street hawkers, entertainers, panhandlers,
homeless, drug dealers, prostitutes, and street preachers with signs
and bullhorns. Traffic was thick, with sirens blaring and horns
honking all the time. I couldn't afford to be out of tune and not
filled with God's light. The Enemy could see me and knew why
I was there. With all I was seeing, hearing, and experiencing, the
game had been dramatically intensified. I now saw God's wisdom
in preparing me through the New York, horse farm, and other
assignments. If I didn't stay saturated with God every day, I risked
being taken out—and not only in a spiritual sense.

The Hollywood/Los Angeles area is a very strategic place that
God really has His eye on. As the global center of the American
film and TV industry, this region affects and influences the entire
world with regard to lifestyles, music, culture, and fashion, and
even attitudes, morality, opinions, and language. Consequently, it's

obvious major prize of the Enemy, who wants it kept in his stronghold to spread his evil influence, ways, and control throughout the world.

However, as I walked the star-lined sidewalks, I was more deeply impressed with what God was feeling and saying about Hollywood. God *loves* Hollywood. He repeatedly calls the town "His." It's His will for His Spirit and kingdom to infiltrate and overtake it in a mighty way. His will is not about judgment, like some think; it's all about releasing His great mercy, grace, love, light, and freedom over its inhabitants and strategic industries. He wants His heart, His creative ideas, and heaven's influence poured into Hollywood and then poured out to touch the world.

God is in the redemption business. Everything He does is for the purpose of redeeming what's been stolen and perverted by the Enemy, and restoring it back to Himself. He wants the world to know Him as He really is, and moving in and through Hollywood is a key tactic to do that in an exponential way.

Day after day, my initial assignment was to casually walk miles and miles of the city's boulevards. I even crisscrossed the side streets and back alleys, discerning everything God was showing me in the spirit, and praying and releasing whatever He was saying over each area. Then I'd go back to the motel room to spend hours alone with Him in worship and prayer. After I'd rest in Him and get tuned back up and filled to overflowing with His light, I'd head back out again.

God wouldn't allow me to do anything else during this period. I didn't talk much to anyone. He wasn't allowing that yet. Over time, though, many people came to recognize me as I repeatedly strolled by. Their reactions varied, from friendly hellos, to stern looks of suspicion and mistrust, to violent cussing, cursing, and threats. Some of those poor, chained-up souls God so loves would react without even knowing why. But I knew. The spirit on them couldn't stand the Spirit on me.

Many witches on the streets in Hollywood could outright

"see" me too, and we both knew it. They would try to their curses and spells on me. Prostitutes and drug dealers tri solicit me, and thugs sometimes followed me. But God's prese was strong on me wherever I went. I felt His beautiful peace over me, and I could see my two big angels right behind me. He had me well protected and wouldn't let anyone touch me.

I had to keep my discernment sharp at all times. God had me seeing and knowing everything that was going on, and He continually refreshed me by showing me what He was doing in Hollywood from heaven's perspective. But He was also showing me the spiritual conditions, and I could even hear people's thoughts as I passed.

I continued on without fear, mindful that God was teaching me how to pray. The rest were all really just distractions that tried to intimidate me, knock me off course, or hinder what He was doing. I was thankful that God had spent a long time preparing me, and I focused my mind on the good God was doing instead of allowing the evil to get to me.

When our time at the bed bug motel thankfully ended, we were out of money. Tee went to stay with some believers and help out with their ministry in a nearby town, but I couldn't leave my assigned post. So I asked God what to do next. Right then, I received a call from my friend Beau back in Pittsburgh. I had given him all my painting equipment before I left, and he wanted to know how I was doing and said he really wanted to help me out.

God had pointed out a low-rent hotel called the Las Palmas Hotel, right off Hollywood Boulevard. With God's supply through Beau's timely and generous offer, I paid the first two weeks' rent. I was kind of hoping for something nicer, but I'd learned not to question God's instructions. The old hotel room was very small and modest, with peeling blue paint on the walls, a dilapidated bed, a plain wooden chair, and a tiny, dirty bathroom. It was at least bedbug-free, though, and really, it had all I needed. I could also see right onto Hollywood Boulevard from my second-story window.

urist businesses, nightclubs, bars, and hordes of visitors ourists surrounded the hotel day and night. Police and fire ns screamed by regularly, with constant traffic, honking horns, ople fighting over parking spaces, and droves of clubbers. Soon after moving in, I realized among my hotel's other weekly rent occupants were many drug addicts, prostitutes, and witches. God had placed me right back in the thick of the surroundings I'd lived in for thirty-five years of my life. There was much He was up to, and He assured me that had me right where He wanted me.

Soon the new hotel room became a sanctuary of heaven. Often the light of heaven would fill it and the presence of God would overtake me. I was filled with His light from all the time I spent in total closeness with Him there, so much that I would literally see it glowing out of my body. That's when I knew I was ready to go back out and release again.

After a few months of my in-and-out routine, God changed things up a bit and asked me to stay in my room just to hang out with Him and talk and worship. I'd stay in for eight to ten hours just to start the day. The entire room would get saturated so thick with His glory that I was giddy-drunk in it and could barely stand or walk. Angels would come, filling the room, and they'd playfully push me around just for kicks as we all laughed and enjoyed the atmosphere of heaven together.

One day, after several hours interacting with the Lord like this, I asked Him, "Now what do you want to do?" In a playful mood, He replied, "Go to your window and pray over everyone who walks by down on the sidewalk." So I went to my window, and as He showed me what the people passing by needed, I prayed and released over them different words He gave me.

Soon it became such a comical game of fun. Everyone who walked by under that window, as soon as I released whatever God said, would stumble, swerve, or nearly fall as He power-whacked them with His glory presence. None had a clue what was hitting them. But God was snapping spiritual chains and bars of the

Enemy off people while releasing His life, freedom, and destiny over them. We both laughed like two boys up to mischief, though He was also wowing me with His outta-control love for the people of Hollywood.

After about nine hours spending time with the Lord like this on one particular day, He said, "Let's go get an ice cream." God knew I loved ice cream, and He was satisfied with my willingness to spend all my time alone with Him. I hadn't eaten all day, and He wanted to take me out for a treat. "Okay!" I responded. I put my shoes on and headed down to the local McDonalds for one of my favorite chocolate-dipped ice cream cones.

This particular McDonalds right on Hollywood Boulevard was always busy, filled with people and tourists, and this day was no exception. The triple-wide line to the order counter stretched all the way out the double doors onto the sidewalk, and I couldn't even see up to the counter. But as soon as I walked up to the end of the line to wait, something amazing happened. The entire line of people ahead of me parted to the sides like the Red Sea and a wide-open corridor opened all the way to the counter. I could see the order-taker kid standing there looking straight at me like he was waiting for me. He signaled me to come give him my order since nobody else was approaching him. I looked at the lines of people on either side of me and felt God physically nudging me forward. So I walked right up to the counter and ordered my ice cream with no delay.

What a God of favor He is for those who love Him. His presence was so heavy on me that day that I'm sure the people didn't even know why they parted—but God and I did. In fact, on my walk to and from the McDonalds, people I passed fell, stumbled, or veered out of the way all around me as they were glory-whacked by the King of Heaven's heavy presence with me. I was still drunk in it myself and amused with silly laughter, watching this happening the whole way there and home. It was like God had laid out His red carpet just for Him and me in the middle of Hollywood, and He was giving me first priority that day.

In 1 Corinthians 6:9, Paul tells us that with open doors come many adversaries. Just like he experienced, I found that the greater the mission, the greater the potential opposition. But I know that when God opens a door and sends us through it, we have all of heaven's backing as long as we stay in Him. On my walk with God, I had also learned that when we know we're doing the will of God and strong opposition may come, it's often just a telling sign that we're right on track. We can't let it distract, intimidate, or detour us.

Daily I ran into various levels of opposition. From my first day in Hollywood, attacks in both the spirit and the natural came my way. Because the Enemy could see me and knew who I was and why I was there, he did everything in his power to try to deter me in my mission. At times on my walks, I'd see hideous demons manifest as plain as day, crouching in side alleys or waiting for me around corners. They were taunting, hissing, and snarling at me with contemptuous, seething hate.

When you know you're where you're supposed to be, you just can't let evil get to you. You need to know who you are, whose you are, and that you're "sent," or at least in a place that's in the center of God's will for your life. Furthermore, you need to stay in God's "secret place," hidden right inside Him. It's the place where He'll keep you "anesthetized" to all of it in His presence. There you don't even care about "danger" or "death threats" anymore. You can literally laugh you're way through anything and stay in the peace, fun, and confidence of heaven. Truly, it's the only way to make it through—and the best way to live.

Are you where you're supposed to be? Are you doing what you're supposed to do? Do you always ask God, or do you end up in places you shouldn't be and in battles you're not supposed to fight? That's when you can get a bit "beat up." And I don't necessarily mean physically; I also mean spiritually and emotionally. You can experience the "beatings" and "buffetings" whether you're on track with God or not, just as Paul did (2 Corinthians

6:4–10; 1 Corinthians 4:11; 1 Peter 2:2). The difference is, wh
God has directed you to do it and you stay on course, heaven wi.
back you up and bring you through to where you're supposed to
be. Then once you've done what you're supposed to do or released
what you're supposed to release, leave. The grace lifts, and the job
is done. Move with His cloud (Exodus 13:21–22).

One evening as I was quietly prayer-walking busy Hollywood
Boulevard, I passed two huge men standing at the sidewalk's edge.
One must have been six feet five and the other almost seven feet
tall. As I approached them amid many others walking the sidewalk, they singled me out and stared me down with intimidating
looks. As soon as I passed, they started hurling insults and cursing
at me for no obvious reason. I walked on, trying to ignore them,
but they followed me. Soon their threats turned to loud rant-
ings on how many ways they were going to murder me. I glanced
back over my shoulder and plainly saw one of my big angels close
behind me. I stayed tuned in to God and walked on in confidence.

This went on for another couple of blocks. It seemed I was
now walking alone with no one else daring to come near the scene
going on behind me. Finally, with the men still following and now
threatening with hand movements and sometimes yelling right up
into my ears, I entered the open door of Joe's Pizza, my favorite
place to eat on the boulevard. I stepped inside and walked past a
man who sat at a table eating his meal. As soon as I passed him
on my way to the order counter, he looked at me and commented
with a knowing smile, "Hmm. A prophet in blue jeans."

The men stood outside the window, still ranting threats and
waiting for me. I placed my order and went to sit on a stool at the
window facing the sidewalk. Right then, a big white glory cloud of
God's presence came into the pizza shop and filled the place floor to
ceiling. It surrounded me so thickly that I couldn't even see out the
window anymore. It stayed there for a while, and I just basked in the
rich, protective peace and presence of God. *Yeah. Cool!* I thought.
When I could see out the window again, the men were gone.

The Devil doesn't want to lose one inch of territory that he's on to himself. But I'm so glad that when great darkness starts to rise, God sends in His greater light to overcome it. Especially when He has His people praying and interceding for His kingdom to come and His will to be done on earth as it is in heaven (Matthew 6:10).

There are many who have been interceding for Hollywood and the "City of Angels" (Los Angeles) for untold years. God has a mighty "air force" in place, doing just that. They've prayed and interceded faithfully in alignment with heaven's will, knowing that God inspired those prayers and that He has been at work moving things into place for the right time. He's also been sending in foot soldiers and relief crews, as well as touching and preparing hearts for more. He even has people that are His already hidden in important key positions in various high places. Some of them own or control those high places while others He's revealing and bringing forth to unleash His precision power.

Many of these people have already been through years of backstage training by the Spirit of God. They've come through their own crucibles in varying degrees and have been found faithful, as they've passed difficult tests of love and loyalty to Him. They've learned that staying in the love relationship with God means more than anything the world has to offer. Now they're ready for frontstage time, the unveiling of their destinies, and the uncovering of their hiddenness planned by God from the beginning.

God is in the business of constantly seeking, finding, redeeming, and restoring all who've strayed or been lost because of the lies, devastation, and destruction of the true enemy of mankind. This will one day include restoration of creation itself also. It will be the restoration of *all* things back to Him, in their full intended glory and good purpose. The kingdoms of this world are destined to become the kingdoms of God. All things will be under His feet, and He will govern it all (Ephesians 1:22; Revelation 11:15). That's because He's the only one capable. He alone is trustworthy

and able to reign over all of it in truth, justice, and righteou.
ness. And it will be a kingdom of freedom, fun, great pleasure,
and peace for His people.

God wants to be known to the world like never before—as
He *really* is. He's releasing revelation of Himself to multitudes
through tangible demonstration of Himself bringing redemption
and restoration of lives one by one.

Heaven's angelic forces are here in Hollywood. I know; I see
them all the time. So many. I see them hanging out on or above
the streets in various places, sometimes in large numbers. At times
I see groups of angels swirling the presence of heaven around and
around, up and down the boulevards in various places. Their
colors vary—green, blue, or shining white—and some carry
gold. They all bear specific plans, orders, and impartations from
God's throne for release here. The trusting prayers of God's kids
immensely help that release.

God is up to something *big* in Hollywood, and even I don't
have the whole big picture of it yet. I just do the part that He's
instructed me to do. He's had me strategically prayer-walking,
prophesying, and releasing His blessings and His heart's desire
around and on specific people and places the whole time I've been
here. This includes the many homeless, poor, and broken, as well
as the businesses and media-giant industries.

Hollywood's streets are filled day and night with tourists and
visitors, but living among them are a population of runaways, street
kids, and homeless who are hurt, lost, abandoned, and destitute.
They survive the only way they know how. Many have come to
Hollywood with stars in their eyes, seeking fame and fortune, only
to run out of money and real opportunities; their utopian dreams
are broken and they have no means to get out or go back home.
They live on the streets right alongside the high-rise empires, cul-
tural icons, and the famous, powerful, and wealthy.

God loves them all and is calling every one. He pours out His
mercy and grace on this place, not the judgment that some profess

through bullhorns or with signs. Jesus came to save the world, not condemn it. This is still the time of untold grace and the time for His kingdom age to come in. God's love for Hollywood is outrageous, and His eye is on it for good. He wants to bring everyone who will come, into His kingdom where there's unparalleled life, freedom, and fun.

God even sends me to dangerous areas of Skid Row in L.A. to release there, and He often sends me there late at night. Some say L.A. has the largest population of the homeless in the United States. The homeless and hopeless range from addicts and junkies, to prostitutes, drug dealers, and alcoholics, to the mentally ill, disabled, and those who have simply hit rock bottom. All ages, young to elderly, live on those streets, sleeping on the sidewalks, in stairwells, and on pieces of cardboard and in makeshift pup tents. The missions and social service organizations planted there fill up quickly and overflow with the thousands in desperate need. It's heartbreaking to see, and it's heartbreaking to God.

After I'd been in Hollywood for ten months, God allowed me to begin speaking with people and releasing some of His miracles. I got to know many people along my routes, and some of the homeless, drug dealers, and prostitutes became familiar acquaintances who I'd engage in conversations as God led me. I just stayed purposed to instill hope, reveal the love of the Father, and release whatever He gave me at every opportunity. God encouraged and healed many, and I saw Him do great miracles that blew me away.

I met one woman who was severely ill from a ruptured appendix. After being seen in a clinic, she didn't have funds to go to a hospital and was in agony. God healed her with one prayer. The next time I saw her, months later, she was looking for me again because she had come down with the flu. She asked me to pray for her again. When I did, the illness instantly left. Many drug addicts and alcoholics became instantly sober when I prayed over them. Though I didn't try to be known, word spread on the streets and more people searched me out.

Late one night, my cell phone woke me. I was surprised t find the caller was a drug dealer who had become an acquaintance. He told me he had been attacked by muggers and was down on the sidewalk on Sunset Boulevard in terrible pain, unable to move with a broken back. "I hear you're some kind of healer," he groaned through clenched teeth on the phone. "Can you come and help me?"

Trying to wipe the sleep from my eyes, I responded groggily, "Well, I'm not a healer, but I know the Healer."

"Well, what do you do?" he asked. "Do you pray or something?"

"Yeah, that's what I do," I replied.

"Well, who do you pray to?" His voice sounded cautious.

I couldn't help the laugh in my voice. "I pray in the name of Jesus."

"Good then," he shot back. "Please come down here and help me!" Then he rattled off his exact location, moaning in pain through the whole conversation.

I glanced at the clock. It was 2 a.m., and I was tired from walking miles all day. I didn't feel like getting up, but I asked God what He wanted me to do. "Go!" He responded. I dragged myself out of bed, pulled on my jeans, shirt, and shoes with strings still untied, and began the walk in the dark to a place about a mile from my hotel (I couldn't take my car because parking would have been impossible with all the busy clubs in the area).

When I found him, he was on the ground, hunched over on the edge of the curb, breathing heavily and groaning in intense pain. He couldn't move and would scream out whenever he tried to. Through the back of his T-shirt, I could see his grotesquely disfigured spine poking out in odd places. It was truly a scary and pitiful sight.

As soon as I got there, the sidewalks filled up with people coming over to gawk. They weren't there to help, and they seemed to crowd and block me, with loud shouting on one side of me while others tried to interrupt and talk to me. Some tried to pull my attention away with crude, filthy talk.

I glanced up from the downed man and my eyes were drawn across the street. Standing there on the sidewalk in the dark shadows were a couple of witches. They were looking right at me, already trying to throw their hand-signal hexes and spells while shouting threats and curses at me.

As the distractions and their volume grew in intensity, I had to shake myself back to the real task at hand. I knew what was happening. I was deep in the middle of late-night enemy territory, and all of it was being used to try to confuse me and thwart what God was so readily about to do. Consciously shutting out all the noise and interruptions fighting for my attention, I refocused on the man in front of me. I laid my hand directly on his back, and it felt like pieces of his spine were turned all over the place. I actually shuddered as I touched him and he groaned in pain. "Father, heal him in the name of Jesus!" I cried out, feeling His intensely compassionate heart as I ran my hand quickly down the length of his back.

He screamed and jumped up to his feet like he had been hit by a lightning bolt. "Wooo-ah! What was that?" he shouted. "I just felt something lift right off my back!" He twisted, bending and feeling around at his back with a look of shock on his face. Then he smiled brightly as he jumped around, ecstatic. His pain was gone and his spine had perfectly realigned. "Thank you, man! Thank you! Thank you so much!"

"Don't thank me. Thank God," I said, chuckling. And with that, I left him to God and began the trek back home.

The next day as I prayer-walked around the Capitol Records Building at Hollywood Boulevard and Vine Street, I heard a voice shouting to me from across the street. It was the drug dealer. He recognized me and ran over to show me again how he could move, bend, and twist with no pain. "Praise God! Pah-raise God!" he shouted unashamedly as he raised both hands to the sky acknowledging the true healer.

"Yes! Praise God!" I chimed in, feeling crazy joy. I was thrilled for him as we enjoyed another moment together in wonder of

God and His amazing mercy and love. The man had gotten the point; he had been introduced to the King and His kingdom in an astounding way on one of his darkest days. We talked for a short while and then went our separate ways. I believe there was a reason for such a great miracle of God on that man's life. I just knew he too had a great destiny on his life.

God performed another miracle with a woman who lived in the "Palmies" hotel where I stayed. She was one of the practicing witches who lived there. A couple of times, from my upstairs window, I'd caught a glimpse of her walking in ceremonial circles around my car with some of her friends. They were chanting and moving their hands and fingers in their silly witchcraft symbols, obviously trying—unsuccessfully, of course—to put hexes and curses on my car. I never said much to this woman other than a cheerful hello when we occasionally passed in the hotel's hallways, but I knew she and her friends could "see" me to some extent. They eyed me suspiciously, as if I was some kind of a big threat.

One day God showed me a big black misty ball in the center of this woman's belly, and I knew she was struggling with some sort of sickness. Over time, compassion overwhelmed me as I felt God's heart for her. Knowing He wanted to show her His love and heal her, I waited for Him to open an opportunity.

Toward the end of my eighteen-month stay at the Palmies, that day finally came. I ran into her in the hotel's front lobby and struck up a conversation with her. God nudged me, saying, "This is it!" and I told her how God had pointed her out to me and how much He loved her and wanted to heal her sickness. She protested, saying she didn't believe there was any power stronger than hers, and God told me that black ball I was seeing inside her was diabetes. I called it out to her. Stunned, she finally relented and allowed me to pray for her.

As soon as I repeated the words God gave me, an angel came, reached into her belly, and pulled the black ball right out her. Then it flew away with it. She nearly fell over when the power of

God's love touched her; she could barely stand. She kept repeating, "Whoa! Whoa! Whooooa!" with her eyes closed, teetering there and basking in it. She'd never felt *this* power before!

I enjoyed watching as God just did His thing. She was awestruck by the overwhelming touch of His love and goodness, which she'd never known before. It was another holy moment as God gave her a great introduction of Himself.

There were times out on my prayer walks when God would tell me to get down on my knees right there on the busy sidewalk, lift up my hands to Him, and decree His blessings and words of love and mercy over the area out loud. To be honest, I found this a bit hard to do at first, so I began by half-obeying—getting down on one knee and pretending to tie my shoelace as I released what He said in a low voice.

I'd often go back and forth in conversation with Him about this, questioning it all, but I was really just trying to evade it. He didn't let me off that easy. It was His invitation to dive right off another cliff in total trust, to let go of any self-preserving pride I had left and dare to look like a fool for Him in the world's eyes. To me, a man who once had a pretty big ego, it felt like the very last straw of self-preservation. So many times I'd told God I'd do anything He asked of me—no matter how hard, unreasonable, or uncomfortable it seemed—because I wanted more of Him. He'd surely then throw some test my way to see if I was really serious.

God always tests and tries the heart. We can get so nervous about things that are really trivial in the big-picture scheme of things. God is relaxed and confident about everything—and really, it's often just amusement to Him watching all the silly, stupid stuff we go through trying to avoid Him and the great things He wants to do in our lives. We just need to humble ourselves and not care if we're called a weirdo by some people while He's just waiting to pour out a great, big God-reward full of His miraculous power when we just obey. What's more important—especially when we're having fun with Him?

Finally, I stopped caring how I looked. I let go, and whenever he prompted, I'd drop to my knees, raise both hands, and cry out whatever He moved me to say for Him. Usually it was amid hundreds of people walking by. With all the crazy happenings on the boulevards of Hollywood, I'm sure many thought I fit right in. But I'd come a long way in my walk with God and fully realized that all that truly mattered was what God and heaven thought of me. And when I obeyed in this, really a rather small thing, the miracles on the streets of Hollywood really broke out. While it blessed me immensely, it blessed Hollywood even more.

Around November 2011, while still on assignment in Hollywood, God began to point out the Capitol Records Building every time I'd pass it. He'd had me praying over it along with many of the other major studios and media headquarters in Hollywood, but He surprised me one day when I walked by it. "That's where you're going to record My songs!" He declared.

I couldn't believe it! "What? Me? Record…at Capitol Records?" I said. I had to wonder if I'd heard him right. I couldn't fathom how that would ever happen—apart from Him, that is.

20

WALK TOWARD DESTINY

You gotta have relationship to have faith.
You gotta have faith to reach your destiny!
– TIM EHMANN

It had by now been almost twelve years since God had pulled me out of hell, given me new life, and been training me in His ways through my love relationship with Him. With the revelation about Capitol Records, I remembered back to that fateful day on September 1, 2000, when God pulled me up into heaven with Him and spoke in so much detail about my destiny. *Is this it?* I wondered. *Is He finally ready to bring me into the beginning of it?* His promises that I'd been waiting for stirred within my heart in renewed excitement.

Over the years, I'd recorded a couple of prophetic albums, but they were my own attempts at jumping the gun trying to make it happen. I was so intent on getting to what He'd shown me, but nothing had really panned out at the time. God instead kept me on the necessary backstage progression of the faith walk, wanting to fully ground me in relationship and trust in Him. I'd learned there was no forcing God's hand before His time and that He couldn't successfully bring forth any destiny without a heart being thoroughly tested, tried, and proven to be fully sold out to Him— to not chance losing the person.

Now here I was, brought to a place where I had finally given up on my own efforts, even my own opinions. God's plan and timing were all that were important. It had cost the person I used to be everything, but I knew all that stuff was worthless. All that mattered was that I loved and trusted Him enough to give Him my whole heart and life and do anything He asked of me.

Our walk with God is all a walk of faith. Faith is just another word for "trust." The more we get to know the one who's trustworthy, the more our trust can grow in Him. It's won through entering into that love relationship, then giving our time, heart, and attention to it. It's a relationship of perfect and faithful love.

Without faith, it's impossible to please God (Hebrews 11:6). Faith requires risk taking. In our journey with God, He often asks us to step off "cliffs"—just so He can show us how He's going to catch us and that we're going to soar with Him. God says it takes only simple faith like a child's (Mark 11:6). You gotta have relationship to have faith, and you gotta have faith to reach your destiny.

I was reminded of the story of Abraham and his barren wife Sarah, who waited about twenty-five years after God's promise that He would give them a special child. Despite Sarah's condition, they believed God, but waiting for so many years took her long past the time of childbearing and proved too much to understand by natural reason alone. They tried to do it on their own too, jumping the gun with their own thinking that they'd "help" God along a little. Sarah decided perhaps their promised child was meant to come through her young handmaiden whom she chose to give her husband as a second wife just for that purpose. They too temporarily veered off track on a self-made detour of their own natural reason and efforts.

When the promised child, Isaac, finally came just as God said he would, Sarah and Abraham were ninety and one hundred years old. I believe God purposely waited to get them to a place of complete impossibility in the natural, just so He could show Himself off, proving He's the God of the impossible and always faithful to His promises. God *loves* to show off! It was all exactly in His planned timing from the start. He kept His end of the promise when He dramatically performed the impossible once again (Genesis 18:1–13, 21:1–7). And don't forget, Abraham is called the "Father of Faith" by God to this day. Somehow, he still never gave up the expectation that God would eventually be good on His word.

Knowing this aspect of God's character myself, I stepped up my prayer-walking around the Capitol Records Building to almost daily. I was releasing His beautiful words of grace and blessing over it and its principles, employees, recording artists, and influence on the world. Then one day, God opened my eyes to see a huge angel that had stationed itself right on top of the tall, circular historic building. The angel stood about fifty feet tall and had liquid-gold-like oil dripping off its white garments and down the sides of the building. I could even feel it dripping on me as I walked by the building in certain areas. Though I wondered what God was up to and how He was going to get me in to record there, I knew He was always good on His word. That was good enough for me.

Since it had been twelve years that I'd been walking with God, it also had been twelve years since I'd dated a woman. Considering my background, I think that proves what God can do for those He calls and graces. I'd asked God about dating many times over the years, but He'd never allowed it. The time had not been right, he said, because "there's too much we have to do together first."

God had also told me that He would one day give me a wife and it would happen before this next phase of my destiny. I was now fifty-five and had never been married. Resolved to stay walking with Him, I had finally become content and didn't even think about it much anymore. Then God surprised me one day when He started pointing out to me the woman He said He had chosen to be my wife.

In the natural, she and I seemed an unlikely match of different personalities and backgrounds, and we really had no romantic interest in each other. I was surprised, a bit confused, and extremely caught off guard, even concerned that maybe I wasn't hearing Him right. He brought it up when I was no longer even asking or looking for it. I couldn't understand what God apparently saw and knew, and I asked Him to give me some sort of confirmation.

A couple of weeks later when I was sound asleep in bed, Jesus came and pulled me up in the spirit into heaven. We walked together on a narrow walkway in a beautiful, well-manicured garden—His private garden. Beautiful fountains with carved-out places to sit abounded, and its plants, shrubs, and flowers literally pulsated with life. Even the very soil of the garden, every little particle, was illuminated and reverberating with life.

As we walked along the garden's path, I noticed faceted-cut gemstones of different sizes, shapes, and colors here and there, in the soil among the plants and flowers like they'd been planted there. Jesus walked me up another path and over to the largest gemstone in the garden. He stopped, pointed at it, looked at me, and said, "That's your wife. That's your wife's heart."

I was awestruck. It was the most amazing gemstone I'd ever seen, absolutely radiant and sparkling! Pulsating and alive, it moved with swirling, living hues of brilliant pink, amber, and purple. Its light emanated throughout the whole garden, leaving me speechless with wonder.

Much later, I learned that God had spoken to each of us about the other in this way, and both of us were surprised. We had been already on our own separate faith walks with God. He alone truly knows and sees the heart. We also both sensed that a marriage would be much more than a marriage for marriage's sake; God was matching together specific hearts, callings, giftings, and talents, in the natural and spirit, for His ministry too.

If you wait on God's perfect timing, He will bring you the right person. Don't settle for just a "good" choice; wait for the "God choice." His choice puts together a chosen team that will have fewer hindrances and will take off on an accelerated track that brings heaven's impact to what He wants to do—and it blesses and honors both the couple and Him.

I married my beautiful wife in September 2012. Now I had a God-chosen partner who prayer-walked the boulevards and places of Hollywood with me. We continued together in ministry to the homeless, the destitute, and street kids, but God also opened new doors by allowing us to minister His life and love to key artists and principles in the media and entertainment industries.

Then came the day when God miraculously opened the door to recording sessions at Capitol Records. He supplied the right people and brought in the means through others. I couldn't believe it. It was finally about to begin just as God had said it would. I was overwhelmed but eager and ready, looking forward to my first session that was to start the very next day.

Late that night as I lay sound asleep in my bed, something coldcocked me so hard in the nose that it jerked my head back across the pillow. I woke up startled and frantic, trying to see through my watering eyes what—or who—was in my room. Afraid of another blow, I shielded my face with my arm. But there was no one in the room.

I felt warm liquid rolling down my face and onto my chest as I stung from the pain of the hard blow. I got up and turned on the light. Blood poured out of my nose and had puddled onto the pillow and sheets. I checked every room of the apartment and ensured the doors and windows were still locked.

No one was there, so obviously I had been hit by some unseen force. I had to wonder if it was something that wanted to stop me from crossing the threshold toward my destiny. I went into prayer as I cleaned up my face and tried to stop the bleeding. I blessed and prayed over the whole house as I nursed my stinging nose (which was bruised and sore for an entire week).

As I said before, with open doors come many adversaries, just like the apostle Paul said and experienced (1 Corinthians 16:9). Only God could have opened this door to me, and I knew the

Enemy felt threatened and was not about to let any coveted territory go without a fight. This opposition always comes from the spiritual realm, whether it comes through people being influenced by it or through the dark spirits themselves. But it was also a sign to me that I was right on track. God was about to take me into something much bigger for Him—in the heart of Hollywood's "Capitol"—and I knew it was time to recruit more prayer intercessors who could assist me in prayer covering.

Interestingly, about a month prior to this, a new tenant had moved into the apartment across from mine. Strange things had been happening since he arrived, and I'd plainly seen the dark spirits around him from the start. Without fail, every time I exited or entered my apartment, he would be right there in the hallway. He would greet me, starting some friendly small talk and prying for information about me. The conversations went from his wanting to hang out with me, to repeated offers to be a musician in my band, to even talk about how much he "loved the Lord" and wanted to help me with whatever project I was working on.

I knew something else was off, though I couldn't put my finger on it at the time. God kept subtly telling me not to talk about any of it, but that only made my too-friendly neighbor more pushy each time I'd run into him. I kept politely declining his repeated hunts for information, and then I tried to avoid him. Even so, he showed up everywhere—the parking lot, the hallway, wherever. He seemed to have an uncanny ability to "know" when I'd be coming or going.

The man loved to keep his door open, so I couldn't help but notice he was up all hours of the night. He drank like a fish, played loud music all night long, lured unsuspecting young women into his apartment "to come and hear him play his guitar," and acted like he was everybody's best friend. But one night, I heard what sounded like strange muttering mixed with occasional shouting coming from his apartment. I couldn't sleep due to the noise, so I went to look out my front door to see what was going on. My friendly neighbor stood in his living room with arms raised high as he shouted praises to Satan, paced the apartment speaking in satanic "tongues," and cursed and denounced the name of Jesus Christ out loud. I knew he meant for me to hear it all.

This guy had been circling my place doing that same muttering at all hours of the night for weeks, but I couldn't hear what he was saying before. That's when I knew it was all a game of deception, and I was reminded that I wasn't the only one who had been sent on targeted assignments.

I prayed for him because I knew he was just another soul bound, chained, and deceived by the Enemy. I couldn't help but wonder if, in some way, I'd let my guard down while distracted by what was right ahead of me. It was a reminder to me to stay alert, keep my discernment up at all times, and stay filled with God's light and tuned in to what He was saying. But as the familiar distractions and intensity rose, it was obvious that I was nearing God's big open door.

My first day at Capitol Records finally arrived. I first set up in their big Studio A. I was so emotional about it, realizing I was in the place where history was made, where so many "greats" had and still recorded. What happened in these studios went out to influence the world.

I blessed the place up from the inside and invited God's presence to saturate my surroundings. Angels came and filled the studio, and the awe of God descended all around as we got recording. God had already given me some of the music ready to track, but I still had no idea what I was supposed to sing. Again, He gave me the words only when I stepped up to the mic in those recording sessions. What flowed from there was all God's heart and what He wanted to say to the world as I released and recorded from there. But God made it clear that this wasn't just a recording opportunity for me; this was my next assignment, and it lasted almost three years.

My wife and I had the opportunity to speak into many lives

there, including key executives, producers, and artists. It was an open door to release the kingdom of heaven and make many new friends in the industry. Soon, God brought in key support in other kingdom-minded artists, musicians, and ministers to assist with the project. And He brought in prayer intercessors to help cover the mission in prayer.

Key strategic gates in the heart of Hollywood had been opened—and I knew the King of Glory had come right in. As of this writing, this is only the beginning of this new chapter. One of the latest albums that I recorded at Capitol I've titled "Crushed Diamonds." It signifies the beautiful gems God creates from lives that once were totally broken and lost. The music and inspired songs were created to speak to those in places I came from and to incite open invitation to step into the reality, freedom, and fun of God and heaven, all set to great-beat rock 'n' roll.

We look forward to taking what God's heart is currently saying out on tour in wild, free, and fun rock fests and freedom concerts to a world in great need of meeting and experiencing Him by unexpected encounter. This was all God's idea from the start, not mine. He wants to reveal Himself to people not even looking or asking for Him, just like He did with me, and He is doing it all.

We're also in planning stages of ultimately establishing and supporting partnered prophetic mentoring centers in various cities. They'll be for those whom God finds and draws to Himself through our concerts. We want to have places ready to encourage people to get grounded in the most important thing of all: recognizing, hearing, and discerning God's voice for themselves.

This has always been the real vision of my heart since God first showed me all He planned to do in the personal commission He gave me fourteen years ago: "Timmy, I saved you. Now you go and save my children. Just bring them to me, and I will do all the rest." God is yearning for *all* His children still out in the world to come home to Him. Many have never encountered Him and don't realize that they're called and already destined to be His. God is the real Rock Star. Like I said, He loves to show Himself off. Time is short and things are accelerating. He is determined the world will know Him and that He'll get front and center stage on a platform where He'll get to do His thing. I know many will experience Him, hear Him, and even see Him for themselves just as I have.

"And I, if I am lifted up from the earth, will draw all peoples to Myself." (John 12:32)

The Hollywood chapter of my story has been the most challenging of all so far, as it's all been a walk of complete trust with God. It began with the faith to give my house away, and then the faith to jump in the miracle car with over two hundred thousand miles on it and drive across the country with only five hundred dollars to my name. Then the faith to walk and minister on the streets of Hollywood for a year and a half through anything and everything…and then the faith that God would one day get me to the destiny He'd shown me.

From the day He burst brilliantly into my car when I was in my twenties and announced, "You've got to do this!" to today, it's all been part of the calling I've been walking in and the destiny I've looked forward to ever since. I can't wait to see all that God alone can do. My life is a miracle story. It began with miracles, and they've continued all the way through.

Why me? I don't know. I was one of the worst of the worst. But God doesn't see us as we are; He sees us as He created us to be and calls us to step into that. All I know is that God is so full of tender-loving mercy and grace and His love is always outta control. Above all else, He desires relationship with us. God will accept and use any who are willing to answer His call and walk in relationship with Him toward their own unique and amazing destiny. The rest in life is really only distractions.

Come and step into Him just as you are. Spend time getting to know Him daily. He's the one who cleans you all up and teaches you along the way. He's the God who does it all. Jesus already paid the price for the world to be saved and doesn't want anyone to miss out on Him or heaven. You're made to be dependent on Him, the only source and sustainer of life. It's a relationship of love, freedom, fun, and new adventures in His kingdom.

No one wants to go to the dark, awful, and *real* place called hell and live an eternity of never-ending regret and torment, lost forever without Him. There's nothing there that has anything to do with life, joy, freedom, fun, or "partying," like some mistakenly believe. It's a place completely opposite all that, because what's good only comes from God. Hell is a place absent of life, joy, peace, or comfort, and it has an inconceivable intensity dreadfully contrary to the likewise inconceivable greatness of heaven. It allows people to realize how many of God's blessings, so often taken for granted here, extend already to both the righteous and the unrighteous in this life.

God doesn't send anyone to hell. People go of their own free-will choice when they reject Him and so great a free salvation, instead believing they have enough of their own "righteousness," means, authority, and power to save themselves on their own or by some other way. I personally had to learn the hard way: Jesus Christ is the only one who holds the keys to hell's gates and is the only door into heaven. The Father planned it that way, just for you and me. He's already madly in love with us. He's given us the Way, the Truth, and the Life. Jesus Christ is the Savior of the World who's already done all that's necessary for us to step into eternal life and heaven right through Him—the Open Door. I urge you, just receive Him.

What's written in this book are only some of the things God personally taught me about Himself. There is *so* much more to God.

Maybe you've felt your heartstrings being tugged as you read my life story. I hope so. Those are God's nudges and another way He speaks to you and calls you to Himself. Hear and recognize His voice. Ask and challenge Him to show you how He's real and who He really is. He can take the challenge, and He *wants* you to know Him. Step into the love relationship He already has for you. Let Him teach you personally. Always use spiritual discernment on your journey. Most importantly, make your life a love affair with the Lord.

And walk toward destiny.

EPILOGUE

It's vitally important that you understand that heaven and hell are *real*. I know without a doubt that one of the reasons God did such a great miracle of bringing me back from hell is so I can be a witness to you—to tell you that hell *is* a real and horrifying place. And it's forever.

I was given this incredible opportunity to warn you, even plead with you, that you don't want to go there. To be alive today and so mercifully sprung from that eternal dark prison is certainly something I didn't deserve. He released me from death and hell's grip, while good friends of mine who I thought much better than me will never have any escape. Their wails of eternal torment and regret will be something I'll never forget. And they remain there still.

In the same way the Lord Jesus called Lazarus from the dead, He did the same for me. All it took was an encounter with the powerful voice of the Living God. It's the hearing of His voice that calls us to life.

"Most assuredly, I say to you, the hour is coming, and now is, when the dead will hear the voice of the Son of God; *and those who hear will live*." (John 5:25 NKJV, emphasis mine)

This miracle of new life is all God—and every one of us needs it. We can't produce it by any effort of our own. God doesn't patch up or re-dress the old person; He can't use any of that. Instead, He makes us a totally new creation from the moment we hear His voice and receive Him. Through Him, sin loses its strength and death has no power over us anymore. This is Him, the

"Resurrection and the Life" Himself that all born-again believers receive, and it can happen in one decided moment.

Raising the dead is God's specialty. I'm not a "special case." All who have heard His voice and received this new birth through Jesus Christ have been raised from the dead too. This is a necessary first spiritual resurrection, and then one day God will also raise our mortal bodies to new glorified bodies just like He did Jesus' body. This is what Jesus referred to in John 3, when He told a seeking religious ruler that he must be born again in order to enter the kingdom of heaven. It takes the supernatural intervention of God Himself to call forth this life by means of hearing His voice.

Through our first father, Adam, the natural-born man has been corrupted by an inherited sinful nature that leads to death. People, left in this fallen natural state alone, cannot enter into or even see heaven. But God in His great love and plan for us has not left us in this state with no remedy.

We have this one life to get this, and God will make opportunities for you to hear Him. Don't miss your time of visitation. Today is the day of salvation. When you hear His voice, don't resist your greatest call. It's Love Himself calling you, and He wants you to experience real life and soar in Him. It's all His work from start to finish, and no one else can take the credit for any of it. He has to do it all for it to be real.

Satan and his fallen angels don't have redemption available to them. Christ's sacrifice doesn't pertain to them. They have no chance in eternity to be redeemed, and their final judgment to be thrown in the lake of fire is forever sealed. Redemption only pertains to you and me, and not any other created being. We alone are special, made in God's very image and likeness, and are of great value to Him. We're the very focus and desire of God's heart and all of heaven. He even made His powerful angels for primary assignment just to fight, protect, and minister to us.

Jesus took onto Himself all our sins and their exacting penalties that lead to death, so we could be set free of having to pay what we truly owe. Then He was raised from the dead because death could not hold Him, and He took His seat back at the right hand of the Father in heaven. Yet He remains changed, clothed in glorified human flesh, having committed to looking like us forever. We are His beloved brethren now and for eternity and made part of all the called sons and daughters of the Father in His family.

The Father loves us just as He loves His Son, Jesus. He sees us as clean, righteous, and holy as Jesus Himself through the cleansing instantly provided when we enter through His Son, the Door. That's because only Jesus, the sinless Lamb of God, qualified to be the perfect sacrifice once and for all. He alone has the everlasting power to take all sin completely away. His holy blood that He willingly offered on our behalf is what makes us instantly clean and fit for heaven when we receive Him. That's something we could never do on our own. He lives forever as our continual advocate and redeemer. There is, and will be, no other who could do this for us. Our salvation remains forever sure in Him, and you can be assured and even know *right now* that you do not have to fear death anymore!

Jesus Christ didn't come to condemn the world; He came to save it. His mercy triumphs over judgment, and this one life is the allotted time we have to get this. God's holiness requires this provided purification for unhindered relationship with Him and heaven. Sin, filth, and death have already been judged—not us. His necessary cleansing is to make and keep us pure and free for entry to heaven.

Life is like a university. Yes, there are hard knocks we have to go through and learn from, but that makes the masterpieces God is creating of us that much more valuable and eternally rewarding. When we choose to put our trust in a faithful God who is true to His word and promises, press through these priceless lessons, pass the tests of our hearts despite the seeming hardships, and never let Him go, it even brings awe to the host of heaven. God and heaven honor us above any other creatures He's made, because none have been tried, tested, and proven like we have. When we come through the refiner's fire, meant for our good, and the end result of overcoming and being found *completely* in Him, none can appreciate and love Him back like we can. What value and eternal reward we gain from it. Though we may not fully understand it now, the rest is nothing in comparison.

God already owns everything there is. He is almighty. He is rich beyond measure. He is the Most High and He is King of Kings. Yet His heart aches for something He wants more than anything else—us. God doesn't just want us beside Him; He wants us right *in* Him, just as the Father, Son, and Holy Spirit are one in each other as separate persons yet one God. We're invited to jump right in too. It's the greatest invitation ever offered to any created being.

Jesus, the Son of God, agreed to set aside the immeasurable riches of heaven to step down from His eternal majestic throne, lower Himself to take on human flesh, live a sinless life, and suffer and die to do what had to be done—just to bring us back to Him. God Himself laid down His own life for us. It didn't come cheap. In fact, it's as priceless as we are to Him. We're so much more than we may think we are. We only need to receive His words and believe and obey them to light up what He already put in us, then He'll give us more.

Heaven is invading earth like never before, and God provided everything you need so you can be a leader for this generation. He wants you filled with His Spirit and light—the very kingdom of heaven residing and operating from within you for release through you into the world. He wants you to manifest Him to a world in great need. It's not religion, and it's not for confinement in some building. It's for wherever you go and wherever you are. You were made to operate from heaven's authority, abundance, and supply right now. You were made to rule and reign with Him, take dominion as His fully authorized son or daughter, and release His kingdom into every area and sector of society, nature, and life. He wants all things restored back to Him.

It doesn't matter how deep your problems are. He can save, heal, and deliver you. It doesn't matter how far you've fallen. There is nowhere you can go where He can't find you. You can't do any of it on your own. Just like it was with Saul (later the apostle Paul) who ran hell-bent completely on the wrong road, and just like it was with me, it took only one decided moment of hearing the mighty voice that calls all to life. All that's left is "now get up and go!" (Acts 9:6 NIV).

I urge you, don't miss Jesus and don't miss heaven. Come home to Him, obey His voice, let Him clean you all up, and give Him your heart today.

ACKNOWLEDGEMENTS

I have many to acknowledge and thank in my life. They were not only loving and merciful, but also great encouragers to me in one way or another.

Of course, with all that is in me I thank my God, without whom I would be eternally lost and banished from Him and His amazing goodness and life forever. There's no one like You, my awesome Friend!

I must thank my precious sister, Maryanne, who never gave up on me. Her prayers, support, and constant tough love made a big difference in my outcome. She hung in there with me through the darkest of times, tenaciously unwilling to stand aside and let me go without a good, hard fight. Her husband, Carl, was also an integral support in that. You're the best.

Also, to my beloved brother: You're always in my heart. You put up with quite a lot from me. Please forgive me and thank you.

I'm so grateful for Mom and Dad, who loved me the best they knew how and never gave up praying for me and trusting God no matter how bad it got. I believe praying parents are often the biggest reason many of us rebels ever make it home. Never discount the power of praying parents. I love you always and forever.

I thank my precious children, who are also on their way to great destinies in God. I love you.

To all the ministers, pastors, prophets, and friends who know God's heart and voice and supported and encouraged me with such life-giving and wise words along my journey, I appreciate you.

And most of all, I'm thankful for my wonderful wife, Dana Ehmann, who spent long months and many late hours steadfastly writing, dependent upon God's anointing and revelation to sweetly relay my story to you in just the way God wanted it told so I could get it out to the world.

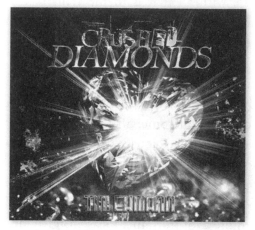